Small-Town Martyrs and Murderers

Religious Revolution and Counterrevolution in Western France, 1774-1914

Edward J. Woell

Small-Town Martyrs and Murderers

Religious Revolution and Counterrevolution in Western France, 1774-1914

MARQUETTE UNIVERSITY PRESS

**Marquette Studies in History
No. 1
Julius R. Ruff, Series Editor**

© 2006 Marquette University Press
Milwaukee, Wisconsin 53201-3141
All rights reserved.
www.marquette.edu/mupress/

Library of Congress Cataloguing-in-Publication Data

Woell, Edward J., 1965-
  Small-town martyrs and murderers : religious revolution and
counterrevolution in western France, 1774-1914 / Edward J. Woell.
    p. cm. — (Marquette studies in history ; no. 1)
  Includes bibliographical references and index.
  ISBN-13: 978-0-87462-311-6 (pbk. : alk. paper)
  ISBN-10: 0-87462-311-1 (pbk. : alk. paper)
  1. Machecoul (France)—History. 2. Machecoul (France)—Religious
life and customs. 3. France—History—Revolution, 1789-1799
—Atrocities. 4. France--History--Revolution, 1789-1799—Religious
aspects. 5. France—History—Wars of the Vendée, 1793-1832
—Atrocities.   I. Title. II. Series.
DC195.M23W64 2006
944'.167—dc22
                                                              2006003245

♾The paper used in this publication meets the minimum requirements of the
American National Standard for Information Sciences—
Permanence of Paper for Printed Library Materials, ANSI Z39.48-1992.

MARQUETTE UNIVERSITY PRESS
MILWAUKEE

The Association of Jesuit University Presses

Acknowledgements

As I am apt to tell my long-suffering students, historians are little more than glorified storytellers. And as any good storyteller knows, narratives rarely emerge out of thin air. They are usually received, occasionally borrowed, sometimes even stolen, from others. Like most narratives, therefore, this one bears the imprint of helpful historians, mentors, and friends kind enough to share their own stories with me. To them I am grateful not only for what they have helped me say here but also for their contribution to the larger narrative that is my life.

I must begin by thanking Marquette University, whose financial support enabled me to conduct on-site research for my dissertation and to write much of it as well. In 1994 and 1995 a Smith Family Fellowship provided funding for my travel in France, and the following academic year a Reverend John P. Raynor Fellowship afforded me the opportunity to write what became the seed bed for this story. While in France a number of scholars were extremely generous with both their time and energy on my behalf, frequently opening doors that otherwise would have remained closed. I received much assistance from Marcel Launay, Jean-Clément Martin, and most notably abbé Jean Garaud, the pastor of Trinité of Machecoul, who graciously allowed me to stay and conduct unrestricted research in his parish's *presbytère*.

Since that first trip to France I have been fortunate enough to present numerous papers at the annual meetings of several distinguished academic organizations, where more experienced and accomplished colleagues have commented on my work and provided much needed scholarly advice. Though these commentators may little remember me, to say nothing of my papers, they played no small part in the shaping of this story. In this regard I recognize and thank John Markoff, Gail Bossenga, Cynthia Bouton, Thomas Sosnowski, William Logue, William Olejnizcak, Dale Van Kley, and other scholars who have been willing to critique my writing and research.

Seeing this narrative to its completion was no doubt a labor of love, but for several years my teaching obligations prevented me from giving this story its due. During that time, however, a number of colleagues and administrators encouraged me to persist with the work. For such support I thank Thomas Wermuth of Marist College, as well as Larry Balsamo and all my other colleagues in the history department at Western Illinois University. Once I produced the rough draft of this narrative, several individuals assisted me in revising the manuscript and producing the finished product. I am particularly indebted to Lisa Kernek, Sterling Kernek, and above all, Fronia Simpson. Each carefully read the manuscript and provided suggestions, but more vitally they helped me become a better writer and a stronger storyteller. I am likewise grateful to Naomi Linzer and Andrew Tallon for their indispensable contributions to this project. In spite of these individuals' worthy efforts on my behalf, any errors found here are mine alone; I take full responsibility for each and every one.

As valuable as those named above were to this work, there remain two scholars especially deserving of my sincere gratitude and deepest appreciation. The first is Jeffrey Merrick, who also did much to shape what follows. Providing many insightful comments and suggestions, Jeff encouraged me to make more connections between what I found in the archives and what other scholars in our field have been arguing in recent years. I thank Jeff for his thoughtful counsel and for the scholarly insight that has informed it. The second is Julius Ruff, who, as his many former students and colleagues can attest, is the consummate professor: an accomplished scholar, a devoted teacher, a wise and prudent advisor. The generosity that Julius has extended to me over the years has been boundless. I am proud to call him my friend. As I go about trying to emulate Julius in my career, I continually marvel at what he has accomplished and hope—albeit in vain, it often seems—that I can maintain the high standards that he has consistently personified.

Still, there is one person who most influenced what I have become as well as what I have written; it is my father. Above everyone, therefore, I owe what I write here to George E. Woell and I dedicate this to him. He remains the greatest storyteller in my life, for through him I first came to understand that a narrative is more than just whimsically entertaining or politically coercive; it is invaluable for making sense of a senseless world, for bringing meaning to collective anarchy and individual chaos. Many of the stories my father told me emphasized honesty, compassion, and perseverance. Even more important, his life showed me how to practice them. Dad, I hope the stories I tell, not to mention the life I lead, are as genuine and meaningful as yours.

Table of Contents

Illustrations

Abbreviations for Notes

Depositories

ACM　　*Archives collégiales de Machecoul. Machecoul, France.*

ADLA　　*Archives départmentales de la Loire-Atlantique. Nantes, France.*

AEN　　*Archives épiscopales de Nantes. Nantes, France.*

APM　　*Archives paroissiales de Machecoul* (Trinité). Machecoul, France.

AN　　*Archives nationales (CARAN). Paris, France.*

Published Sources

AP　　*Archives parlementaires de 1787 à 1860; recueil complèt des débats législatifs et politiques des chambres françaises, première série* (1787-1799). Vols. 60-92. Paris: Centre national de la recherche scientific, 1869.

MU　　*Moniteur Universel* (also entitled *Gazette National*). Paris, 1789-1810.

SRN　　*Semaine religieuse du diocèse de Nantes. Nantes, 1865-1914.*

All religions are guilty of massacre.

Jacques-Louis Ménétra[1]

Introduction

Though many details of the episode are in dispute, the basic facts are not. On March 11, 1793, a crowd of more than one thousand people—mostly poor peasants—converged on Machecoul, a small town in western France. After quickly overrunning about one hundred national guardsmen, these insurgents began killing local officials and other prominent citizens. They also took numerous municipal officers, soldiers, national guardsmen, and other public functionaries as prisoners and confined them to a former women's monastery. As many as thirty of the town's inhabitants met violent deaths over the following two days, while others had their homes ransacked and pillaged. Witnessing the death of fellow Machecoulais and the destruction of their property, many townspeople fled their homes and took refuge in other area communities.

With Machecoul under their control, the insurgents became better organized and saw their numbers swell. Using it as their base of operation, they then attacked other small towns, including nearby Pornic, on March 23. Their invasion and takeover of that community initially seemed successful, but shortly thereafter government forces counterattacked and killed about two hundred rebels. In a reprisal for what was viewed as an unjust bloodletting at Pornic, insurgent leaders concluded that many of their prisoners held at Machecoul should be put to death. Beginning on March 27 and continuing for about four weeks, they periodically passed judgment on their prisoners and condemned many to death. Most of these, led out of their confinement in the old monastery and tied to a rope that passed under their arms, faced a firing squad just outside town. Other prisoners experienced a more gruesome fate; at least one was hacked to death and had his corpse dismembered. Others probably died of their wounds in prison. Still unclear is how many were killed at Machecoul before government forces recaptured the town on April 26, though the most recent research suggests that at least 160 died.[2]

While the killings at Machecoul were remarkable, they were not altogether exceptional during the French Revolution. Indeed, if the most recently figured body count is correct, the bloodshed in this small town appears diminutive compared with the savagery sanctioned by France's revolutionary leaders throughout 1793 and 1794. Still, few if any acts of violence during the Revolution had as disproportionately immense repercussions as these small-town murders, making this singular episode among the most momentous during the French Revolution. What explains the seeming paradox? Much of it was a matter of timing. The Machecoul massacres occurred at the precise moment when the Revolution was most in doubt. France was at war with the rest of Europe and found itself all but encircled by enemies. Fragilely constituted only a few months earlier, the republican government was still in its infancy but was already riven with legislative and administrative factionalism. Religious unrest had been pervasive throughout the country for several years and showed no sign of abating. Many former nobles had fled the country and from nearby states were exerting political pressure and funding efforts to bring down the republic. Economic problems associated with inflation, food shortages, and government debt were rampant and made even more acute by the war. Thus, when numerous "patriots" were spectacularly murdered in an innocent small town, the Revolution reached perhaps its most critical juncture—especially since these massacres marked the beginning of a counterrevolutionary insurgency that henceforth became known as the "War of Vendée."[3]

The many layers of crisis facing the French republic at that moment shaped the revolutionary government's response to the Machecoul massacres and the greater insurgency it ignited. Initially members of the National Convention reacted with shock and disbelief at the news of the killings in Machecoul, but not long thereafter most concluded that their young republic was the victim of a conspiracy forged among France's external adversaries, noble expatriates, and the "enemy within."[4] The massacres activated, then, a collective paranoia responsible for the most infamous episode of the entire Revolution, the Terror. Sending special envoys into the provinces, officials in Paris encouraged the silencing or elimination of those showing even the slightest sign of opposition to the National Convention. Nowhere was the ferocity of republican repression more felt than back where the trouble first began, western France.[5] Indeed, the state's reprisals in the west that followed these small-town murders were, as the eminent historian François Furet put it, "the greatest collective massacre in the Revolutionary Terror."[6]

This episode did more, however, than bring unparalleled repression to western France; the Machecoul massacres also augmented political breaches among revolutionaries themselves. Instead of uniting the National Convention around a common cause, the massacres and the broader War of Vendée that they came to symbolize only widened divisions between legislators. Guided by their ideological differences as well as their mutual fear and suspicion, the factions of the Mountain and the Gironde within the National Convention and their supporters beyond it grew more divided than ever, rendering any kind of republican consensus impossible. In the ensuing months the fractious divide resulted in the Girondins' forced expulsion from the Convention as well as numerous "Federalist" revolts in key provincial cities.[7]

Yet the massacres' reverberations did not end there. Even after the Terror subsided with the death of Robespierre, and rampaging republican troops crushed the remains of the organized Vendéen army, the massacres, the wider insurgency, and the harsh reprisals had produced a prolonged bitterness that precluded any kind of civil reconciliation, much less any democratic compromise. In Paris the republic's government continued to founder, in part because the political factionalism arising out of events in 1793 and 1794 was never overcome. Brigandage, banditry, and sporadic acts of terror, spurred on by political vengeance and countervengeance, troubled many regions of the nation and brought the government's administrative system to the brink of collapse. Meanwhile, in western France a drawn-out guerilla war from 1794 to 1800, commonly known as *chouannerie*, demonstrated that the regional civil war that had first exploded at Machecoul was far from over.[8]

Although Napoleon helped restore order beginning in 1799, the specter of the massacres and the civil war that it triggered continued to haunt the French polity not only during his regime but throughout the nineteenth century. The prospect of yet another insurgency in western France contributed to the crumbling of Bonaparte's empire in 1814, and the outbreak of revolt near the town during Napoleon's brief comeback in 1815 required him to commit troops in the west that were badly needed elsewhere. Later, in 1832, the legitimist duchesse de Berry covertly entered Machecoul's region with the hope of fomenting a new revolt and toppling the Orléaniste monarch, Louis-Philippe.[9] Like all previous insurgencies, it failed, but during that regime as well as the ones that followed the ideological divide created by the massacres and their reprisals remained pivotal, often dividing the French body politic. During the Third Republic, for example, deputies of the National Assembly from the West constituted one of the most important blocs of the conservative "Regime of Moral Order," which in the 1870s engaged in a struggle with anticlerical republicans and socialists for the soul of the French nation.[10]

So prolonged have been the repercussions of the rebellion and the massacres that "Machecoul" reappeared in the nation's political lexicon as recently as 1989. As France celebrated the bicentenary of its great revolution that year, a political maverick from the department of the Vendée, Philippe de Villiers, became prominent by proclaiming that the celebration was a sham because it marked the fall of the Bastille but failed to commemorate the alleged republican extermination of peasants in 1793 and 1794.[11] When Villiers and the leftist pundit Max Gallo engaged each other in a nationally televised debate over the issue, Gallo recalled the Machecoul massacres in an attempt to show that the civil war in western France had been as much a tragedy for local republicans as it had been for Vendéen insurgents.[12] Similarly, a communist champion of the Revolution, Louis Oury, was working on a novel about the massacres during the bicentenary. The title of his work, *Les chapelets de Machecoul* (The rosary beads of Machecoul) was a reference to the town's prisoners being led to execution while tied together, like beads on a string, by seemingly sadistic Catholics.[13] In several articles in a leftist magazine, Oury suggested that because insurgents struck first in committing the massacres, they bore the blame for all tragic events that followed.[14] Almost two hundred years after the fact politicians and pundits were still recalling these small-town murders, and doing so in partisan terms.

Still, the massacres' salient roles in the revolutionary chain of events and in postrevolutionary politics constitute only a shadow of the episode's historical import. For although they make up only one local incident in a civil war confined to merely one region of France, the Machecoul massacres have a universal relevance—in no small part because of their capacity to teach broader lessons about what revolutions mean for ordinary people caught up in them, how and why revolutions take on lives of their own, as well as why revolutions live on in the memory well after they are over in reality. The murders not only raise the most fundamental, profound, and perplexing questions that scholars have sought to answer, but they also embody the quintessential themes of the French Revolution. In what way?

One might start with the broader historical process of which the massacres were certainly a part. The French Revolution, akin to all political revolutions, did not unfold in a theoretical void; it became defined not only by the ideology that inspired it but also by the context in which it occurred. An implicit part of that context was counterrevolution: an active opposition to revolution, particularly among those who lost much in the creation of a new order. Once the French Revolution is put in proper context, "counterrevolution" is more than just an accessory to the main event; it is as fundamental to France's historical path as the Revolution itself. Both revolution and counterrevolution should be regarded, therefore, as interrelated aspects of the same historical process. Each shaped the other's identity, as one constantly informed the character and direction of the other. Once a clearly defined counterrevolutionary movement emerged, it radicalized the Revolution and propelled politics into new and unforeseen directions. As the Revolution became more radical and uncompromising, moreover, a counterrevolution grew even more entrenched and all the more defiant toward the new regime. Perhaps nowhere was this revolutionary-counterrevolutionary dynamic more apparent than in the Machecoul massacres. The killings in this small town, at their simplest level, constituted a counterrevolutionary backlash against the revolutionary reforms and reorganization implemented in the region between 1789 and 1793.

That revolution and counterrevolution in France were complementary and interrelated historical forces has not been lost on scholars, especially among those who have recently written about the Revolution. In identifying the common threads of revolutions in France and Russia, for example, Arno Mayer argued that "there can be no revolution without counterrevolution," that they are "inseparable, like truth and falsehood," and that the two make "for a 'historical motion, which is at once dialectical and driven by necessity.'"[15] Well before Mayer wrote this, Donald Sutherland had already surmised that both the French revolutionary and Napoleonic regimes were characterized by "a struggle against a counterrevolution that was not so much aristocratic as massive, extensive, durable, and popular."[16] Somewhat echoing Mayer and Sutherland, Jean-Clément Martin labeled revolution and counterrevolution in France "the cogs of history"—suggesting that both operated together, with the one constantly driving the movement of the other.[17] Given this scholarly emphasis, the instructive value of the Machecoul massacres becomes even more clear; they vividly portray revolution and counterrevolution operating together and paced in unison. Or to borrow Martin's metaphor, the murders show how the cogs of revolution and counterrevolution actually turned, particularly among ordinary people and in everyday life.

Since revolution and counterrevolution were intrinsically irreconcilable, their dialectic often culminated in violence—yet another theme central to both the Revolution and the Machecoul massacres. Whether justified or not, the French Revolution has become a synonym for violence. The storming of the Bastille in Paris introduced a pattern of both political and popular violence, not only in the killing and wounding of some who attacked the prison, but also in the crowd's brutal murdering of the Bastille's commander and Paris's chief magistrate.[18] Violence then broke out in the countryside, as many peasants attacked landlords and destroyed their property.[19] Still, such tumult was modest compared with the more expansive violence of war, civil no less than international, that confronted the nation from the spring of 1792 through the end of the revolutionary decade. Violence on the battlefield and occasionally in the nation's streets (as was the case at Machecoul) became the basis for a massive mobilization of both human and material resources.[20] The threat of a violent and rampaging enemy spawned unprecedented political centralization in France, and yet with it came an unrivaled state coercion best evidenced in the Terror. Indeed, of all the notions that persist in popular thinking about the French Revolution, none is more common than that of the guillotine's prevalence during the Terror. That perception may be more caricature than reality, yet the Terror's reliance on the threat, if not the enactment, of state-driven violence is well established.[21] Much like this infamous period, the Machecoul massacres offer a meditation on the origins, meaning, and effects of bloodshed and death in the midst of political upheaval and social disruption.

Violence has become one of the most popular topics taken up by contemporary historians of the French Revolution. Some scholars, seeking to link that violence to the massive death and destruction of the twentieth century, have returned to questions of why violence emerged during the Revolution, what it meant within the revolutionary context, and how it became justified.[22] Such questions pushed historians like François Furet and Keith Michael Baker into the realm of "political culture," specifically the language and rhetorical devices employed by political theorists such as Jean-Jacques Rousseau and subsequently embraced by revolutionaries in sanctioning violence.[23] Other specialists, including Olwen Hufton and Colin Lucas, focused on the role of the crowd in revolutionary and counterrevolutionary violence, thereby uncovering important aspects of riot behavior related to crowd activity during the Old Regime, gender roles, and other cultural factors.[24] Influenced by cultural anthropology and psychological theory, still other historians considered what violence meant to those who perpetrated or witnessed revolutionary bloodshed. Lynn Hunt, for example, showed how revolutionaries understood and interpreted the death of Louis XVI, as well as the "martyrdoms" of Michel Lepeletier and Jean-Paul Marat.[25] Similarly, in analyzing the dying of seven prominent figures of the Revolution, Antoine de Baecque argued that the Terror could be best contemplated through the "discourse of corpses." Baecque characterized a French populace preoccupied with death during the Terror—a period that in his words "produced real corpses on top of real corpses" among people having "sensibilities that multiplied [corpses] in their imagination."[26] This trend in recent scholarship suggests that the Machecoul massacres are a timely topic, yielding as they do even more insight into the origins, practices, and representations of revolutionary and counterrevolutionary violence.

The Terror, or for that matter the violence that accompanied it, was not forgotten once it had ended—far from it. The trauma as well as the political polarities that it had produced left an indelible mark on national psychology, to such a degree that it showed little sign of fading throughout the nineteenth century. For this reason, the "memory" of the 1790s among the French constitutes another theme applicable to the Machecoul massacres and the Revolution alike. Although the revolutionary generation gradually passed away in the nineteenth century, the remembrance of the Revolution persisted among subsequent generations. Such memory frequently expressed itself in "places of remembrance" that included an array of signs, symbols, rituals, and stories—not to mention actual spaces and edifices. For those who saw much good in the French Revolution, memory often took the form of the tricolor flag or Marianne, the personification of Liberty. Their memory was also embodied in public commemorations, like that marking the storming of the Bastille on July 14 or, just as importantly, in scholarly narratives about revolutionary events. But for those for whom the Revolution was an abomination, a counterrevolutionary memory was conveyed through symbols such as the royalist fleur-de-lis or the Catholic Sacred Heart of Jesus. Public or liturgical commemorations marking the death of Louis XVI, Marie-Antoinette, and insurgent military leaders also became poignant acts of remembrance for royalists, as did stories about the French Revolution underscoring the anarchy, death, and destruction supposedly wrought by it. As much as the French at large had good reason to remember the Revolution, for the Machecoulais it was a virtual necessity; the trauma of the massacres and subsequent republican reprisals changed the community forever, thereby requiring its reckoning with a troubled past.

A recent wave of scholarship has taken great interest in how the French remembered their past. Through the pioneering efforts of these specialists a completely new avenue of research associated with *mentalités*, that is, how people from the past understood and interpreted their world, emerged.[27] In this respect, Jean-Clément Martin made one of the most important contributions to the study of French memory. In considering counterrevolutionary remembrance, Martin demonstrated how in the nineteenth and twentieth centuries the memory of the War of Vendée became integral to the collective identity of those living in the region where the insurgency had been fought.[28] Martin argued more broadly that the "counter-memory" found in the Vendéen region has been as vital to France's national identity as the "official" revolutionary memory promoted by state officials and institutions during the modern republican era.[29] Martin also conducted a pointed study of the Machecoul massacres, partly out of his recognition of their contentious status within the realm of French memory.[30]

Although memory, violence, and the revolutionary-counterrevolutionary dynamic are variegated themes, at one point they all seem to converge. Standing at the crossroads of all of these themes is religion.[31] Whether considered a social institution, a collective belief system, an assembly of ritualistic practices, or some combination of all three, religion is the most integral of the themes shared by the Revolution and the Machecoul massacres, and it is far from difficult to see why. With regard to the revolutionary-counterrevolutionary dynamic, for example, few other issues polarized political opinion more during the French Revolution than religion. Although peace and reconciliation are perennial religious ideals, history shows—as recently as September 11, 2001—that religious belief can facilitate and justify violence as much as any secular ideology. Given its heavy reliance on sign, symbol, ritual, and narrative, religion is also inherently capable of forging memory, particularly among its adherents.

To anyone even remotely familiar with France in the eighteenth century, that the Roman Catholic Church fostered political polarities, fomented violence, and influenced a people's conception of the past should come as no surprise. The only rival to the Catholic Church's power during the Old Regime was that of the state. The Church's personnel comprised less than one percent of the French population in 1789, but in theory the clergy constituted one-third of the political order in the kingdom and in reality held no less than one-tenth of the land. The Catholic Church also exercised pervasive cultural influence. Given the many dialects, weights and measures, and social customs in Old-Regime France, perhaps the only common cultural thread was the observance of Catholic beliefs and practices.[32] Yet all was not well with the institution as political unrest was rapidly coming to a head. By 1789 the French were exhibiting a crisis of confidence in Catholicism, thus ensuring that the Revolution would make the Church a prime target. Here again, the story of the Machecoul massacres is symptomatic of a larger development. Similar to much of France at the time, the Church's political and cultural potency was keenly felt in this small town before 1789. But also akin to the kingdom at large, this power was fast becoming a source of cultural and political disagreement among the townspeople. Indeed, fundamental divisions over the Church's institutional status, beliefs, and practices go a long way in explaining what led to the Macheocul massacres, just as they help make sense of what happened during the Revolution as a whole.

Over the past thirty years scholarly consensus about religion's significance to the French Revolution has only grown. Dale Van Kley, for example, argued that the long and drawn-out political and ecclesiastical conflict over Jansenism created the political fault lines during the Old Regime that made the revolutionary eruption possible.[33] Michel Vovelle showed how "baroque" religious devotion already seemed to be in decline by 1750, thereby shedding new light on popular religious attitudes as the Revolution drew near.[34] John McManners and Bernard Plongeron also contributed to a more complete picture of a Church increasingly subject to contentious political and theological struggles during the late Old Regime.[35] Several other scholars demonstrated the salience of religion in the unfolding of the Revolution itself. Perhaps no study is as seminal in this regard as Timothy Tackett's examination of the Ecclesiastical Oath of 1791, which highlighted one of the key turning points in modern French history.[36] Arguing for the persistence of religion as a viable cultural and political force throughout the revolutionary decade, Suzanne Desan showed how the laity—proponents of the Revolution no less—adhered to Catholic beliefs and practices even after churches were closed and clerics defrocked.[37] By no coincidence, these topics—ecclesiastical structures and personnel, theological politics, popular religious beliefs, the oath crisis of 1791—are integral to the Machecoul massacres, as the rest of this story will make clear.

Invoking the themes of religion, memory, violence, and the revolutionary-counterrevolutionary dialectic is necessary in this context not only because they frequently appear *within* this narrative of the Machecoul massacres, but also because they shape *how* the story itself is told. But more than just embodying what others have already said about such matters, the following story develops and refines these themes, often adding shades of subtlety and nuance. Indeed, this account of an underappreciated episode in the French Revolution represents a unique opportunity to explore these themes further—in no small part because the narrative approaches them in a somewhat novel way. Instead of discussing the entire insurgency region or the broad phenomenon of popular counterrevolution, this story focuses on a single town, Machecoul, albeit over the relatively long period from 1774 to 1914.

To be sure, local narratives like this one are nothing new in the field of French history. Usually, however, they cover a department—one of eighty-three administrative units created during the Revolution and still in use. As heuristic as departmental studies have been to scholars, they have also become highly redundant, particularly regarding a topic like popular counterrevolution in western France. In explaining the origins of the Vendéen insurgency, for example, Charles Tilly examined the department of the Maine-et-Loire.[38] Donald Sutherland, in a parallel work, examined the entire Ille-et-Vilaine to gain better insight of *chouannerie*.[39] Also seeking to explain the origins of insurrection in the west, Paul Bois studied virtually all of the Sarthe.[40] These analyses have enabled scholars to understand vital social and economic trends, especially with the help of the statistical methods they utilized. But while such studies do well at explaining tendencies, they often fail to show what happened on the personal and intimate level—arguably the point where for most ordinary people "real life" occurred. For those seeking to discover cultural intricacies, a departmental study may pose as many obstacles as it seeks to overcome.

Or so say the proponents of "microhistory"—a methodology first developed by scholars writing for the Italian journal *Quaderni storici* and the approach utilized here. Like those in *Annales* school of French social history, microhistorians seek to penetrate the lives of ordinary people from the past, but they differ from *annalistes* by relying less on statistical methods and focusing more on the minutiae of the historical record.[41] Carlo Ginzburg pioneered the effort to uncover the most subtle and hidden aspects of the past in a qualitative manner, though only through severely limiting the parameters of his studies. Instead of focusing on an entire country or an expansive region, microhistorians like Ginzburg were more inclined to analyze one event, one community, or even one individual.[42] In doing so they paid attention not so much to the most dramatic or largest aspects of their subject but rather to the small and seemingly insignificant details, many of which appear opaque or anomalous to the contemporary observer.[43] They especially sought to trace convoluted social, economic, and political relationships within small communities.[44] Hence the story here of just one town.

The decided advantage of using a microhistorical methodology lies in its ability to uncover elements of religion, violence, and memory among ordinary people. Such themes, after all, involve more than just people from the past; they concern their *mentalité*. To be sure, departmental studies are often helpful in illuminating certain aspects of ordinary people's cosmology. The anthropologist Clifford Geertz and the historian Robert Darnton showed, nonetheless, that unraveling symbolic or representational systems was especially effective when done at a minute, intimate level.[45] Reconstructing *mentalités* is a microhistorical preoccupation, particularly when it involves "lost peoples"—those from the past who left few written records or material artifacts.

A microhistory is fitting for this topic for another reason as well. As parochial studies in French history have grown in volume, so has the recognition of local agency. Gone are the days when historians view a development like the French Revolution as a "top-down" phenomenon whereby policy and procedures are set in Paris and then are implemented and heeded in the provinces. Recognizing the diversity found throughout many regions of France, as well as the complexity of relationships between central and regional authorities, scholars now realize that even within a centralizing event like the Revolution, local peoples deviated from the national norm—sometimes markedly. It would be no exaggeration to say that a locality's circumvention or alteration of centralizing efforts has become as vital to the story of France's past as the more celebrated development of national unification. Perhaps even more so than departmental studies, microhistories underscore the relevance of local agency, yet in this they also highlight a common tendency found throughout all of French history.[46]

No doubt some will perceive this microhistory as having little scholarly value precisely because of its narrow parameters. Even if much is revealed about religion, violence, and memory at Machecoul, the argument might go, there is no way to prove that the town was germane to other communities in France.[47] Such criticism, however, misses the point. The critique might be valid if this story claimed to be an overarching analysis of religion, violence, and memory, much more a comprehensive explanation of the revolutionary-counterrevolutionary dynamic. But it does not. More than anything this microhistory calls attention to greater degrees of subtlety and complexity. True, Machecoul's take on the themes of religion, violence, memory, and the revolutionary-counterrevolutionary dialectic may be either commonplace or extraordinary, but in any case what follows inevitably contributes to understanding them a little more. For all these reasons, this story of a singular community is less trifling than it may initially appear.

Paradoxically, the only way to prove that the Machecoul massacres have broader significance is to dwell on the trifles, that is, the details of fact surrounding these murders, and to arrange them into some coherent order. That is what readers will find here. Chapter One depicts the town's geographic, social, economic, and political conditions shortly before the massacres, thus setting the stage for the drama that followed and indicating why the story's major themes matter. The most important of these themes—religion—is taken up in Chapter Two. In assessing the town's religious complexion before 1789, this chapter outlines how and why religion divided the community, thus revealing the foundations for the revolutionary-counterrevolutionary dialectic that polarized the town during the Revolution. Addressing the first three and a half years of the French Revolution, Chapter Three considers the dialectic itself. It centers on three catalysts of conflict: the 1790 Civil Constitution of the Clergy, the 1791 Oath Crisis, and establishment of the town's Constitutional Church from 1791 to 1793. Chapter Four includes the center of the story, the massacres, and more generally considers the theme of violence. It recalls two versions of the murders—complete with the dramatic discrepancies between them—and shows how the memory of the massacres became contested even before the Revolution came to a close. Chapter Five dwells even more on the theme of memory by showing how Machecoul's Catholics remembered their turbulent past in the nineteenth century and what effects such a memory had. The chapter suggests that the town's memory of the Revolution was evident in religious symbols, rites, and teachings between 1801 and 1914, yet also manifested itself in the townspeople's political actions. Finally, the epilogue puts the story's major themes into present perspective, by locating both the continuities and ruptures of religious culture and memories of revolution and counterrevolution in and around contemporary Machecoul.

Readers will also discover a "moral" to the story, which perhaps is best captured in the title, "small-town martyrs and murderers." That moniker refers not just to Machecoul's Catholics between 1774 and 1914 but also to the argument made about them here. Central to this story is the notion that religion facilitated, if not instigated, popular conflict and violent revolt at Machecoul, though not necessarily in the way that some historians have claimed, and much less for the reasons that most have provided. Given that the revolutionary-counterrevolutionary dialectic arose from disparate religious cosmologies, and that the violence enacted in the town arose from elements of religious belief and practice, in no small way the town's fervent Catholics, revolutionaries and counterrevolutionaries alike, can be held culpable for the murders in their community. Similarly, those Machecoulais killed during the civil war, regardless of the side they chose in the conflict, were truly martyrs since an acute religious division all but motivated their murders. In another sense, though, "martyrs" is an especially fitting name for those counterrevolutionaries killed—at least according to the memory of the town's Catholics in the nineteenth century. Indeed, the cornerstone of such memory was that the insurgents had embodied divine obedience and providential purpose by revolting in 1793, and as such were worthy of imitation in the century that followed. Although such a memory seemingly faded in the town after 1914, elements of it, along with those of a competing republican memory, were still evident in France as recently as the end of the twentieth century.

This argument should not detract, however, from what is supposed to be simply a good read. While many may consider this a study or an analysis, an effort has been made—to the extent that it is possible—to tell a story. Perhaps the distinction is little more than an exercise in semantics here, but there are broader implications to consider. If there is a crisis involving the relevance of history today, it is due not so much to what one historian has called the "pigmification" of history, but rather to a widening gap between the way historians are now writing and what many, scholars and nonscholars alike, seek to read.[48] Postmodernism and other recent academic trends have done much to destroy the historical narrative by claiming the meaninglessness of anything beyond the language used to describe it.[49] As valid as this point is, very few of its proponents have offered a palatable alternative to what they have dismantled. In their attempts to discuss discursive practices, cultural matrices, and problematizations, many scholars have left a reading public in the dust. Such academics may have succeeded in undermining traditional narratives, but even they are left with mere stories of the past to tell. The only question is whether such stories will be heard, let alone understood, by those all too eager to listen. Can the chasm be crossed any more? This story seeks to breach that abyss.

Notes

[1] Jacques-Louis Ménétra, *Journal of My Life*, trans. Arthur Goldhammer (New York: Columbia Unversity Press, 1986), 352.

[2] Jean-Clément Martin, *Révolution et contre-révolution en France 1789-1989: Les rouages de l'Histoire* (Rennes: Presses Universitaires de Rennes, 1996), 33-47. Martin's chapter in this book on the Machecoul massacres first appeared as a journal article, "Histoire et polémique: les massacres de Machecoul," *Visions Contemporaines* 7 (1993): 156-91.

[3] For a more thorough understanding of the revolutionary context in which the Machecoul massacres occurred, see William Doyle, *The Oxford History of the French Revolution* (New York: Oxford University Press, 1989), 197-271, 295-317.

[4] Martin, *Révolution et contre-révolution*, 38.

[5] Doyle, *The Oxford History*, 252-59.

[6] François Furet and Mona Ozouf, *A Critical Dictionary of the French Revolution*, trans. Arthur Goldhammer (Cambridge: Harvard University Press, 1989), 174.

[7] Martin, *Révolution et contre-révolution*, 39.

[8] A good summary explanation of *chouannerie* is found in Roger Dupuy, *Les chouans* (Paris: Hachette Littératures, 1997).

[9] For more on the Vendéen revolts of 1814, 1815, and 1832, see Jean-Clément Martin, *La Vendée de la mémoire* (Paris: Editions du Seuil, 1989), 37-50, 95-99.

[10] This and other political struggles during the Third Republic are analyzed well in Jean-Marie Mayeur, *La vie politique sous la troisième République, 1870-1940* (Paris: Editions du Seuil, 1984).

[11] Stephen Laurence Kaplan, *Farewell Revolution: Disputed Legacies, France, 1789/1989* (Ithaca: Cornell University Press, 1995), 85-111.

[12] Martin, *Révolution et contre-révolution*, 29.

[13] Louis Oury, *Les chapelets de Machecoul: histoire et legendes en pays Chouan* (Paris: Temps actuels, 1993).

[14] Kaplan, 89; Louis Oury, "La second mort de Joseph Bara," *Révolution* 471 (March 10, 1989): 58-63; Oury, "Les chapelets de Machecoul," *Révolution* 488 (July 7, 1989): 20-24. Both of these articles were a response to Reynald Secher's claims that republicans were responsible for a genocide in western France during the Terror. See Reynald Secher, *Le génocide franco-françaises:*

La Vendée-vengé (Paris: Presses universitaires de France, 1989). The English edition of this highly polemical work is *A French Genocide: The Vendée*, trans. George Holoch (South Bend: University of Notre Dame Press, 2003).

[15] Arno J. Mayer, *The Furies: Violence and Terror in the French and Russian Revolutions* (Princeton: Princeton University Press, 2000), 45.

[16] Donald Sutherland, *France 1789-1815: Revolution and Counterrevolution* (New York: Oxford University Press, 1985), 10.

[17] Martin, *Révolution and contre-révolution*, 7-15.

[18] Mayer, *The Furies*, 85.

[19] Doyle, *The Oxford History*, 114-16.

[20] See T. C. W. Blanning, *The French Revolutionary Wars, 1787-1802* (London: Arnold Publishers, 1996).

[21] For a short but comprehensive discussion of the Terror, see Hugh Gough, *The Terror in the French Revolution* (New York: St. Martin's Press, 1998).

[22] See Michel Vovelle, "1789-1917: The Game of Analogies," in Keith M. Baker, ed., *The French Revolution and the Creation of Modern Political Culture*, 4 vols. (Oxford: Pergamon Press, 1994), 4: 349-78.

[23] François Furet, *Interpreting the French Revolution*, trans. Elborg Forster (New York: Cambridge University Press, 1981); Keith M. Baker, *Inventing the French Revolution: Essays on French Political Culture in the Eighteenth Century* (New York: Cambridge University Press, 1990).

[24] See Olwen Hufton, "Counter-revolutionary Women" and Colin Lucas, "The Crowd in Politics," in Peter Jones, ed., *The French Revolution in Social and Political Perspective* (London: Arnold, 1996), 285-307, 420-50.

[25] Lynn Hunt, *The Family Romance of the French Revolution* (Berkeley: University of California Press, 1992), 53-88.

[26] Antoine de Baecque, *Glory and Terror: Seven Deaths under the French Revolution*, trans. Charlotte Mandell (New York: Routledge, 2003), 10.

[27] See Pierre Nora, ed., *Les lieux de mémoire: La république, la nation, les France*, 3 vols. (Paris: Gallimard, 1997).

[28] Martin, *La Vendée de la mémoire*, 227-29.

[29] Jean-Clément Martin, "La Vendée, région mémoire: Bleus and blancs," in Nora, 1: 519-34.

[30] Martin, *Révolution et contre-révolution*, 29.

[31] Note how much emphasis Arno Mayer places upon religion in his discussion of violence in the French and Russian revolutions. See Mayer, 141-67.

[32] Peter McPhee, *The French Revolution 1789-1799* (New York: Oxford University Press, 2002), 13-15; Doyle, *The Oxford History*, 33-36.

[33] Dale Van Kley, *The Damiens Affair and the Unraveling of the Ancien Régime, 1750-1770* (Princeton: Princeton University Press, 1984); *The Jansenists and the Expulsion of Jesuits from France, 1757-1765* (New Haven: Yale University Press, 1975); *The Religious Origins of the French Revolution: From Calvin to the Civil Constitution, 1560-1791* (New Haven: Yale University Press, 1996).

[34] Michel Vovelle, *Piété baroque et déchristianisation en Provence au XVIIIe siècle* (Paris: Editions du C.T.H.S., 1997).

[35] John McManners, *Church and Society in Eighteenth-Century France*, 2 vols. (Oxford: Oxford University Press, 1999); Bernard Plongeron, *Théologie et politique au siècle des lumières (1770-1820)* (Geneva: Droz, 1973). See also Dale Van Kley, "Christianity as Causality and Chrysalis of Modernity: The Problem of Dechristianization in the French Revolution," *American Historical Review* 108 (October 2003): 1081-104.

[36] Timothy Tackett, *Religion, Revolution, and Regional Culture in Eighteenth-Century France: The Ecclesiastical Oath of 1791* (Princeton: Princeton University Press, 1986).

[37] Suzanne Desan, *Reclaiming the Sacred: Lay Religion and Popular Politics in Revolutionary France* (Ithaca: Cornell University Press, 1990).

[38] Charles Tilly, *The Vendée: A Sociological Analysis of the Counterrevolution of 1793* (Cambridge: Harvard University Press, 1964).

[39] Donald Sutherland, *The Chouans: The Social Origins of Popular Counter-Revolution in Upper Brittany, 1770-1796* (Oxford: Clarendon Press, 1982), 218.

[40] Paul Bois, *Paysans de l'Ouest: Des structures économiques et sociales aux options politiques depuis l'époque révolutionnaire dans la Sarthe* (Paris: Flammarion, 1971): 292-94.

[41] Edward Muir and Guido Ruggiero, eds., *Microhistory and the Lost People of Europe*, trans. Eren Branch (Baltimore: Johns Hopkins University Press, 1991), vii-xxviii; See also Jacques Revel, "Microanalysis and Construction of the Social" in Revel and Lynn Hunt, eds., *Histories: French Reconstructions of the Past* (New York: The Free Press, 1995), 492-502.

[42] See, for example, Carlo Ginzburg, *The Cheese and the Worms: The Cosmos of a Sixteenth-Century Miller*, trans. John and Anne Tedeschi (Baltimore: Johns Hopkins University Press, 1980).

[43] Carlo Ginzburg, *Clues, Myths, and the Historical Method*, trans. John and Anne Tedeschi (Baltimore: Johns Hopkins University Press, 1989), 96-125.

[44] Carlo Ginzburg and Carlo Poni, "The Name and the Game: Unequal Exchange and the Historiographic Marketplace," in *Microhistory and the Lost Peoples of Europe*, 1-10.

[45]See Clifford Geertz, *Negara: The Theater State in Nineteenth-Century Bali* (Princeton: Princeton University Press, 1980); Robert Darnton, *The Great Cat Massacre and Other Episodes in French Cultural History* (New York: Random House, 1985).

[46]For an example of the scholarly recognition of local agency in the French Revolution, see Peter Jones, *Liberty and Locality in Revolutionary France: Six Villages Compared, 1760-1820* (New York: Cambridge University Press, 2003).

[47]This particular criticism is expressed, for example, in Valerio Valeri's review of Ginzburg's *The Cheese and the Worms* in the *Journal of Modern History* 54 (1982): 139-43.

[48]Muir and Ruggiero, *Microhistory and the Lost Peoples*, xx.

[49]For more on postmodernism and its impact on the historical discipline, see Richard J. Evans, *In Defense of History* (New York: W. W. Norton, 1999).

1

Where the Spirit Dwelt

I still remember my first visit to Machecoul. It was on a fall day when the weather along France's western seaboard was all too typical; gray clouds and intermittent rain, ranging from light drizzle to an occasional heavy downpour, gave the sky a dark and depressing hue. Such monochromatic gloom did little to dampen my excitement, though, as I boarded a bus in Nantes to travel about twenty miles to this small town. Traveling first over the murky Loire River and then past Nantes's southern suburbs, I soon caught a glimpse of a mysterious terrain that the French call *le bocage*. I had first come across this term as a graduate student when reading about the War of Vendée. For the first time I saw the *bocage* with my own eyes: the muddy, rain-soaked fields, some of which were still lined by trees and various thickets. I tried to imagine what it had been like for the ragtag bands of rebels to march over the moors or hide in the heavy brush. Before I knew it I reached my destination, where I found a whole new world—both past and present—waiting for me.

Among the reasons why I recall that trip so well is that it allowed me to develop a "sense of place" regarding my research. But it did not happen all at once, least of all when I first stepped off the bus. Despite the celebrated reputation of the massacres, I found a relatively sleepy community showing no sign of the bloody vengeance that unfolded in 1793. Still, I learned more about that town during my week-long stay there than I did in all the years that have followed. My thoughts about what may have happened in the town during the insurgency and why this was so have changed with the passing of time. Ever since my arrival in Machecoul that day, however, one belief about the episode has stayed with me: understanding the massacres requires an intimate sense of the setting in which they occurred.

That conviction shapes this portion of the story. In establishing the broader milieu in which the murders took place, this chapter serves several purposes. Since the massacres have been subject to perennial scholarly debate, the key issues framing the discussion—including the town's geography, social composition, economic exchange, and political status during the late Old Regime—must be understood. Examining these factors clarifies the debate and puts various interpretations about the origins of popular counterrevolution to the test. Because the massacres in and of themselves are quite complex, moreover, it follows that an extensive description of the town, particularly as it stood just before the Revolution, can illustrate that complexity as well as what accounts for it. But perhaps most important for this story, paying a visit to this town will allow readers—if only in their minds—to walk the town's streets, to encounter the characters along the way, to gain a sense of where this story unfolded. For, as with any other topic in history, learning about this episode demands a journey to a different time and place.

Debating "Why"

From the moment they unfolded, the Machecoul massacres have been mired in controversy. A relentless debate has raged not only about what unfolded in the town in March and April 1793, but just as importantly about what may have inspired those events. Immediately after the massacres became known, republican officials were quick to blame the insurgency on local members of the Catholic clergy, many of whom had defied the new regime and thus enjoyed wide support among the rebels.[1] This explanation continued well into the nineteenth century, particularly among writers sympathetic to the Revolution. In 1824, for example, Julien-Marie Savary maintained that eighteenth-century missionaries in western France inspired the revolt; according to Savary, "it was to the activity of their zeal, to their underhanded plots, to their tireless and secret preaching that we must attribute the disposition of a great majority of people."[2] At midcentury Jules Michelet called the insurgency inexplicable, for peasants took up arms against a government that was supposedly working in their best interest. He could only comprehend the incomprehensible by means of a religious conspiracy theory:

> The woman and the priest, there was everything, the Vendée, the civil war, . . . The woman's place was in the home, but it was also in the church and the confessional. This somber oak closet, where the woman, on her knees, in the midst of tears and prayers, received,

repeated, more ardently, the fanatical spark, was the true home of the civil war. . . .[3]

Writing near the end of the century, Charles-Louis Chassin rejected the conspiracy theory, but he too put much of the blame on the Catholic clergy, concluding at one point that it had "prepared the nucleus of the insurrection, and, over the years, reviving the sacred fire, kept the popular gunpowder ready to explode."[4]

But at the same time that pro-republican writers contended that clerics were responsible for popular counterrevolution, a small but influential group of notables and scholars sympathetic to the insurgency wrote opposing narratives that cast the Catholic clergy in a different light. The marquise de La Rochejaquelein, a wife to one of the insurgency's leaders, defended her husband and the insurgents in general by explaining that "this war, was not, as some say, excited by the priests. . . . There was no plan, nor plots, nor secret intelligence. All the people rose up at once."[5] These and similar memoirs claimed that rural life in the west during the late Old Regime had been happy and peaceful, and that the peasants had exhibited great deference toward nobles and priests, who had protected and looked after the simple rural inhabitants. The Revolution, they claimed, had destroyed this paradise by imposing a new and foreign order in western France. They also maintained that although peasants may have been inspired by religion, by no means was the rebellion due to priestly coercion. As J. Créteneau-Joly concluded in the early nineteenth century, "the inhabitants of the west were attached by heart and conviction to the religion they received from their father and to the gospel which sustained them in the midst of the ordeals of life."[6] The theme continued in the twentieth century in the work of Emile Gabory, who claimed that in spite of the insurrection occurring among diverse peoples of the west, "the same traditionalist spirit reunited these men from disparate backgrounds. . . . A great religious wind circulated from the hills to the sea."[7]

In the 1960s, however, a new view of the insurgency began to emerge. Utilizing the quantitative techniques made famous by the *Annales* school of social history, Charles Tilly, Paul Bois, and Marcel Faucheux emphasized social and economic factors in explaining the origins of the insurgency. For Tilly, whose study centered on the region in the west called the Mauges, the insurgency could be explained in terms of an "urbanization"process whereby town-based officials were rapidly expanding their control over traditional rural elites and the social structures supporting them.[8] Similarly, Bois found that economic interaction between towns and the countryside largely determined the political opinions of peasants in the Sarthe. Though not altogether dismissing the religious factor, Bois believed that religion merely buttressed choices made for primarily economic reasons.[9] Faucheux saw the economic distress of peasants as the key to the revolt. He contended that poverty in the west, which he showed had been pervasive before the Revolution, was the basis for insurrection.[10] Thus for all three of these authors, religion took a back seat to social and economic rationale.

The numerous socioeconomic interpretations convinced a generation of historians that religious matters were merely peripheral to popular counterrevolution, but by the 1980s some specialists began to exhibit a degree of doubt. Jean-Clément Martin, Roger Dupuy, Claude Petitfrère, and Donald Sutherland refused to dismiss the importance of social and economic factors, but they tended to see counterrevolution as being multilayered in its origins, thus bringing religious issues back into play.[11] Sutherland, for example, argued that peasants had supported the clergy because in many rural parishes the priest had personified the traditional peasant community; defense of the clergy was primarily related to the maintenance of peasant cultural identity and collectivity.[12] In 1989 François Furet, France's most influential historian of the Revolution at that time, went so far as to repudiate all socioeconomic interpretations and instead returned to the traditional view that religion was key to the crisis:

> The great issue, the heart of the conflict from the Civil Constitution on, was the religious question. The insurrection of March 1793 was preceded by a series of local incidents stemming from the compulsory oath and the division of the Church between two warring clergies. All indications are that the principal source was religious and not social nor simply political; … military heroism in the insurrection—when there was heroism, for the Vendean army was also subject to panics—was inspired by religious fanaticism and the promise of paradise. This communal devotion to the old faith and the old Church, perceived as inseparable and both threatened by the Revolution, transcended the limits of the conflict between town and country.[13]

With Furet's declaration the interpretative pendulum seemed to swing back to where it began. Yet by no means did he settle the issue once and for all.

These competing interpretations underscore the value of comprehensively considering Machecoul during the late Old Regime. As a review of the historiography shows, one of the most critical issues involving the massacres is whether the town's geography, social composition, economic exchange, and political activity were somehow responsible for the murders, or whether religion largely authored the violence. What elements of the town's broader milieu helped facilitate conflict before the Revolution and in what way? Were rivalries prevalent in and around the town before 1789, and if so on what were they based? In what ways might the Revolution have exacerbated preexisting factionalism within the town? These questions cannot be answered without considering the local context in which the massacres took place. The long-standing debate about the origins of these murders provides all the more impetus for taking a good look at the town itself.

Contrasting Landscapes

What is Machecoul? Although it is casually called a "small town" here, properly speaking it is a municipality (in French, a *commune*) located about twenty-four kilometers south-southwest of Nantes, the *chef-lieu*, or administrative seat of its department, the Loire-Atlantique (called the Loire-Inférieure before 1957), and immediately north of the department of the Vendée, as indicated in Figure 1.1a & 1.1b (see p. 38-39). Since the Revolution the municipality of Machecoul has comprised 6,659.5 hectares (66.6 square kilometers) of land, which is quite large for a commune, even for the prodigious municipalities found in the western province of Brittany. The climate and weather patterns affecting Machecoul are what one would expect for a community located close to the North Atlantic coast. The municipality is completely landlocked, yet the ocean is located only about six kilometers from its western border, meaning that the Atlantic shapes Machecoul's mild climate. Most notably, the ocean's moisture provides fine but voluminous rain along the coast, with most of it falling in the autumn and winter.[14]

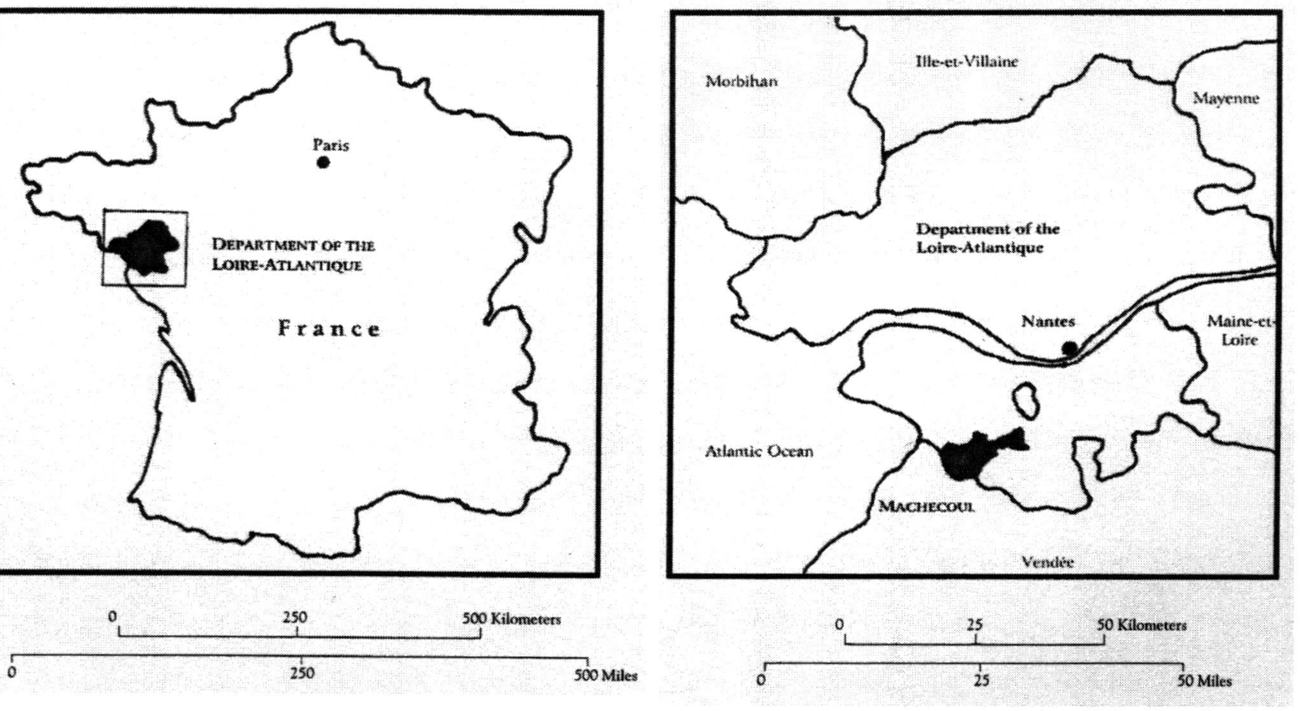

Figure 1.1 Machecoul from a National Perspective

As part of the vast French coastal plain slightly above sea level, Machecoul is largely flat and has two small rivers winding their way through the commune.[15] The homogeneous appearance is somewhat deceptive, however, since the municipality included five diverse habitats in the eighteenth century. Figure 1.2, which is based on an 1850 agricultural map, illustrates these habitats.[16] During the late Old Regime two of these were part of the *marais breton-vendéen*, a treeless, monotonous marsh in the western part of the municipality that constituted about 40 percent of its land.[17] One part of the *marais* included meadows that usually served as pastures, while the other part consisted of *salants* containing numerous rectangular salt-water ponds interconnected through canals and ditches linked to the Atlantic Ocean.[18] On the other side of the municipality stood two other habitats: a forest and a small plain. Broken by a number of pastures and fields in the eighteenth and nineteenth centuries, the forest comprised twelve square kilometers of land in the municipality, making it one of the largest forests in the region at that time.[19] Unlike the marsh, the Machecoul Forest was mostly confined to the commune, extending only a little into its neighboring municipalities.[20] Oaks, beeches, hornbeams, and chestnuts were the forest's dominant tree species, and wild boars, stags, deer, and even wolves inhabited it as late as 1800.[21] The plain, located in the approximate center of the commune, was called Les Chaumes. Its name literally meant "thatch," perhaps a reference to the grain stalks that grew there in great abundance. Les Chaumes produced much more grain than any other area in the municipality, probably because of the presence of a limestone that neutralized the prevailing acidity in the region's soils.[22]

The remaining area of the commune, the northern and southeastern sections occupying about 30 percent of its area, consisted of small fields frequently lined by tall hedges of trees and bushes. A zone cut by sunken, hedge-lined roads and numerous brooks and streams, this *bocage* was the predominant geographic pattern in the southern parts of the provinces of Brittany and Anjou, as well as northern Poitou.[23] Generally, the quality of the soil in the *bocage*, composed of large quantities of clay and sand, was mediocre at best. Many fields could grow low-quality grains only once every two years and were otherwise left fallow. Some fields were so unproductive in the *bocage* that they could serve only as pastures for cattle.[24] Those historians emphasizing the social and economic origins

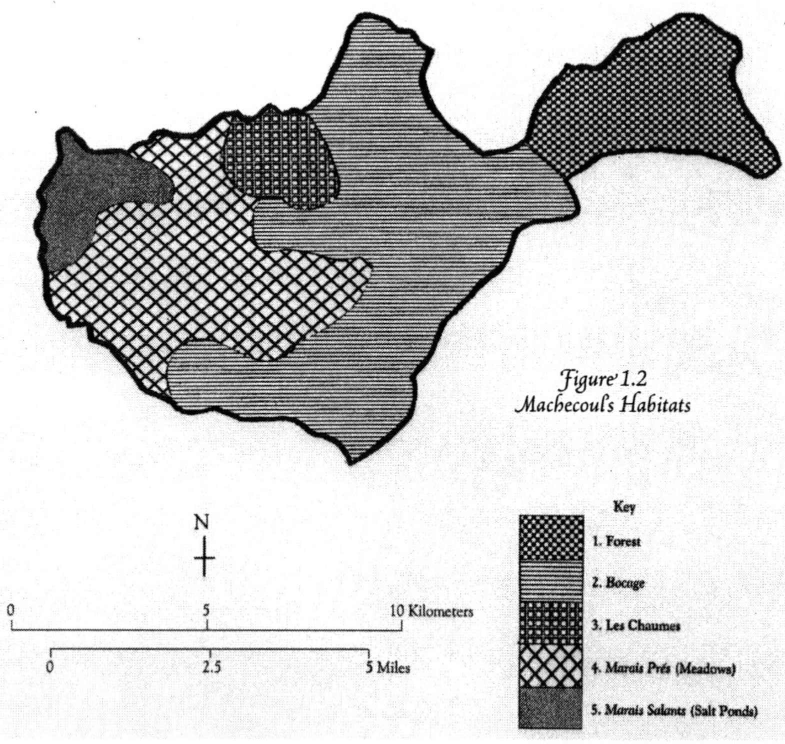

Figure 1.2
Machecoul's Habitats

of the insurgency have often seen the *bocage* as especially conducive to counterrevolution, particularly because its habitat provided such meager economic opportunities.

Due to such interpretative emphasis, many have falsely assumed that the entire area where the insurgency erupted was dominated by the hedge-rowed fields of the *bocage*. The reality, though, is that many environmental variations marked the zone of popular counterrevolution. Machecoul perfectly illustrates this variety, and the commune's diversity underscores the problem of attributing the rebellion to a specific type of habitat in western France. Whether the habitats of the *marais*, forest, and *bocage* inherently fomented revolt remains unclear, but what seems certain is that they all became formidable barriers to outsiders once the insurgency began. Indeed, these habitats explain why rebel forces experienced initial success in the region, including the prolonged occupation of Machecoul while the massacres took place. In trying to reclaim the region, republican troops and state officials encountered not only a rebel army entrenched in its own backyard, but also an environment deterring formal military movement and coordination.[25]

Where Town and Country Converged

The varied habitats in and around Machecoul were the source for a diversified economy in the 1770s and 1780s. No doubt the most important economic activity in the commune was agriculture, particularly the growing of wheat.[26] But in the late eighteenth century the *bocage* of southern Brittany and northern Poitou was also home to crops aside from wheat, including rye, buckwheat, millet, peas, cabbages, beets, potatoes (beginning in about 1770), and grapes.[27] Given the mostly poor soils of the region, however, the cultivation of crops like wheat and rye also had to be supplemented by another endeavor: the raising of some kind of stock. The meadows in the marsh, along with many fields in the *bocage*, served as pastures for herds of work cattle, beef cattle, milk cows, horses, pigs, sheep, and smaller livestock.[28] In the late eighteenth century a tenant farmer in the region typically had anywhere from fifteen to sixty head of cattle raised for either work, beef, dairy, or some combination of these. Machecoul's part of the *marais* also supported horse raising.[29] Almost all affluent landowners in the *marais* possessed a team of horses, and since there were no trees in the marsh, horse manure sufficed as a combustible fuel for peasants residing there.[30] Various kinds of small livestock, above all pigs, raised in the meadows of the marsh were also fundamental to the local economy.[31]

Another economic activity associated with the *marais* during the late Old Regime, namely that closest to the ocean, was the production of salt. The *sauniers*, or peasant salt-makers, dug out large rectangular basins along the coast, gave them foundations of insoluble clay, and then partitioned them off into small compartments. These ponds received ocean water through canals originating at the Atlantic Ocean during the rainy season from October to April. In May the salt-makers blocked off the canals and the salt water in the ponds evaporated through the summer. By September, if the weather cooperated, the water evaporated in the ponds, leaving plates of salt that were broken up, processed, and sold.[32] The fields and forests within the commune were integral to the local economy in other ways as well during the late Old Regime. Brushwood

from the forest provided local workshops and households with much
needed firewood, and the larger trees were sought for carpentry and
woodwork. Woodcutters would work in the forest, supplying material
for the town's coopers, shoemakers, and lathe makers, among others.[33]
Many fields on the outskirts of town were also home to the production
of flour at mills powered by the wind. In 1789, according to one account,
approximately forty-eight mills were situated around the town.[34]

But milling was only one of a myriad of professions or crafts practiced
in or around the town during the late Old Regime. While few records
from the town before the Revolution exist, a census of Year IV (1796-
97) shows that Machecoul was probably a longtime center of economic
transaction for the greater area. The professions listed on this census
reveal that the fulfillment of the most basic human needs—food, shelter, and clothing—was the source of most commerce conducted in the
town.[35] The census also suggests that the town was largely self-sufficient
at the end of the eighteenth century, and there is no reason to believe
that the situation was any different just before the Revolution.

Yet there was also much interchange between Machecoul and the
outside world at that time. Indeed, the town was the site of a number
of *foires*, or market fairs, during the year, which likely drew large numbers of inhabitants throughout the region. If these Old-Regime fairs
resembled those held in the nineteenth century, a wide choice of goods
and products, such as clothing, cattle, tools, and domestic utensils,
would have been bought and sold.[36] But these fairs aside, fluctuations in
recorded baptisms, marriages, and deaths in Machecoul during the late
Old Regime suggest that much regional migration occurred, particularly
within a thirty-kilometer radius around the town. Marriages between
a Machecoulais and someone from a peripheral town or village were
common—yet another confirmation of economic interaction between
the town and surrounding communities.[37]

While Machecoul's economy during the late Old Regime was heavily
dependent on agricultural production from the surrounding countryside,
urban commerce was also integral to its economic life. Not unlike the
municipality's habitats, therefore, no one economic activity defined the
town; it was a hub of both agrarian production and artisanal output. How
might this fact relate to the violence that erupted in 1793? Competing
economic interests of town and countryside came together at Machecoul,

quite likely spawning tensions and some hostility between inhabitants. But at the same time, the merging of urban and rural economic activities allowed many—in town and countryside alike—to benefit materially and in some cases even prosper; more than a few gained from such interaction. In other words, the town's economy during the late Old Regime reveals as much about commercial collaboration as it does about conflict. True, some inhabitants did better than others economically, but this was nothing new for Machecoul in the 1770s and 1780s, or in this vein for any other small town in France during the same period.[38]

Being Machecoulais

Determining how many Machecoulais were a part of this thriving and diverse economy during the late Old Regime is an inexact science, largely due to the absence of reliable records from the period. Still, most extrapolations have put the municipality's population at about four thousand inhabitants in 1789.[39] While it is true that the population in France was rapidly growing in the 1770s and 1780s, due in part to a decline in mortality, there is little indication that Machecoul's own population was significantly increasing as the Revolution approached. Like much of France, mortality in the municipality was likely decreasing, yet this trend may have been offset by less fertility as well as migration, meaning that the total number of inhabitants hardly changed. Despite the apparent demographic stability, though, complaints about high unemployment and increasing indigence in the town during the 1780s were on the rise—as they seemed to be throughout much of France.[40]

Where did these four thousand Machecoulais live? A typical community in the *bocage* during the Old Regime consisted of a small town, surrounded by secondary villages, numerous hamlets, and, finally, isolated farms.[41] In most respects the settlement of Machecoul in the nineteenth century, as seen in Figure 1.3, fits this pattern, and there is little reason to suspect that the settlement before the Revolution was altogether different.[42] Town officials frequently referred to their community as a small *ville*, but it probably closely resembled more what was called a *bourg*: typically a small market town where one could find not only artisans and shops, but also liberal professionals like doctors, notaries, or schoolteachers.[43] Although the urbanized center was the most demo-

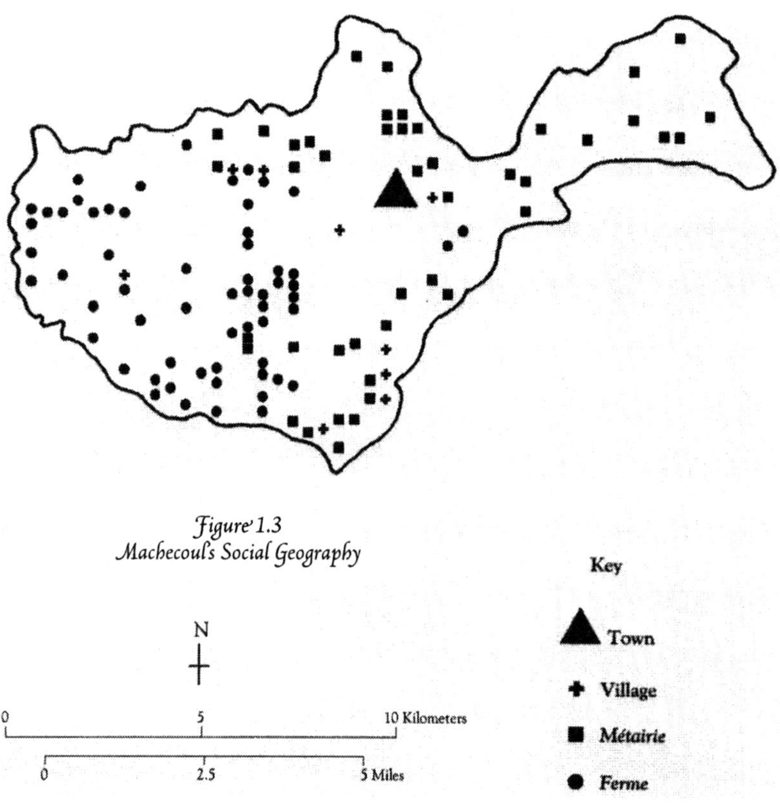

Figure 1.3
Machecoul's Social Geography

graphically dense part of the commune (with approximately half of the population situated there), the Machecoulais were likely scattered over the municipal territory during the late Old Regime.[44] Most population centers immediately outside the town itself were quite small, and were called villages, or *faubourgs*, even though they more resembled what in most of France were called hamlets.[45] The remaining settlements in the municipality, little more than isolated farmsteads, were either very small hamlets or what was called a *ferme* or *métairie*—the latter two being the residence of a tenant farmer who rented the land that he worked.[46] Before the Revolution such tenant farms or small hamlets frequently had one, two, or three households, yet the number of inhabitants was rather substantial. In one *métairie*, for example, there existed two houses, with five separate couples living there.[47]

The population's location is indicative of Machecoul's socioprofessional organization during the late Old Regime, which was—as throughout much of rural France at that time—bottom-heavy.[48] At the top of this formation were the few (about 4 percent of the local population) *propriétaires fonciers*, *grands propriétaires*, and *rentiers*, the large landowners or individuals solely living off their property rents.[49] In the eighteenth century many landowners near the town were of noble origin, although such nobility might have been recently acquired. They usually possessed vast tracts of land, that is, the great bulk of the *métairies* in the *bocage* and the *fermes* found on the plain or in the *marais*. Prestige among the ranks of landowners in and around Machecoul was based not so much on the origin of one's fortune, but on the length of residence in the area.[50]

These large landowners were followed by, though often indistinguishable from, an urban elite, which made up about 8 percent of Machecoul's population during the Old Regime.[51] This elite included, first of all, administrative officials and petty bureaucrats: tax collectors, judges, inspectors, scribes, prosecuting attorneys, and bailiffs. Also a part of this grouping were the so-called liberal professionals: notaries, lawyers, doctors, veterinarians, teachers, and engineers. These were joined by those in the upper echelon of commerce: larger retail merchants or wholesale merchants and an occasional entrepreneur. Social ascent was possible and indeed was accomplished by those within this category in a variety of ways. But to assure real prestige among the urban elite in western France, one's profession had to be accompanied by a certain degree of landownership; control of two or three *métairies* guaranteed respectability, permitted one the right to hunt, and during the late Old Regime provided a small share of agricultural yields produced during the year.[52]

The minor nobles and the urban elite of Machecoul deserve special attention because of their pivotal role in this story. They exercised a disproportionate amount of influence over the town, and as such figured large in developments leading up to the massacres. But even more significantly, many are counted among the murdered in the spring of 1793, and a few among those who murdered as well. Still, little is known about them due to the lack of documentation. From what few records do remain, their professions are their only identity. François-

Michel Robin, for example, was a lawyer and a *sénéchal*, that is, a civil and criminal judge for the Duchy of Retz. Alexandre Plantier declared himself a doctor in medicine. Réné Caviezel, Pierre Claude Fleury, and Jean Seigneuret were lawyers in the Parlement of Brittany, the powerful provincial court located in Rennes. François Le Bedesque was a retired infantry officer, and Jacques Garreau was an artillery officer for the coast guard. Pierre-Mathurin Couédélo identified himself as a notary and a prosecuting attorney. Pierre Blanchard, Jacques Vrignaud, and Hyacinthe Musset were all self-proclaimed surgeons. Etienne Gaschignard was the principal of the town's secondary school. François Charruau and Jean Beziau were scribes. These fourteen individuals were but a small sampling of the urban elite, but a disproportionate number of them (nine) can be verified as victims in the Machecoul massacres.[53]

Below the urban elite stood small shopkeepers and artisans who engaged in a trade or offered their services to the commune's inhabitants. These small-time merchants and workers, making up a little less than 40 percent of the town's population, were responsible for the "preindustrial" labor like weaving, spinning, and milling. They frequently provided services associated with agriculture, as in the case of gelders, saddlers, and coopers, or provided the most customary kinds of products, including those sold by butchers, bakers, and shoemakers.[54] Occasionally a few of these artisans' names (most likely shopkeepers) also appear in political correspondence: André Charriau, a tanner; François Bret, a saddler; Louis Maulouin, a tinner; Marie Coignard, a tailor. A significant number of them, moreover, show up on lists of those murdered in the massacres as well: the tailor François Chiffoleau; the cooper Charles Fouquet; the glazer René Fortineau; the butcher Henry Reignier; and the carpenter Augustin Villeneuve.[55]

The largest socioprofessional grouping—about one of every two inhabitants in and around the town—included those living in the countryside and most who labored in the agricultural sector. They were agriculturalists by trade but were most often called *paysans*: peasants. Cleavages within this grouping were based more on a relationship to the land than to income. Those owning even a little land, no matter how poor, were called *propriétaires*. Thus it followed that the first among this group would be the small landowners or *petites propriétaires*, who worked their own holdings and were commonly found in areas where the agricultural land was extremely bountiful (which is why there were very few in the *bocage*).[56] The great majority of agriculturalists in and around the town were tenant farmers, but distinctions were made between them—at least by census takers, notaries, and other officials in the eighteenth and nineteenth centuries. The *cultivateurs* and the *laboureurs* usually held and worked more land and thus were required to own several teams of oxen and to employ an appropriate number of hired hands to work the soil. The *fermiers* and *métayers*, on the other hand, were "middling tenants" who cultivated perhaps twenty to thirty hectares, usually with fewer oxen than the *cultivateurs* and *laboureurs*. Renting even smaller portions of property were the *bordiers*, virtually all of whom worked the fields with poor soil in the *bocage*. At the bottom of the agricultural category stood a number of workers whose lives bordered on destitution. These included the *journaliers* and *domestiques*, temporary workers hired by tenant farmers, and the *laboureurs à bras*, day laborers.[57]

The lopsided socioprofessional structure at Machecoul was ascribable to the landownership scheme that dominated western France during the late eighteenth century, in which only a few actually owned land and rented it out to a large number of tenants. But this was far from a case of "nobles" looking over their "peasants"; in reality it was more complicated, especially once the urban elite began to acquire land in the area. As early as 1750 a transfer of wealth and property was occurring between nobles and this urban elite. Merchants, investors, and entrepreneurs at Nantes became quite wealthy through transatlantic trade (including that of slaves) and, armed with this wealth, bought land in the countryside around Nantes. Indeed, at the end of the Old Regime, according to one count, the urban elite was actually ahead of nobles in landownership in the Machecoul region.[58]

When taken together, Machecoul's demography, settlement, socioprofessional organization, and landownership on the eve of the Revolution were typical for much of France or, at the very least, a wide region of the west.[59] There was no marked difference between its settlement pattern and those of most other small towns in the west, and the same can be said of its socioprofessional organization. Perhaps the most unexceptional development was that the urban elite was becoming increasingly indistinguishable from the nobility, at least as far as economic status was concerned. Indeed, instead of dividing the few nobles from members of the urban elite, it would make more sense to describe all of them as Machecoul's "notables."[60] But if the town appeared typical in most respects, it is then all the more puzzling why horrifying massacres would take place there only a few years later, instead of another French town of its size. Certainly there must be more to the story than the social factors reviewed here.

A Rising Political Angst

As unremarkable as the town's social or economic structure may have been, Machecoul saw more political unrest than likely was the case in such communities during the late Old Regime. In the 1770s and 1780s most of what would become the Machecoul municipality was within the boundaries of the Comté de Nantes, a jurisdiction drawn up by Breton nobles in the eleventh century. The Nantes *comté* was further subdivided into two duchies and five baronies, each of which possessed the right to be represented at the Estates of Brittany, the local provincial assembly. The town was within the Duchy of Retz and in fact was the old capital of this territory comprising the southwest corner of the Nantes *comté*. Administratively, the community was part of the Old Regime's Generality of Brittany, led by the *intendant* Germain-François Dufaure de Rochefort in 1789. The *intendant* in turn was assisted by twelve subdelegates within the Nantes region, including one at Machecoul.[61] The town's own political status was complicated, however, by a division of authority and jurisdiction within the area that became the municipality. One section of the future commune belonged to an unusual political arrangement called *les marches communes du Poitou et de Bretagne*. Figure 1.4 shows the territory that comprised the *marches*, revealing that the southern edge of the community, specifically all land south of the Falleron River, belonged to this unique administrative entity. During the late Old Regime the territory was granted its own officers, who represented and defended the interests of the *marches* communities to *intendants* and their underlings in the provinces of Poitou and Brittany. Perhaps the most significant aspect of this arrangement was that the inhabitants of the *marches* were exempt from the old indirect taxes, which gave them a financial advantage over inhabitants beyond

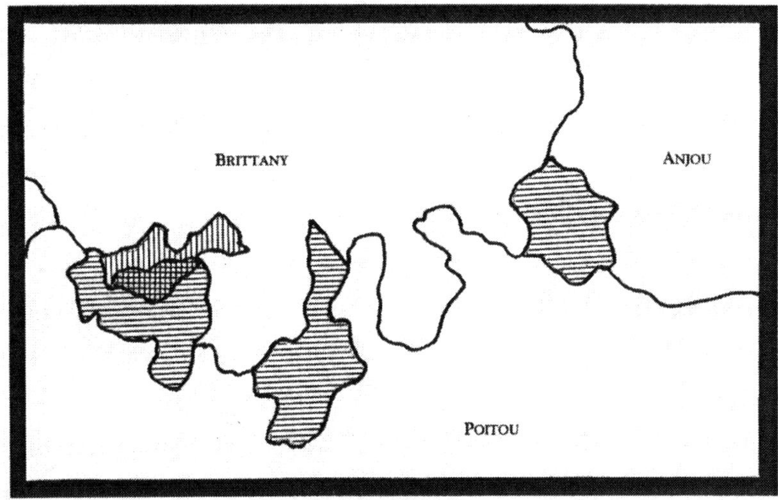

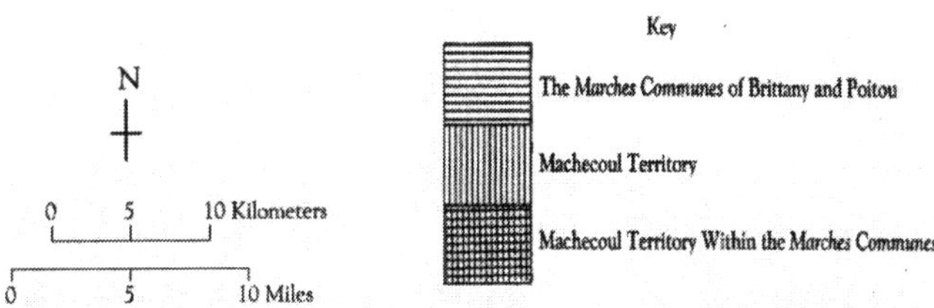

Figure 1.4
Machecoul and the Marches Communes of Brittany and Poitou

the *marches*. These economic and political privileges of the *marches* were confirmed as late as 1777, when Louis XVI outlined them in a royal order.[62] Such an arrangement was likely a source of political tension within the community, in part because officials in the town had little political control over the *marches*.

But the *marches* were only one of several sources of political discontent in and around the town during the late Old Regime. As in much of France, local institutions like the Estates of Brittany, the Breton Parlement, and the Chamber des Comptes at Nantes increasingly challenged the power of the *intendant*. The conflict between the royal administration and provincial authorities became apparent in 1787, for instance, when the Nantes municipality, supported by Breton provincial institutions, opposed the royal decision to name a subdelegate of the *intendant* as the new mayor of the city. Although Machecoul was not directly involved in this dispute, no doubt sides were being taken throughout Brittany over this issue. One other political matter, though, was even more pressing for the town. The marquis de Brie-Serrant purchased the Duchy of Retz in 1764, but shortly thereafter he sold large tracts to new nobles and members of the urban elite. The marquis sold so much land that, in 1787, the duchy lost its seat in the Estates of Brittany, meaning that the town was no longer represented in this powerful provincial institution.[63]

By the end of the Old Regime, therefore, most notables at Machecoul found themselves embroiled in political disputes on several levels. These struggles involved, among other things, overlapping local authority, rights and privileges, turf wars between the crown and provincial authorities, and the town's representation in provincial assemblies. But here again, such disagreements were not necessarily remarkable in Old-Regime France; they were ubiquitous, and thus the town's purely political conflicts seem comparatively mundane.[64] What sometimes made these disputes more acute, however, was that they coincided with differing theological and ecclesiastical perspectives—making local religious institutions and personnel sources of contention and thereby exacerbating political conflict.[65] Whether this was true for Machecoul will be addressed later, but in any case the close tie between political and religious politics during the late Old Regime should not be overlooked, especially since the link had far-reaching ramifications once the Revolution began.

As significant as these political squabbles were, they probably had little effect on the rest of Machecoul's milieu—at least not in the short term. There likely continued to be a stable but often migratory population, economic winners and losers from both town and countryside, a bottom-heavy socioprofessional organization, and significant political discontent, complete with the resentment and passive aggression that all these matters generated. Such a scenario may strike many today as somewhat dire, yet conditions like these were all too common throughout many regions of France in 1789.[66] Indeed, on the face of it Machecoul seemed no more predisposed to murderous rage than any other small town at that time. What seems just as significant is what one fails to find here; undoubtedly there had to be more to a town that exploded in unparalleled violence in 1793.

The inability to identify prerevolutionary geographic, socioeconomic, or political roots for the Machecoul massacres helps explain why the origins of the Vendéen insurgency have been so fiercely debated. In keeping with the character of that debate, this chapter has mostly muddied the waters, raising at least as many questions as it has answered. To be sure, one can understand how certain conditions in the 1770s and 1780s could generate or perhaps accommodate conflict. But no glaring geographic, political, social, or economic factor can be seen as a motivator for murder. If anything, the lack of an obvious causal condition suggests that religion—the other factor often cited as a basis for the violence—merits much more consideration in this story.

This is not to claim, however, that a clear line separated the town's religious character from the attributes described here. On the contrary, such an artificial dichotomy has existed only in the minds of scholars. Factors like social order and political structures likely determined how religion manifested itself within the town, especially since politics and religion were closely aligned during the late Old Regime.[67] Similarly, religious beliefs and institutions inevitably shaped the community's collective life, particularly given the Catholic Church's political and cultural pull at that time.[68] In all likelihood, the relationship between Machecoul's milieu and its specific religious structures, beliefs, and practices was entirely reciprocal during the late Old Regime.[69] But even so, the town's general characteristics can only *imply* that religion somehow mattered in the massacres; it cannot establish how or why this was the case. This chapter, therefore, has set the stage for the rest of the story. Readers may now know "where the spirit dwelt," but what that spirit was remains to be seen.

Notes

[1] Martin, *Révolution et contre-révolution*, 45.

[2] Quoted in Claude Petitfrère, "Les causes de la Vendée et de la Chouannerie: Essai d'historiographie," *Annales de Bretagne et des pays de l'Ouest* 84 (1977): 76-77.

[3] Quoted in Petitfrère, "Les Causes," 80. For more on Michelet's perspective on the Vendéen insurgency, see, *Histoire de la Révolution française*, 2 vols. (Paris; Gallimard, 1962).

[4]Charles-Louis Chassin, *La préparation de la guerre de Vendée 1789-1793*, 3 vols. (Paris: Imprimerie Paul Dupont, 1892); Petitfère, "Les Causes," 81.

[5]Quoted in Petitfrère, "Les Causes," 83.

[6]Ibid., 86.

[7]Ibid., 89-92.

[8]Tilly, *The Vendée*.

[9]Bois, *Paysans de l'Ouest*, 292-94.

[10]Faucheux, *L'insurrection vendéene*, 369-83.

[11]See, for example, Jean-Clément Martin, "La religion et les débuts des insurrections de l'Ouest (mars-avril 1793)," in Martin, ed., *Religion et Révolution: Colloque de Saint-Florent-le-Vieil* (Paris: Anthropos, 1994), 77; and *La Vendée et la France* (Paris: Editions du Seuil, 1989), 85-87; Roger Dupuy, "Ignorance, fanatisme et contre-révolution," in François Lebrun and Dupuy, eds., *Les résistances à la Révolution: actes du colloque de Rennes* (Paris: Imago, 1987), 37-42; Claude Petitfrère, "The Origins of the Civil War in the Vendée," in Jones, *The French Revolution in Social and Political Perspective*, 340-58.

[12]Sutherland, *The Chouans*, 218.

[13]Furet and Ozouf, *A Critical Dictionary*, 173.

[14]Jean Renard, *Les évolutions contemporaines de la vie rurale dans la région nantaise: Loire-Atlantique, bocages vendéens, mauges* (Les Sables-d'Olonne: Éditions Le Cercle d'Or, 1975), 111.

[15]ADLA, 1 Fi. Loire-Atlantique 18 Pl. XXVI. Canton de Machecoul, 1850. Map of Pinson and de Tollenare.

[16]Michel Le Mené and Marie-Hélène Santrot, eds., *Cahiers des plaintes et doléances de Loire-Atlantique 1789: Texte intégral et commentaires*, 4 vols. (Nantes: Édition du Conseil Général de Loire-Atlantique, 1989), 2: 749-50. Marcel Launay describes the nineteenth-century Loire-Atlantique as "une terre de contrastes." See Launay, *Le diocèse de Nantes sous le second empire: Monseigneur Jaquemet, 1849-1869*, 2 vols. (Nantes: CID Éditions, 1982), 1: 23.

[17]René Bourrigaud, *Le développement agricole au 19e siècle en Loire-Atlantique* (Nantes: Centre d'Historie du Travail de Nantes, 1994), 24.

[18]Danielle Naud, "Les structures familiales en Vendée au XIXe siècle," Mémoire de maîtrise, directed by Y. Durand (Nantes: Université de Nantes, 1976), 23-24; Bourrigaud, 21-25.

[19]Le Mené and Santrot, 2:750.

[20]Renard, 4.

[21]J.-B. Huet, *Recherches économiques et statistiques sur le département de la Loire-Inférieure* (Nantes: M. Malassis, An XI [1802-03]), 88.

[22]Huet, *Recherches*, 13; Le Mené and Santrot, 2: 749-50.

[23]Jean Renard calls the region "un pays d'arbres sans forêts," a country of trees without forests. See Renard, 4; Tilly, *The Vendée*, 28, 83-85.

[24]Naud, "Les structures," 25.

[25] Naud, 18-19. The marquise de la Rochejacquelein described the roads in the *bocage* as "bourbeux en hiver et raboteux en été," in Launay, *Le diocèse de Nantes sous le second empire*, 34. Fernand Braudel also emphasizes the social and economic implications of the roads in the *bocage*. See Braudel's *The Identity of France*, trans. Siân Reynolds, 4 vols. (New York: Harper Perennial, 1993), 1: 136-37. Claude Petitfrère makes this precise point in "The Origins of the Civil War in the Vendée," in Jones, *The French Revolution in Social and Political Perspective*, 357.

[26]J.-B. Huet, *Statistiques du département de la Loire-Inférieure* (Paris: Imprimerie des Sourd-Muets, an X [1801-1802]), 1.

[27]Yves Chéneau, *Les marches communes du Poitou et de Bretagne et leurs paroisses au XVIIIe siècle* (Cholet: Imprimerie Farré et Freulon, 1950), 26.

[28]Tilly, *The Vendée*, 114-15.

[29]Le Mené and Santrot, 1: 107.

[30]Naud, 24.

[31]Chéneau, *Les marches communes*, 26.

[32]Naud, 23. Le Mené and Santrot, 1: 108-09. There was no salt tax, the *gabelle*, assessed in Brittany and the price of salt was relatively low there, probably because the mineral was so readily available. However, most provinces surrounding Brittany, including Normandy, Maine, and Anjou, had a very high salt tax, which deterred Bretons from legally exporting it and encouraged salt smuggling. See Marcel Marion, *Dictionnaire des institutions de la France aux XVIIe et XVIIIe siècles* (Paris: Éditions A. and J. Picard and Compagnie, 1969), 247-50.

[33]Huet, *Recherches économiques*, 88.

[34]Le Mené and Santrot, 2: 756; 4: 1642.

[35]Fabien Mille, "La population de Machecoul pendant la Révolution d'après l'état civil," mémoire de maîtrise, directed by J.-C. Martin (Nantes: Université de Nantes, 1997), 44. The variety of artisans listed in 1796-97 census correspond well to that in the censuses of the nineteenth century. See ADLA, 2 Mi 507 R1, 2, and 3. Censuses of 1836, 1861, and 1911.

[36]Eugen Weber, *Peasants into Frenchman: The Modernization of Rural France, 1870-1914* (Stanford: Stanford University Press, 1976), 407; Bourrigaud, 94.

[37]Mille, 34-37.

[38]George Huppert shows that urban-rural hostility was common throughout the early modern period, not just in France but throughout Europe. See Huppert, *After the Black Death: A Social History of Early Modern Europe*, 2d ed. (Bloomington: Indiana University Press, 1998), 14-18.

[39]Mille, 38-40.

[40]Mille, 30-33. The *recteur* at Machecoul complained to provincial authorities shortly before the Revolution that "it would be desirable that there be more work and that someone established manufacturing. There would be less poverty and thus better morality." See Jean Aoustin, "Répurcussions démographiques et économiques de la Révolution dans la région insurgée de Machecoul," Mémoire principal pour le diplome d'études supérieures d'histoire, directed by J. Bois (Nantes: Université de Nantes, 1966), 35. Arthur Young echoed these complaints as he traveled France just before the Revolution. See Young, *Travels in France during the Years 1787, 1788, and 1789*, ed. Constantia Maxwell (Cambridge: Cambridge University Press, 1950).

[41]Tilly, *The Vendée*, 85.

[42]The same names of *fermes* and *métairies*, for example, appear both in the parish registries from the Old Regime and the population records from the nineteenth century.

[43]Braudel, 1: 162-66.

[44]Mille, 41; Volume Annex, 117.

[45]Ibid., 1: 130, 135, 137, 180; ADLA, 1 M 2 Mi 507 R1. Census of 1846.

[46]By the late eighteenth century the terms of *fermier* (tenant) and *métayer* (sharecropper) had become all but interchangeable in most of western France, since most *métayers* paid their rent with money and not with crop shares. See Bois, *Paysans*, 184-89; Tilly, *The Vendée*, 72, 123.

[47]Mille, 41-42. Censuses from the nineteenth century indicate generally the same pattern. The 1846 census listed five *métairies* in one sector of the commune that had a total of six houses (*maisons*) along with six households (*ménages*) at these *métairies*, and a total of sixty-two inhabitants. See ADLA, 2 Mi 507 R1. Census of 1846.

[48]Naud, 98. A small number of Machecoulais, though, did not fit into any category mentioned here. Guards, *gendarmes*, musicians, sacristans, fishers, coach workers, students, and soldiers were among those who made a living yet were not wealthy enough to be considered among the urban elite nor had a specific skill or performed a service that would deem them artisans. See Tilly, *The Vendée*, 348-49. For a broad perspective on rural society just before the Revolution, see Annie Moulin, *Peasantry and Society in*

France since 1789, trans. M. C. and M. F. Cleary (New York: Cambridge University Press, 1991), 4-23.

[49]The percentages provided here are taken from Aoustin, "Répurcussions," Table 45.

[50]This is why, in part, a sizable number of landowners in the region during the eighteenth century were not absentee landlords who lived in Nantes or in Paris, but instead residents of extravagant estates located on the land that they owned. As residents, landowners frequently assumed prominent political positions or became patrons of charitable institutions like those connected with the town's parishes, which served to sustain the deferential treatment that they expected and received from their inferiors in rural society. See Renard, 167; Tilly, *The Vendée*, 119-22.

[51]I consciously choose not to use the term, bourgeoisie, here, in part because it has become thoroughly amorphous, and in part because it is loaded with Marxist connotations, many of which have been proven to ill fit French society during the late Old Regime. See Alfred Cobban, *The Social Interpretation of the French Revolution* (Cambridge: Cambridge University Press, 1964).

[52]Renard, *Les évolutions*, 167. Usually, each town in this part of France was dominated by three or four eminent families, whose impressive residences were often surrounded by yards and were situated on the town's main street. But because Machecoul was one of the larger towns in the region, it probably had a larger urban elite than neighboring communities. See Naud, "Les structures," 100.

[53]Le Mené and Santrot, 2: 749, 761; Martin, *Révolution et contre-révolution*, 47-50.

[54]Naud, 101; Mille, 43-44.

[55]Le Mené and Santrot, 2: 749, 761; Martin, *Révolution et contre-révolution*, 47-50.

[56]Renard, 167.

[57]Tilly, *The Vendée*, 71-73; Naud, 101.

[58] Renard, 171.

[59]McPhee, *The French Revolution*, 6-9. Among the better local studies about French society before the Revolution are Thomas Sheppard, *Loumarin in the Eighteenth Century: A Study of a French Village* (Baltimore: Johns Hopkins University Press, 1971); and Patrice Higonnet, *Pont-de-Montvert: Social Structure and Politics in a French Village, 1700-1914* (Cambridge, Mass: Harvard University Press, 1971).

[60]Fabien Mille points out that many times a member of the wealthy urban elite was referred to in parish registries as "noble homme." See Mille, 45. This point is most powerfully made in George V. Taylor, "Noncapitalist Wealth

and the Origins of the French Revolution," *American Historical Review* 72 (1967), 469-502.

[61]Le Mené and Santrot, 1: 15-16.

[62]AN, K 1151. *Arrêt* of the Council of State of the King, 24 June 1777.

[63]Le Mené and Santrot, 1: 16-18, 25-26.

[64]For more on the most salient political conflicts of the late Old Regime, see Doyle, *The Oxford History*, 36-43.

[65]Dale Van Kley makes this point when he discusses the transition from religious to ideological "parties" during the late Old Regime. See Van Kley, *The Religious Origins*, 249-302.

[66]For a comprehensive description of poverty in both towns and the countryside before the Revolution, see Doyle, *The Oxford History*, 14-22.

[67]Emile Durkheim first articulated the notion that society shapes conceptions of the sacred. See Durkheim, *The Elementary Forms of Religious Life*, trans. Karen E. Fields (New York: The Free Press, 1995).

[68]That religion can broadly define a society is the guiding force behind Max Weber's "Protestant Work Ethic." See Weber, *The Protestant Ethic and the Spirit of Capitalism*, trans. Talcott Parsons (New York: Scribner, 1957). For an elucidation of Weber's argument, see Marcel Gauchet, *The Disenchantment of the World: A Political History of Religion*, trans. Oscar Burse (Princeton: Princeton University Press, 1997).

[69]To understand how both Durkheim and Weber's ideas can be applied to French religious and political history, see Van Kley, *The Religious Origins of the French Revolution*, 10.

2

The Good Old Days

The story now turns to religion, but first in an encounter with fiction more than fact. With the 1867 Lenten season approaching, Monseigneur Alexandre Jaquemet wanted to reinforce the faith of flock. Like many priests at that time, the bishop of Nantes complained about the depravity of his own day and recalled a better time: an "autrefois." Perhaps the best English equivalent for this term is "the good old days," but in this case it meant the supposedly idyllic period before the French Revolution when, according to the bishop, belief in Christ in his diocese had been universal and obedience to the Church had gone unquestioned. Aware that his people's historical memory was strong, Monseigneur Jaquemet invoked a mythic *autrefois* in an effort to make Catholics in his diocese turn away from the vices of the present and embrace the virtues of the past. He commanded his flock "to rebuild all those crosses to which the Christian traveler happily bowed in the *autrefois* on your roads, on your hills, at the entrance of towns and *bourgs*, in your fields and on a great number of your homesteads."[1] Though his sentiments were no doubt sincere, Jaquemet's perception of the past was more wishful thinking than good history. The Catholic Church enjoyed great influence in western France during the late Old Regime, yet in no way did all Catholics support this political and cultural potency, much less were swayed by it. Indeed, many in this rural society frequently resented the Church and were critical of its clergy. And though religious participation was pervasive in the diocese of Nantes before the Revolution, the Church's attempt to instill the beliefs, values, and rites emanating from the Catholic Reformation met with only partial success. Truth be told, in "the good old days" Catholic adherence among the faithful was mediocre at best.

Machecoul was emblematic of such mediocrity, as this chapter will show. During the twilight of the Old Regime, the community had a convoluted religious climate; it possessed an impressive array of Catholic institutions and numerous Church personnel, yet many within the town refused to subscribe to the beliefs and teachings endorsed by the local clergy. Most significantly, pronounced disagreements over the meaning of Christianity and the role of the Church were present within the community, above all among an educated elite. In other words, during the 1770s and 1780s Machecoul had not one religious culture, but several. While not suggesting that these cultural disparities, in and of themselves, led to the 1793 massacres, this chapter proposes that religious differences during the late Old Regime provided the fertile ground for a more acute divide that arose in the town after 1789. Few may have realized it at the time, but Machecoul's precarious religious situation—an elite religious culture at odds with a local clergy that exercised institutional dominance—made for an extremely volatile mix. Fewer still saw that this unstable atmosphere was about to explode.

A Turbulent Backdrop

The religious volatility at Machecoul was largely attributable to the broader political and theological struggles in France during the Old Regime. As late as the 1770s and 1780s the Catholic Church in France was still feeling the effects of religious turbulence dating as far back as the sixteenth century. When the Council of Trent met from 1545 to 1563, it reinforced those aspects of Catholicism most attacked by Protestant reformers, specifically through reaffirming the Church's seven sacraments as the only conduits for salvation and underscoring the central role of the priesthood. The council also called for an ecclesiastical reorganization that would enable the Church to fight off the Protestant challenge more effectively. It concluded that the best means for achieving the council's doctrinal and organizational goals was to strengthen the authority of the pope and to establish more educational institutions for both clergy and laity. Several religious orders, most notably the nascent Society of Jesus, dedicated themselves to fulfilling the council's mandates. Renowned for their allegiance to the pope, the Jesuits came to France amid the political turmoil of the Wars of Religion, yet quickly became influential at the highest political echelons.

But the Jesuit presence in France quickly produced a backlash, particularly among Catholics who favored a "Gallican" Church—one that remained somewhat independent and autonomous from the bishop of Rome.[2] There is no single definition of Gallicanism because those who sought a thoroughly independent French church were often divided over who should hold ecclesiastical power within the kingdom. Some proponents of Gallicanism sought greater ecclesiastical control by the king, others wanted the French episcopacy to have more authority, while others wanted the lay *parlements* to possess such power.[3] Still others, most notably Edmond Richer, contended that the most important leaders of the French church were parish priests, and that bishops and other high church officials were no more than representatives of the priestly will.[4] As numerous and powerful as Gallicanists were, though, the divisions among them allowed the Jesuits to make significant inroads in implementing Trent's reforms during the seventeenth century.

Yet another reason for the growth of Jesuit influence in the 1600s was that it complemented the French monarchy's simultaneous quest to gain greater political control over the kingdom. Despite this, ecclesiastical and popular opposition to the Society of Jesus continued to mount, eventually gaining a theological coherence through the writings of Cornelius Jansen, a bishop from the Netherlands and fierce Jesuit opponent. Jansen accused the Jesuits of moral laxity and overemphasizing the role of free will in Christian salvation; he championed what the Society of Jesus purportedly lacked—moral purity and a recognition of the supreme role of God's grace in human salvation. For their part, the Jesuits called these "Jansensists" crypto-Calvinists, not only because of their alleged support of predestination but also because their insistence on moral purity supposedly denigrated the role of the sacraments and, by extension, that of the priesthood. But probably the most critical issue dividing the Jansenists from the Jesuits was political and ecclesiastical centralization in France. Opposing the consolidation of ecclesiastical and political power long advocated by Jesuits, the Jansenists became a thorn in the side of an increasingly centralized monarchy by the beginning of the eighteenth century.[5]

That is why in 1713, at the urging of Louis XIV, Pope Clement XI intervened in the dispute by issuing the bull *Unigenitus*, which condemned positions taken by Jansen and his supporters. But by that point Jansenism had been firmly implanted among both the clergy and influential members of the laity, thus assuring that a long struggle would ensue among Catholics throughout France. The fight indeed unfolded over several decades, ultimately becoming injurious not only to the church but to the monarchy as well.[6] In the 1750s the Jansenist-Jesuit divide became as much a political showdown as an ecclesiastical schism, often pitting the Jesuit-friendly monarchy against the pro-Jansenist, provincial *parlements*. Ultimately, the *parlements* succeeded in expelling the Jesuits from France by 1763, yet with its primary goal achieved, Jansensim quickly dissipated as a coherent movement.[7]

The effects of the Jansensist-Jesuit fight were highly evident in France in the 1770s and 1780s, both within the Catholic Church and beyond it. Many ecclesiastical issues around which this struggle centered—including the implementation of Tridentine reform, the establishment and control of social institutions, and the role of papal, episcopal, and priestly authority—continued as contentious matters within the church. To a degree this struggle resulted in a highly varied ecclesiastical geography in France during the late Old Regime. Some regions possessed a large cadre of secular and regular clergy, numerous institutions like schools and hospitals, and in some cases a more devoted and active laity. Other regions, however, had very few priests and members of religious orders, a small number of Catholic institutions, and often more spiritual indifference among the people. But even within this varied geography, Catholic officials—to say nothing of the educated laity—were keenly divided over how the church should be governed and what was the best means of fulfilling its mission.

Such a backdrop underscores the significance of religious ideology and practice apparent at Machecoul during the late Old Regime, hopefully making the remainder of this chapter a little less opaque. In the 1770s and 1780s both local ecclesiastical officials and many of the town's notables were well versed in these struggles; some were even veterans of the political maneuvering that these ecclesiastical issues had provoked. Thus, both the clergy and the elite laity would have taken sides over these issues and formulated opinions about them. In other words, political experience and the ideological formation arising from it required a religious engagement on the part of both clergy and notables during the late Old Regime. For these Machecoulais, therefore, "politics" was never a purely secular phenomenon. Questions about what it meant to be a Catholic and why the church mattered often stood at the heart of the most serious political problems in France, which is why those who were politically aware in the town also had a strong religious consciousness.

An Unshakeable Foundation

The Catholic institutions and personnel at Machecoul weathered the religious struggles of the Old Regime remarkably well. The town possessed an impressive array of church institutions and a plentiful corps of secular and regular clergy. Yet by no means was this ecclesiastical presence exceptional within the religious jurisdiction of which the town was a part. The diocese of Nantes, whose boundaries closely though not perfectly corresponded to the *comté* of the same name, encompassed 242 parishes on the eve of the Revolution. The diocese consisted of two archdeaconries and five deaneries, including the deanery of Retz—the seat of which was a parish at Machecoul.[8] In 1789 a total of 880 secular priests and 180 men and women in religious orders were within the diocese, a plentiful number for even the larger dioceses of France.[9] These statistics reflect why the Nantes episcopacy may have been among the most important and influential bishoprics, not only in Brittany but in all of France. The bishop of Nantes had extensive control over all the parishes in his diocese, meaning that other high clerical positions (canons, vicar-generals, archdeacons) were economically rewarding and symbolically prestigious, but not always ecclesiastically influential.[10] The Nantes episcopacy seemed especially receptive toward the Tridentine (and typically Jesuit) ideal of doctrinal uniformity, which is why it pursued an agenda of centralization in the diocese during the second half of the eighteenth century. The efforts of Jean-Augustin de Frétat de Sarra, the bishop of Nantes from 1775 to 1783, exemplified these centralizing trends. Twice visiting all the parishes in the diocese during his tenure, Monseigneur Frétat died while trying to complete his third tour. His successor, Charles Eutrope de La Laurencie, sought even more centralization by attempting to implement a uniform liturgy for the diocese.[11]

Yet bishops could not go it alone; they greatly depended on parish pastors to carry out their directives. A pastor or *curé* in Brittany was usually called a *recteur* during the Old Regime, a title signifying the authority and influence that many Breton pastors enjoyed within their communities. Much respect among parishioners in the diocese of Nantes derived from *recteurs* being, as it were, one of their own. In 1789 about 90 percent of the parish clergy was native to the diocese, with the other 10 percent from dioceses bordering it. Socially, most of the diocesan clergy originated among artisan, small merchant, and prosperous peasant families.[12] The *recteurs* received sound intellectual and spiritual formation, both at the various *collèges* located in the diocese and then at the major seminary in Nantes. Their training allowed *recteurs* to fulfill three main duties aside from leading religious services and preaching: to keep track of registries recording baptisms and burials (and thus birth and deaths) for the government; to aid the poor; and to direct local education.[13]

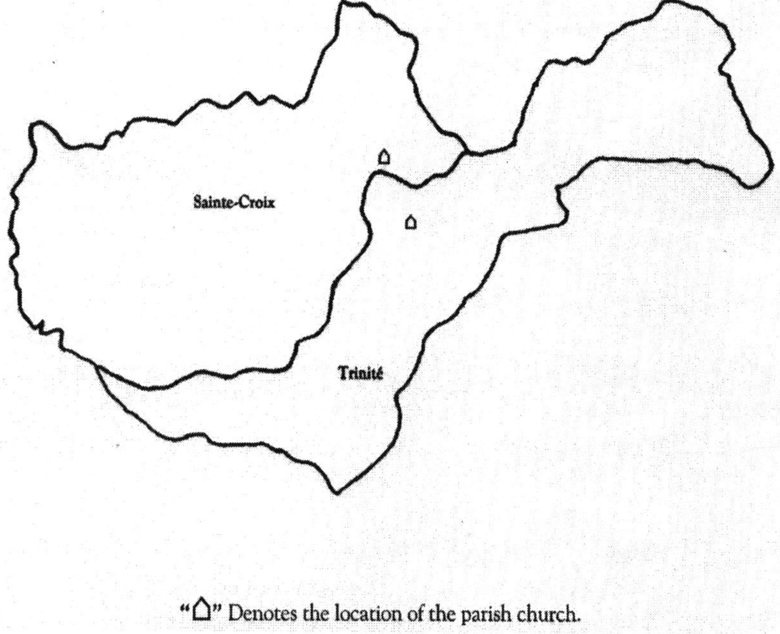

"⌂" Denotes the location of the parish church.

Figure 2.1
Machecoul's Parish Boundaries, 1774-1791

During the late Old Regime the Machecoulais, virtually all of whom were Catholic, belonged to one of two parishes. As seen in Figure 2.1, on the west side of the commune, including the vast *marais*, stood the parish of Sainte-Croix. The other parish, Trinité, covered the eastern territory in the commune, including much of the town itself as well as the privileged *marches* territory. Of the two parishes, Trinité was slightly more populous and noticeably more wealthy and prestigious.[14] Such status was reflected in the physical appearance of the two parish churches. Sainte-Croix's edifice was in serious need of repair, while Trinité's was in relatively good condition.[15] The two *recteurs* who presided over the parishes during the late Old Regime were Simon Blanchard at Sainte-Croix and Roland Hervé de la Bauche at Trinité. Abbé Blanchard, born on the outskirts of Nantes in 1733, was first named a *vicaire* at Sainte-Croix in 1781, then assumed the position of *recteur* in the parish shortly before the Revolution.[16] Trinité's *recteur*, abbé Hervé, was born in 1726 in the parish of Saint-Nicolas in Nantes and was the son of an important city magistrate. Showing great promise as a student, Hervé attained a doctoral degree in theology at the University of Nantes, a rare accomplishment for a member of the low clergy. He became a priest in December 1750 and for the next twelve years served at his home parish. In 1771 he assumed the offices of *recteur* and *doyen* at Trinité, one of the most important posts in the diocese.[17]

A *recteur* like abbé Hervé received no uniform salary in the diocese of Nantes. Clerical incomes varied from parish to parish, depending on a variety of factors.[18] A priest's salary in Brittany was largely dependent on income derived from benefices, which were parcels of land donated to members of the clergy by the faithful.[19] Records from the Revolution show that at least twenty benefices stood within the commune of Machecoul in 1790, a substantial number for merely two parishes.[20] Yet this too was not necessarily unique for western France.[21] Indeed, due to the high number of benefices, Breton *recteurs* usually earned double or even triple the national average for *curés*, thus making them some of the most prosperous members of the low clergy in all of France.[22] In Machecoul, for example, a fiscal summary of the parish of Trinité in 1756 shows that the *recteur* was receiving a substantial revenue of 1,200 livres, a considerable salary at that time.[23] By 1789 both of the town's *recteurs* were earning between two thousand to four thousand livres per year—average to slightly above average for pastors in the diocese of Nantes.[24] The *recteur's* pervasive control over all ecclesiastical revenues in his parish only enhanced his own financial prominence, for during the late Old Regime laypeople in western France rarely had access to parish finances. In 1756 Trinité's building committee or vestry (*le conseil de fabrique*), which was composed of three notaries, was in possession of an annual revenue of only 330 livres.[25]

As impressive as the *recteurs* were, though, their stature was only enhanced by other clergy who stood below them. Parish *vicaires* aided the pastors in leading liturgy, administering the sacraments, and performing other priestly obligations. At the time of the Revolution abbé Blanchard had one *vicaire* under his tutelage while abbé Hervé had two. Another priest, moreover, served as the chaplain of the female Benedictine monastery in town.[26] Two retired priests were also still receiving revenues from benefices while living in the town in 1790.[27] In addition, a tonsured cleric living in the parish of Trinité, René Archambaud, was under the guidance of a tutor in the town at the time of the Revolution.[28] Other kinds of clerics, such as subdeacons or priests serving as teachers, lived in or near the town as well.[29] Having a considerable number of clerics in the two parishes was not at all uncommon in the region; ninety-two parish priests were dwelling in the fifty parishes around Machecoul, or an average of 1.84 priests in each parish.[30]

The sizable number of secular clergy in Machecoul resulted from trends in clerical recruitment in the west during the second half of the eighteenth century. When compared with other dioceses in France, the diocese of Nantes enjoyed abundant sacerdotal recruitment from 1750 to 1789; vocations, in fact, were thriving in the west in comparison with dioceses located in Champagne, Ile-de-France, Berry, eastern Poitou, and the southwest.[31] From 1750 to 1769 an average of twenty-five secular priests were ordained each year in the diocese of Nantes, twenty-one between 1770 and 1779, and twenty-three in the ten years before the Revolution. Steady recruitment to the priesthood in the diocese was probably the result of two factors. The diocese's sound educational structure, for one, proved a most effective conduit for guiding young men toward the priesthood.[32] But perhaps just as significant, massive campaigns in the eighteenth century to evangelize rural inhabitants seemed to bear fruit in the form of increased vocations.[33]

The presence of regular clergy in the diocese of Nantes was also considerable in the 1770s and 1780s, although religious orders there were in decline as the Revolution approached. This drop was occurring, though, more among male than female orders, as evidenced by the closing of three abbeys in the diocese during the second half of the eighteenth century.[34] At Machecoul two religious orders were conspicuous. The first was the Franciscan order of Capuchins, whose monastery was situated on the southwest edge of the town.[35] Though the Capuchins may have been more numerous earlier in the Old Regime, they felt the effects of the severe decline in regular clergy recruitment before the Revolution. By 1789 their numbers in the town had dwindled to five.[36] The second religious order consisted of contemplative and cloistered nuns. The Benedictines of Our Lady of Calvary, commonly called the Calvarians, were renowned for their ascetic rigor and austerity—a clear indication of the influence of Jansenism. The Calvarians refused to repudiate Jansenism until the relatively late date of 1741, and even then it took the strong arm of Jesuits from Quimper to effect the change.[37] Yet even as late as the 1770s and 1780s the Calvarians probably adhered to many austere principles that had characterized Jansen's theology. How many resided at the monastery for its first one hundred years is uncertain, but at the time of the Revolution it had nineteen members.[38] A ledger recording payments to these women during the Revolution includes the names of seventeen of the nineteen women who made up the Calvarian community in 1790. Predictably, the names suggest that many Calvarians were from families constituting the town's urban elite.[39]

The regular and secular clergy's influence over all social and educational institutions was yet another sign of the church's extensive power in Machecoul. Educationally the most prominent establishment in the commune was the *collège*, established well before the Revolution and led by a priest as late as the 1750s. In 1763, however, a layperson and master of arts graduate from the University of Nantes, Etienne Gaschignard, took charge of the institution.[40] Gaschignard employed some priestly colleagues from the university to teach at the school, which had eighty students at the time of the Revolution.[41] There were also several *petites écoles* in the commune, each under the direction of one instructor.[42] Several other educational institutions could be found at the Calvarian monastery. The first was an orphanage under the patronage of the baron de Retz and called Little Calvary.[43] The Calvarians also had a small boarding school and held classes for day students.[44] Very few records about this educational institution remain, but in all likelihood only a few select girls from notable families attended it.[45]

During the late Old Regime the town's clergy also assumed responsibility for poor relief—an arrangement that was fast becoming rare in France at that time. Although some Breton parishes had established charity offices by the late eighteenth century, in Machecoul poor relief largely remained in the charge of the *recteurs*. As such, pastors were called on not only to dispense charity but also to be advocates for the poor.[46] Fortunately for the *recteurs*, a *hôpital* at Machecoul helped supplement relief efforts. Established in 1778 by the local clergy and town officials, the *hôpital* likely served two purposes: a reform school where the poor could be "educated" in manual skills and the habits of hard work, and an infirmary where the chronically and seriously ill who could not work would find a bed.[47] Though members of religious congregations and laypeople probably staffed the establishment, officially it was under the control of a board that included the two Machecoul *recteurs*, among other dignitaries. Ecclesiastical control was also apparent in the stipulation that the board could choose a chaplain to instruct the poor at the *hôpital*, but its choice to be approved by the bishop of Nantes.[48] Financial support for the institution largely fell upon the local community. When the town celebrated the construction of new buildings for the institution in 1785, a cleric noted that it was made possible "through the charity of the Lords of Retz and of la Clartière, by the generosity of the fathers of the poor [the *recteurs*], the gifts of pious individuals, and some inhabitants of the two parishes."[49]

Given the diocese's successful centralization, coupled with the clergy's control over many local institutions, one might think that a strong sense of religious solidarity permeated the town. Ironically, however, Catholic centralization and institutional power divided the community at least as much as they united it. While the Catholic Church exercised a great deal of cultural influence in the town, its sway could antagonize many, particularly community notables who felt that political authorities, not religious ones, should control schools, hospitals, and efforts to care for the poor. This concern over institutional control tended to echo the religious struggles of earlier decades, for it raised questions related to Gallicanism and clerical authority. As divisive as that issue continued to be, however, the church's extensive institutional control in the town provoked an even broader political concern; few opportunities seemed available to Machecoul's notables to question, let alone debate, the church's degree of power.

The Rituals of Reform

As far-reaching as the clergy's institutional grip was, equally remarkable was its authority over religious practice and doctrinal teaching. Clerical supervision over ritual and doctrine was one of the most important principles emanating from the Council of Trent, as well as a notion to which the Breton clergy tenaciously adhered before the Revolution.[50] Much of the clergy's devotion to Catholic reform was attributable to the Order of Saint-Sulpice, whose members taught at the seminary at Nantes from 1728 until the Revolution. Somewhat similar to Jesuits, Sulpicians were noted for their advocacy of Tridentine ideals. Also not unlike many in the Church—Jesuits and early Jansenists alike—Sulpicians embraced a *contemptus mundi*, a notion that emphasized evil in the world and that priests therefore had to remain segregated from their parishioners and aloof from worldly concerns.[51]

The parish clergy's strict adherence to Tridentine Catholicism was attributable to other factors as well. Many priests in Brittany showed much respect for papal authority—a somewhat striking stance since many priests in France tended look to the supervision of episcopal authorities or clerical assemblies.[52] Clerical opinions about papal authority in the Breton province are difficult to determine at Machecoul. Still, in one of the rare entries in the parish registry of Trinité that did not denote a baptism, marriage, or burial, a member of the parish clergy noted that abbé Hervé had obtained a piece of the true cross from Rome in 1777, complete with a plenary indulgence officially approved by Pope Pius VI. The same year the parish celebrated its reception of this relic on September 14, the feast of the Exultation of the Holy Cross. When the parish registry's entry regarding the celebration is viewed in conjunction with subsequent ecclesiastical actions during the early stages of the Revolution, there is much reason to suspect that abbé Hervé and likely other senior members of the lower clergy in the diocese of Nantes not only heeded papal authority, but also may have had vital connections with church officials in Rome.[53]

That Breton *recteurs* like abbé Hervé were inclined to defer to the papacy and other officials in Rome was related to historical developments dating as far back as the Middle Ages. Before the sixteenth century, the dioceses in Brittany were directly under papal obedience. In spite of the 1516 Concordat of Bologna, which gave Gallican authorities great control over the church in France, Brittany retained the title of *patria obedientiae*, a country under papal obedience. Some in the province strongly held to this distinction, in part because it was one of the last manifestations of the region's independence and autonomy. Thus Breton *recteurs* had a strong tradition of heeding papal direction, including the many exhortations in the seventeenth and eighteenth centuries often echoed by Jesuits and Sulpicians.[54]

The Sulpician influence and Brittany's longtime attachment to Rome, moreover, may explain why Jansenism failed to make substantial inroads among the lower clergy in the Machecoul region during the late Old Regime, even though Nantes was one of the most formidable bastions of Jansenism in the seventeenth and eighteenth centuries.[55] Much support for Jansenism within the diocese originated among the Oratorians at Nantes, who assumed a critical role in the city's secondary educational institutions and thus were capable of influencing many of their students.[56] In the 1720s Jansenists in Nantes claimed that miraculous healings were taking place at the tomb of the former Nantes seminary director, abbé de La Noë-Mesnard—much like contemporaneous events unfolding at the cemetery of Saint-Médard in Paris.[57] Later, in 1757 and 1758, Jansenist clergy and laity in the diocese intensified their attack on the Jesuits, accusing one of inciting regicide while he was preaching at a mission.[58] One year before Jesuits were expelled from France, the Parlement of Brittany succeeded in closing all of their secondary schools. Those priests attracted to Jansenism were successful in fostering their cause among the laity, as many notables in Nantes and in small towns of the diocese were won over. Still, the vast majority of parish priests in the countryside remained opposed or at best indifferent to Jansenism. In 1730 records indicate that only about seventy (of a total of about eight hundred) were considered to be Jansenists, most of whom were residing in Nantes.[59]

Tridentine Catholicism placed a premium on ritual, perhaps more so than many Jansenists preferred. Indeed, the Breton clergy insisted that the only way to salvation was through the sacraments, and thus it is no coincidence that the church's sacraments were the focal point of a Machecoulais's religious life. Parish registries indicate that the *recteurs* and *vicaires* of the two parishes were relentless in administering the sacraments and holding funerals during the late Old Regime. Between 1774 and 1789 the parish of Trinité averaged 75 baptisms, 20 marriages, and 92 funerals each year. Over the same period the town's other parish, Sainte-Croix, averaged 72 baptisms, 18 marriages, and 80 funerals.[60] Such numbers were not extraordinary, especially since baptism, marriage, and funerals were rites of passage more or less expected of all French Catholics, regardless of personal religious sentiments. Still, the numbers suggest that typical inhabitants would be well aware of the clerical insistence on the sacraments as a means for salvation.

Services held on Sunday (low mass, high mass, and vespers) were likewise important rituals in keeping with Tridentine Catholic teaching. As in many parts of rural France, these services also had much social significance for inhabitants, since they constituted the centerpiece of communal activity, particularly for peasants. Periodic gatherings at the churches and weekly contact with the *recteur* went a long way in forging the community's identity, particularly given that there were few other opportunities when everyone could come together.[61] As one historian of western France explained, "the Church was the symbol of [the peasants'] small autonomous collectivity, the symbol of their unity, the symbol of their existence." The church activities themselves, moreover, gave the impression to most that the parish leader, the *recteur*, was the singular embodiment of their community.[62]

Although each Sunday offered an opportunity for a Machecoulais to affirm a sense of cohesion, the various holy festivals held throughout the year were perhaps even more significant in this respect. Inhabitants commemorated twenty-two feast days during the late Old Regime, which again was not necessarily unique in France.[63] For the townspeople the most significant of these was the festival for Saint Honoré.[64] Held on May 16 every year, it recognized the community's patron saint, who had been the eighth bishop of Amiens during the sixth century. In the eleventh century a severe drought struck the Amiens area, prompting the people in the area to pray to Honoré and ask for his intercession. When rain returned to the region, enough wheat was produced to end the famine. The Amiens people proclaimed Honoré the patron saint of bakers, and thereafter his cult slowly grew throughout France. Devotion to the saint probably became strong in the town during the early modern era because abundant amounts of flour were produced at the windmills on the plain of Les Chaumes, and thus baking became one of the more common trades in the town. Little evidence about the festival in the town before the Revolution can be found, but according to one local erudite, inhabitants from thirty-two area parishes came to the town for the celebration, particularly for the procession held immediately after the high mass in the morning.[65]

Parishioners would not only witness ritual at such liturgies; they would also be exposed to religious teaching, above all that given in the sermon during mass. Unfortunately, few sermons from the Old Regime exist at Machecoul, but, if they were anything like others given at surrounding parishes, they emphasized obedience—to the Church, to landlords, to parents, and to the state—all of which were considered expressions of obedience to God. Priests frequently would tell the wealthy of the parish to show obedience to God by looking after the poor and being just to them. They called on the poor in the parish to respect their superiors and to follow their orders. *Recteurs* and *vicaires* likely emphasized to the Machecoulais that conformity and resignation were among the most important Christian virtues, and that all revolt was not only useless but ultimately injurious, since it caused suffering within one's self as well as in society.[66] Another predominant theme heard by parishioners in the sermons was that of sin, especially *impurité*, meaning sexual offenses. The preoccupation with sins of the flesh was widespread among the clergy in western France—an indication that the Jansenist accusation of moral laxity among Jesuits and other proponents of Tridentine Catholicism was largely without merit. Other sins, such as drunkenness, anger, and avarice, were frequent subjects of sermons heard by inhabitants on Sundays and feast days as well. Typically priests invoked death and described hell or purgatory in order to motivate their audience to abide by church teaching. The message might strike many today as extremely morbid, austere, and pessimistic.[67]

The themes of obedience and sin were likewise prominent in the catechism taught to Machecoul children. In 1781 Monseigneur Frétat de Sarra approved the distribution of a catechism used throughout the diocese, which was very simple and ostensibly designed to be understood by the mass of inarticulate peasants. The author, abbé de la Noë-Mesnard, was purportedly a Jansenist, yet it may have been precisely because of catechism's moral rigor that the bishop approved its distribution.[68] The catechism emphasized the need to remain pure before marriage, recommending in one instance that during all kinds of recreation boys and girls were to remain separated.[69] The obedience theme, especially with regard to the church, was evident in numerous series of the catechism's questions and answers.[70] The message was simple and unequivocal: the laity must submit to the authority of the church if it wanted to inherit eternal life.

Unfortunately, due to a lack of pastoral visitation records, little else is known about religious ritual and teaching at Machecoul shortly before 1789.[71] From what is known, though, the enactment of ritual at the town's parishes appeared little different from that at many other parishes in France at the time, especially with regard to regular sacramental practice and the observance of holy days. Yet in equal measure, the townspeople would often have been subject to the clergy's insistence on Catholic reform emanating from the Council of Trent, and thus they would have been constantly reminded of the spiritual gravity of religious rituals—perhaps more so than might have been the case in the typical French parish. Consequently, the Machecoulais would have been left with the indelible impression that sacramental rites, together with the clergy who led them, were indispensable to their own salvation.

Efforts to Evangelize

Parishioners became aware of Catholic reform from more than just their parish priests; they also received similar instruction from missionaries occasionally conducting parish revivals.[72] During the seventeenth and eighteenth centuries bishops and priests in the diocese of Nantes frequently asked the regular clergy to conduct these missions at various parishes. From 1728 to 1758, for example, the Sulpicians held thirty-three missions in sixteen parishes in and around the Loire River valley.

Capuchins were particularly active in the small towns of the diocese between 1712 and 1750, and Jesuits held numerous retreats at their house in Nantes up to their dissolution.[73] In the small deanery of Roche-Bernard, located in the northwest part of the diocese, a registry from the seventeenth and eighteenth centuries indicates that 111 missions were held there over the two centuries, most of which were led by the regular clergy.[74]

The most influential missionary in the Machecoul area during this period was Père Louis-Marie Grignion de Montfort (1673-1716). Grignion, a priest based in Saint-Laurent-sur-Sèvre (Vendée), exercised his ministry in the expansive coastal territory between La Rochelle and Vannes.[75] He was gifted at presenting the teachings of the church in a way that illiterate peasants and artisans would understand: making analogies, for example, about the relationship of Christians and Christ to that of a child and a parent, or an apprentice and a master.[76] As popular as Grignion was in life, though, he became even more celebrated after his death. In 1722 some of his followers established an order called the Brothers of the Holy Spirit, whose members popularly became known as the Mulotins. From that point up until the Revolution, the Mulotins conducted at least seventy-eight missions in the dioceses of Nantes, Luçon, Angers, and Poitiers, including at least one at Machecoul. A female Montfortian order also emerged in the 1720s, whose members were called the Daughters of Wisdom. It opened seventy-four houses between 1724 and 1790. One of these was in Machecoul.[77]

To what degree did Grignion, the Mulotins, and other missionaries make an appreciable impression on the Machecoulais? In short, the evidence is contradictory.[78] To be sure, the songs and canticles composed by Grignion probably had a profound effect. In his songs and writings the missionary emphasized devotion to the Holy Cross and to Mary (in the form of the rosary), both of which seem to have taken root among the laity.[79] A third devotion, the cult of the Sacred Heart of Jesus, was very popular among the Tridentine clergy and made an impression on inhabitants of western France during the eighteenth century as well.[80] Some signs of missionary progress became visible. According to the pastoral visitation records from the west that remain, more commemorative crosses appeared along roads of the *bocage*; the laity showed a greater respect for cemeteries, and more retables were created in parish churches. The same records suggest, moreover, a renewed interest in pilgrimages by the laity and a drop in violence, disorder, and debauchery at public festivals and gatherings.[81] Yet clearly not all of the laity heeded the missionaries' message. Missions were periodically repeated, in part because those who attended them often reverted to their old ways.

Still, missionary efforts prompted more than a few Machecoulais to join confraternities, which, like parish missions themselves, were numerous in and around the town's parishes.[82] Indeed, the parish of Trinité had three confraternities in 1756: those of the Holy Spirit, the Rosary, and the Dying (*agonisants*). The Confraternity of the Holy Spirit, which was founded in Trinité in the twelfth century, was the most important and prestigious of all. Holy Spirit confreres in the parish attended services together and prayed for fellow members, living or dead. Two of these confraternities are listed as having the pastor as the head of the organization, while a third was under the administration of a woman notable.[83] Thus even when it came to lay organizations in the town, the parish clergy exercised much influence. As a part of Catholic reform stemming from the Council of Trent, in the seventeenth and eighteenth centuries, priests in France often tried to suppress the Confraternity of the Holy Spirit or purge it of practices that they deemed offensive.[84] But in Machecoul's case the confraternities received not only the clergy's support and approval but ultimately its supervision.

Clerical control over confraternities, in conjunction with the pervasive efforts of missionaries in the Machecoul area, confirms that Catholic Reform was firmly implanted among the town's inhabitants during the late Old Regime. Though parish missions and lay organizations were distinctly different aspects of religious participation, they had one thing in common: they were earnest efforts to evangelize the faithful in and around the town. The commitment on behalf of both the secular and the regular clergies to make the ideals of Tridentine Catholicism a reality, therefore, was an impassioned one. But to what degree the Machecoulais embraced Catholic reform is an entirely different question—and one much more difficult to answer.

Christian Culture among the Elite

In view of the considerable number of services, festivals, missions, devotions, and confraternities at Machecoul, it would seem safe to conclude that religious adherence was strong in the two parishes, and that most were very dedicated to their faith. But in reality, popular religious belief in and around the town was extremely nuanced. Neither the identity nor the precise numbers of parishioners regularly attending mass or receiving Easter communion before the Revolution can be determined, thus complicating any determination of religious adherence in the town.[85] There may be, in fact, only one instance of direct documentation about religious vitality at Machecoul before the Revolution: a statement written in reference to a Montfortian mission conducted there in 1768. One Mulotin involved with the mission inadvertently indicated a complexity of popular belief:

> This mission . . . was excellent for the parishioners of Sainte Croix since the people were submissive. . . . the parishioners of the town were very indifferent. However, the mission exercises were popular and the confessions were numerous. The cross and the *calvaire* were splendid. We gave a retreat for seven days to the nuns at Our Lady of Calvary, an excellent community.[86]

By no means were the townspeople, therefore, of one religious mind and heart. On the contrary, the mission provoked a variety of responses on behalf of inhabitants, probably for a number of different reasons.

The notables at Machecoul are a case in point. The small amount of evidence from the late Old Regime suggests complex religious divisions among the elite in and around the town.[87] To be sure, some notables approved of the church's imposing institutional stature, if not the theological and spiritual assumptions on which it was founded. This may be, in part, because the church played a key role in maintaining a status quo that benefitted the elite.[88] An interesting ritual, documented in the parish registry of Trinité, helps explain why some notables may have seen the church as integral to their own political and economic interests at Machecoul:

> On 10 July 1775 we, Roland Hervé de la Bauche, *recteur* of Trinité
> and Dean of Retz [along with six other *curés* and three *vicaires*],
> the Monsieur Louis Joseph Charette, Knight and Lord of Moulin
> Henriette, Master Joseph Jan Gourraud [Garreau], Lord of la Bar-
> rodière, Pierre Dye, surgeon, Pierre Louis Barreau, surgeon, and many
> other inhabitants and notables from the different parishes assembled
> to proceed to the blessing and implantation of the Cross popularly
> called the Cross of Four Borders ... there has been no contestation
> between us or our inheritors concerning the borders and limits of
> our parishes, and animated by the same spirit of brotherhood and
> peace that our predecessors had, we have unanimously decreed that
> four gray stones will be placed here at the cost of the *recteurs*, the
> faces of which will have the name of each parish [Trinité, Paulx,
> Bois-de-Cené, and La Garnache] engraved upon them.[89]

The brief narrative is rich in implication. The excerpt shows that *recteurs*
and some local notables—including a member of the Charette family,
whose significance will become clear in the following chapters—seemed
closely affiliated during the late Old Regime.[90] The four parishes described
here were part of the *marches*, the privileged border area between Brittany and Poitou described in the previous chapter. The notables who
enjoyed the fiscal and political advantages of the *marches* seemed to
welcome the opportunity to have their distinction confirmed through
a religious commemoration. This ceremony, in short, seems to reflect a
value placed on religion as a means of sustaining the existing political
and social order.

That politics, social status, and religion were frequently tied to each
other, particularly among notables, is confirmed in another way as well.
Important political meetings frequently took place in conjunction with
the Sunday services. An entry from the registry of deliberations for
Trinité parish states that on August 1, 1779, following the high mass
and after the sounding of the bell "according to the custom," the *marguilliers*, that is, the church wardens of the parish, gathered at the church
doors to discuss matters concerning the levying of a tax on a property
within the parish. The office of church warden, at least at Machecoul,
was more of a political position than a religious one, and was typically
held by a member of the urban elite.[91] The inhabitants of the privileged
marches in the southern part of the future commune likewise met at

the doors of Trinité following the high mass to discuss political affairs that pertained exclusively to their unique status.[92]

This is not to say that social status and political power solely determined notable attitudes toward the church. On the contrary, some notable men were very supportive of the church out of spiritual conviction. Yet this may have been even more true for the town's elite women.[93] There is some evidence at Machecoul of a "sexual dimorphism": a gendered contrast in religious belief and practice during the late Old Regime. In the early eighteenth century Jansenism had made an impact on both male and female notables, but arguably by the 1780s the two genders were adhering to different aspects of the same religious ideology. On the one hand, notable women seemed more attracted to spiritual aspects of Jansenism, such as the call for moral purity and belief in the intrinsically evil nature of humanity.[94] Notable men, on the other hand, tended to accept the more politicized facets of Jansenism, especially opposition to the political and ecclesiastical centralization often advocated by Jesuits and Sulpicians. This dimorphism of the late Old Regime may have arisen in part because the more spiritual aspects of Jansenism were much more reconcilable with Tridentine Catholicism than its political equivalents.[95]

A variety of indicators further suggest that elite attitudes toward the church among men often stood somewhere between mild indifference and overt hostility. First, this social group contributed relatively little in terms of vocations to the diocesan priesthood. Compared with other social categories (namely artisans and affluent peasants), there was a marked deficit in the number of priests originating from families of notables in the diocese of Nantes during the eighteenth century, suggesting that parents saw other careers for their children as more beneficial.[96] Inventories of the personal libraries in Nantes taken before the Revolution reveal, moreover, that books on religion and spirituality constituted only a small portion of notable collections. An analysis of wills in the diocese during the eighteenth century also suggests that a typically Tridentine enthusiasm for the sacraments fell among notables, as bequests for masses and donations for Church institutions diminished after 1750.[97]

Another indication that notables in Nantes and in towns like Machecoul were reluctant to adopt Trent's reforms was their enthusiasm for the ideas of the Enlightenment, some of which were obviously incompatible with Tridentine Catholicism.[98] Admiration for the enlightened ideals of American revolutionary leaders like Thomas Jefferson was conspicuous in Nantes during the 1770s and 1780s, and private library inventories list many scientific and philosophical books and treatises written by Enlightenment thinkers. Many notables also supported progressive organizations, such as Nantes' *Société patriotique bretonne*, which was a provincial club championing political reform. The club began in 1785 and by 1789 had an office of correspondence in Machecoul. Seven Masonic lodges were operating in Nantes before the Revolution, and many of these lodges had members or established branches in the smaller towns of the diocese. In Machecoul, for example, many lawyers, doctors, and notaries frequented a Masonic lodge as well as a literary chamber established sometime before 1789.[99]

But there was more to some notables' resentment of the clergy than an enlightened perspective; there may have been some economic enmity as well. Given the large number of benefices located on the outskirts of the town that the clergy enjoyed, priests often had what area notables were often seeking: land. An appreciable 8 percent of the future commune, or 5.3 square kilometers, belonged to either the regular or secular clergy in 1790. Clerical control of this land around Machecoul may have been responsible for additional agitation among those notables seeking more property in the area.[100]

To conclude that those notables at Machecoul who resented the clergy and Tridentine Catholicism were "dechristianized," however, would be unwarranted. Parish registries disclose that some Machecoul notables who later assumed prominent positions in the local revolutionary administrations fully participated in the sacraments and burial rites at both parishes. In February 1784 the lawyer Alexandre Lemeignen went to the church of Sainte-Croix to have his daughter, Marie Marguerite, baptized.[101] About five years earlier he had been married at the parish of Trinité to the daughter of another Machecoul lawyer.[102] In June 1774 the *collège* principal Etienne Gaschignard had his son, Etienne Pierre, baptized at the church of Trinité, and in July of the following year did the same for his daughter, Jeanne Thérèse.[103] In 1781 the *négociant* Pierre-Marie Biclet was married at Trinité and went to the church in August of 1784 for the baptism of his daughter, Angélique Rosalie.[104]

True, attending a baptism was at best a minimal gesture of religious belief, yet the act demonstrates that these progressive notables were in no way totally disengaged from Catholic practice.

Although the evidence is scattered, there are implications that few if any of Machecoul's notables were anti-Christian or inclined toward atheism. Instead, it would be more accurate to say that they did not necessarily subscribe to the Tridentine beliefs and practices espoused by the clergy in western France during the eighteenth century. They especially resented complete clerical hegemony and instead favored a more Gallican church characterized by increased state control of the institution. In doing so, they implicitly rejected the major tenets that Jesuits and Sulpicians had long advanced.[105] Missionary records indicate that notables were often skeptical of parish missions, openly declaring that these revivals were farces and that missionaries like the Montfortians were buffoons.[106] This reaction may have been rooted, above all, in the notables' repudiation of Tridentine orthodoxy.[107] Such a negative disposition toward the missions suggests, moreover, that not only was the Enlightenment guiding their perception but also that Jansenism had informed it as well.[108] To a degree this influence is directly traceable, for some of the notables—Etienne Gaschignard, for example—were educated by the Nantes Oratorians, who had been celebrated opponents of the Jesuits and had taken control of the Faculty of Arts in the University of Nantes in the seventeenth century.

The traces of Jansenism in and around Machecoul are but one of the indicators that a variety of religious cultures existed among notables as the Revolution approached. Some of the elite, seemingly more females than males, accepted the Tridentine model of Catholicism advocated by the parish clergy and area missionaries, no doubt for sincere spiritual reasons. Other notables, however, may have supported the church to assure their political, social, and economic advantage, especially given that religious institutions and formal practices reinforced existing social and political structures. For still others among the elite, though, the church stood as a barrier, not only to their own social and political interests but also to ideals thought to be just as "Christian" as any promoted by Tridentine Catholicism—most notably popular sovereignty and greater social equality. In other words, religious differences among the Machecoul elite were more than a matter of politics or self-interest. As much as this was a struggle about what the church was—its Tridentine character, institutional dominance, and proprietary affluence—it was also about what the church should be. Thus those notables committed to Gallican, Jansenist, and enlightened principles were out not so much to diminish the Church, but rather to reform it on their own terms.

Christian Culture among Commoners

The elite, however, was far from the only social segment with divided religious sensibilities; such differences also existed among those Machecoulais considered commoners. Small shopkeepers and artisans possessed varied religious cultures as well. The Mulotins remarked that in their missionary experience certain professions were not disposed toward religious devotion, namely potters, quarry workers, barge workers, smiths, millers, and salt traders.[109] This is why, before the mission at Machecoul, the Mulotins noted that "the great number of millers" in the parish of Sainte-Croix "was not as bad as we had feared."[110] Why these particular artisans were hostile or indifferent to religion remains unclear, although patterns of sociability among these workers may have been a key factor.[111] In any case, an appreciable number of artisans appeared to adhere closely to the church in the eighteenth century, if the statistics for priestly vocations in the diocese of Nantes are any indication. Of ninety priests whose social background could be determined, fifty-three of them (59 percent) came from the artisan category. Artisan backgrounds were especially notable in the ample number of priests who came from secondary urban centers in the diocese, including Machecoul.[112]

Perhaps the only other indication of the degree to which this middling social group adhered to the tenets of Tridentine Catholicism is found in parish registries that imply prenuptial conception. With regard to babies being born less than nine months after their parents' marriage, the averages for parishes in the diocese of Nantes are noticeably lower than the national average for rural areas. The rare instances of illegitimacy in the west usually occurred among daughters of temporary workers, tenant farmers, or the poorest of artisans—those who were on the edge of indigence or who had frequently lost one or both parents. The birth control method of coitus interruptus, moreover, did not seem to be practiced among artisans in the diocese of Nantes, since most married relatively late as a way to limit the size of their families. The average age for marriage was usually around twenty-seven or twenty-eight near the end of the Old Regime in the parishes studied within Machecoul's diocese.[113]

As for the single largest social group within the parishes of Machecoul, namely the many tenant farmers and other agricultural laborers, the reception of Easter communion was likely unanimous and periodic mass attendance was also probably very high.[114] A variety of indicators confirms that Christian observance among peasants was ubiquitous. Some initiatives on behalf of Grignion de Montfort, the Mulotins, and parish priests may have been successful. Peasants later involved in counterrevolution were known to have recited the rosary in the evenings around campfires, a practice obviously in place during the Old Regime. Although Grignion de Montfort did not introduce this devotion, his emphasis on this form of prayer probably was responsible for making it very popular in the region.[115]

Church attendance and the practice of certain devotions did not necessarily mean, however, that the peasants accepted and abided by all aspects of Tridentine Catholicism. Rather, they likely saw most church ritual as one of several channels of sociability, making little distinction between the mass, celebrated with pomp and solemnity, and profane popular gatherings like the fairs, games played at the cabaret, or dances. Nor did peasants make any differentiation between beliefs and practices sanctioned by the church and those stemming from preChristian cults. Sixteen miraculous fountains and sixty-five pilgrimages, some of which remained animistic in nature, were observed within the diocese of Nantes at the time of the Revolution. Civil authorities, no doubt spurred by the bishop and parish priests, suppressed many such pilgrimages because they often led to disorder and debauchery.[116]

Despite many attempts by *recteurs*, missionaries, and royal officials to stamp out practices clearly not Christian in origin, many "pagan" practices still persisted through the late Old Regime.[117] Jean-Baptiste Huet, a local erudite writing in the early nineteenth century, described a marriage ritual that peasants in the region still practiced:

> On the eve of the wedding, the bridegroom mounts a horse and the bride-to-be sits behind him. They then enter one of the rooms at an inn, followed by the groomsmen. All of them crowd up to the horse

and run around it, and the bridegroom pours a bottle of red wine over his groomsmen. One cannot be but ashamed of such practices, which recall the mysteries of Hymen [the god of marriage] more so than those of Bacchus [the god of wine].[118]

The act certainly had the flavor of a fertility rite and very well could have been Celtic or Gallo-Roman in origin.

Attitudes and practices involving death also went beyond the limits of official Church teaching. Once again, Huet discussed peasant attitudes and actions on the occasion of a death:

> The loss of one of their animals, an accident, a storm, overwhelms them with sadness. Death especially, of which they have made life's torment, death which accompanies all the terrors of superstition, strikes them with anguish and dread. The parents, friends, neighbors, all are in mourning. They pass the night by saying prayers around the dead, holding burning candles; they multiply acts of purification. . . . They still fear that the dead souls still will not be satisfied, and that a vengeful ghost will come to exact the least of forgotten obligations.[119]

Huet's description stresses the importance that death had in the mental world of the Breton peasant. In western France the strong tradition of belief in the Devil and his immense powers was alive and well near the end of the Old Regime. Articles of Breton popular culture frequently abounded with images of demons, whom the Bretons depicted as monsters, dragons, wolves, or simply grotesque individuals. There was also an ongoing belief in a personification of death, a physical and spiritual being who went by the name of *Ankou.* This personage, probably the product of ancient Celtic religion dating back hundreds of years, remained a viable figure in the mental world of peasants well into the nineteenth century.[120] Thus, by 1789 the peasant interpretation of death was, in all likelihood, an amalgamation of Christian and preChristian beliefs that priests, let alone peasants, found difficult to deconstruct.[121]

At times priests may have condoned such beliefs, or perhaps tried to integrate them into Tridentine doctrine. They formally recognized and allowed a ritualistic gathering of family and friends immediately preceding the death of a person, referred to as *l'agonie*, in which the

dying said his farewell to his earthly existence and prepared himself
for the netherworld, as well as a wake or *veillée funèbre*, which was a
social gathering as much as a prayer service. For centuries these rites
had special significance and meaning for Breton people as expressions
of solidarity and cohesion among the community of survivors, not to
mention between the living and the dead.[122] Some historians have gone
so far as to say that death was "the cement of the marriage between
the Church and Bretons," and that because Tridentine Catholicism
and Breton culture spiritualized death in similar ways, the people of
Brittany were able to maintain their cultural autonomy in spite of the
"colonization" of Catholic reform during the Old Regime.[123]

But recently some historians have questioned whether Brittany was
truly unique in this sense. Many other regions of France, after all, had folk
tales that included figures personifying death. Stories about "Godfather
Death," for example, were present during the Old Regime as far away as
Artois and Narbonne.[124] Indeed, church doctrine regarding death was
inextricably mixed with pre-Christian beliefs among people in other parts
of rural France, just as in Brittany.[125] The notion that death assumed a
greater role in Brittany than it did in any other French province is no
certainty. If the Breton province was truly distinct from most of the
other regions in France in terms of Catholic belief and practice, it was
because the church, given its pervasive structural presence in Brittany,
was more capable and effective at preserving a spiritual perspective on
death, but thereby also promoting one aspect of Tridentine Catholicism.[126]

Regardless of whether death and popular beliefs about it were the
key to strong Catholic belief in western France, little proof suggests that
Grignion de Montfort, or other missionaries for that matter, completely
won peasants over to Catholic orthodoxy before the Revolution. Several developments occurring before and during the Revolution tend to
refute the notion that peasants venerated Grignion on any large scale.
Montfortian religious exercises were typically very intense activities that
required believers to express a great deal of emotion and outward affec-
tive action toward God, the Virgin Mary, and the saints. Yet this type
of religious demeanor was alien to peasants in Brittany and Poitou. By
most accounts the peasants in the Machecoul region were typically dif-
fident, extremely reserved, and simplistic. Although some scholars have

concluded that local pilgrimages to the tomb of Grignion de Montfort at Saint-Laurent-sur-Sèvre during the eighteenth century indicated a considerable level of devotion to the missionary among peasants, existing records give no indication of such pilgrimages taking place in either 1791, 1792, or 1793, thus suggesting little enduring attachment to his veneration.[127] Grignion de Montfort and the Mulotins, therefore, probably did not have an appreciable impact on artisans and peasants, at least not over the long term.

Thus, just as notables were divided over religious matters, so too were the commoners in and around Machecoul—albeit for different reasons. Some artisans showed indifference to missionaries trying to implement Catholic reform, while others embraced it at least enough to encourage their sons to become priests. Peasants, by contrast, participated in Catholic ritual and devotion en masse, but not necessarily for the reasons that the clergy would have preferred. Their knowledge, to say nothing of their acceptance, of Catholic reform doctrine was limited, and in some cases it did not deter them from maintaining age-old pre-Christian beliefs and rituals. The conflicting signs regarding what peasants and artisans believed seem to confirm that clear correlations between religious fervor, on the one hand, and distinct social and economic categories, on the other, were untraceable—just as was the case with the notables.[128]

All in all, then, during the late Old Regime Machecoul comes across—beneath the veneer of Catholic unanimity—as a religious labyrinth. True, the church's solid apparatus within the town likely made a great impression on inhabitants. They felt the effects of a highly centralized diocesan hierarchy, a secular clerical corps that was both affluent and numerous, and indisputable clerical control over all of Machecoul's social and educational institutions. Clerical supervision over all aspects of Catholic ritual in the town was total, which, together with the many parish missions being conducted, acquainted the Machecoulais with the ideals of Catholic reform. Yet by no means did the imposing structures and stringent beliefs of the clergy mean that the townspeople fully embraced what the church was offering.[129] Indeed, local dissatisfaction regarding the clergy was apparent as the Old Regime was coming to a close, particularly among progressively minded notables.[130] Many of the urban elite, moreover, increasingly saw the whole system of benefices and other sources of clerical income, which sometimes resulted in vast economic inequities between parish priests and other clergy, as outmoded and in need of fundamental reform.[131]

Well before the Bastille was stormed, therefore, multiple religious divides were prevalent at Machecoul. The most important of these divisions was one that existed among educated notables and even some artisans. More than a simple case of Christians against enlightened doubters, proponents of Catholic reform against its detractors, or Gallicanists against ultramontanists, the division encompassed a wide array of ecclesiastical matters—church structure, wealth, governance, teachings, and perhaps even ritual. Given that the chasm was so multifaceted, it had an especially explosive potential, arguably more so than any other political, economic, or social issue affecting the town during the late Old Regime. But if indeed this breach was so serious and possibly so divisive, why were there no signs of this conflict in the town before the Revolution? The answer, in short, was that there was no forum in which religious ideas contrary to those held by the local clergy could be publicly articulated or ritualistically expressed. Indeed, the lack of any dissident religious expression may have exacerbated the deepening divide between proponents and opponents of the ecclesiastical status quo.[132]

In his magisterial analysis of the Old Regime and the French Revolution, Alexis de Tocqueville argued that the Old Regime's political repression resulted in writers taking up the cause of political reform, in which they proposed radical and somewhat naive initiatives subsequently implemented during the Revolution.[133] Tocqueville's appraisal of the ideological background for the Revolution is closely apposite to the religious life of Machecoul during the late Old Regime. That some in the community could neither express their dissenting (but Catholic) beliefs nor put them into practice during the late Old Regime assured that, when given the chance in the Revolution, the community's subterranean religious fissures would rapidly surface. Thus the seeds of schism, if not outright violence, germinated during the Old Regime not only because of irreconcilable religious perspectives but also because of the town's inability to negotiate these opposing beliefs successfully. In a sad irony, the "Good Old Days" all but assured the town's impending misfortune.

Notes

[1] "Mandement de Monseigneur l'Évêque de Nantes pour le saint temps du Carême de l'an de grâce 1867," *SRN*, March 10, 1867.

[2] William Doyle, *Jansenism: Catholic Resistance to Authority from the Reformation to the French Revolution* (New York: St. Martin's Press, 2000), 1-14.

[3] For more on the distinctions among Gallicanists, see Richard M. Golden, *The Godly Rebellion: Parisian Curés and the Religious Fronde, 1652-1662* (Chapel Hill: University of North Carolina Press, 1981).

[4] The significance of Richerism, especially with regard to the coming of the French Revolution, is underscored in Timothy Tackett, *Priest and Parish in Eighteenth-Century France: A Social and Political Study of the Curés in a Diocese of Dauphiné, 1750-1791* (Princeton: Princeton University Press, 1977).

[5] Doyle, *Jansenism*, 14-44.

[6] See Jeffrey Merrick, *The Desacralization of the French Monarchy in the Eighteenth Century* (Baton Rouge: Louisiana State University Press, 1992).

[7] Doyle, *Jansenism*, 45-67. See also Van Kley, *Jansenists and the Expulsion*.

[8] Le Mené and Santrot, 1: 16-17.

[9] Marius Faugeras, "Le diocèse de Nantes à la veille de la Révolution," *Mémoires de la société archéologique et historique de Nantes et de Loire-Atlantique* 124 (1988): 37.

[10] Le Mené and Santrot, 1: 168-69; Charles Berthelot du Chesnay, *Les prêtres séculiers en Haute-Bretagne au XVIII⁷ siècle* (Rennes: Université de Rennes, 1984), 127.

[11] Yves Durand, ed., *Le diocèse de Nantes* (Paris: Beauchesne, 1985), 142-44. John McManners found that after 1746 the bishops of Nantes did all of their own pastoral visitations in their diocese. See McManners, *Church and Society in Eighteenth-Century France*, 1: 190-91.

[12] McManners, *Church and Society in Eighteenth-Century France*, 1: 328-29.

[13] Le Mené and Santrot, 1: 176-77.

[14] The boundaries of the two parishes at Machecoul can roughly be determined by examining the *lieu de naissance* of those who were baptized, as recorded in the registry for Sainte-Croix in the 1780s. See ADLA, 1 Mi EC 323 R3 État civil. Registres paroissiaux. Machecoul. Sainte-Croix, BMS, 1760-1789.

[15] ADLA, L 659. *Procès verbal* of the election of constitutional priests, Machecoul District, March 27-29, 1791.

[16]O. Pare, *Les pasteurs de Machecoul* (Tarbes [Pyrénées Hautes]: Imprimerie de Saint Joseph, 1975), 55.

[17]Alphonse Jarnoux, *La Loire leur servit de linceul: Les prêtres victimes de la première noyade, Nantes 16 novembre 1793* (Quimper: Imprimerie Cornouillaise, 1972), 157; Faugeras, 38.

[18]Timothy Tackett, "The West in France in 1789: The Religious Factor in the Origins of the Counterrevolution," *Journal of Modern History*, 54 (1982), 720-22. This article also appears in a revised form in Gilbert Shapiro and John Markoff, eds., *Revolutionary Demands: A Content Analysis of the Cahiers de Doléances of 1789* (Stanford: Stanford University èress, 1998), 325-45; Marion, 445-46.

[19]Le Mené and Santrot, 1: 174-76; Faugeras, 38-39. For more on benefices and how they were obtained, see McManners, *Church and Society in Eighteenth-Century France*, 1: 615-46.

[20]ADLA, Q 169. Entry of September 24, 1790.

[21]Charles Tilly also found that the *curés* in the Mauges were also affluent or, in his own words, "men of substance." See Tilly, *The Vendée*, 105-8.

[22]Tackett, *Religion, Revolution, and Regional Culture*, 90-91; Durand, 149-50; Le Mené and Santrot, 175.

[23]ADLA, G 59. *Brevet* of Trinité of Machecoul, June 1, 1756.

[24]Berthelot du Chesnay, 292. For more on ecclesiastical revenues during the Old Regime, see Nigel Aston, *Religion and Revolution in France, 1780-1804* (Washington, D. C.: Catholic University Press, 2000), 25-29.

[25]ADLA, G 59. *Brevet* of Trinité of Machecoul, June 1, 1756. The diminishment of the laity's role in the building committees was also the result of Tridentine reform. See Philip T. Hoffman, *Church and Community in the Diocese of Lyon 1500-1789* (New Haven: Yale University Press, 1984), 116-18.

[26]Although the Calvarian house essentially amounted to a "convent," since the order was Benedictine in origin, the term monastery is more appropriate here.

[27]ADLA, 2 Mi 246 (L 815). The State of Ecclesiastical Public Functionaries, March 30, 1791.

[28]ADLA, Q 32. Adminstrators of the Machecoul District Directory to Machecoul Municipal Corps, 17 October 1790.

[29]ADLA, G 59. *Brevet* of Trinité of Machecoul, June 1, 1756.

30 Berthelot du Chesnay, 82, 341-42.

[31]Timothy Tackett and Claude Langlois, "Ecclesiastical Structures and Clerical Geography on the Eve of the French Revolution," *French Historical Studies* 11 (1980), 361-62.

[32]Berthelot du Chesnay, 512-13.

[33]Durand, *Le diocèse de Nantes*, 148-52.

[34]Le Mené and Santrot, 1: 170-74.

[35] O. Paré, *Quelques documents sur la paroisse de Machecoul* (Tarbes: Imprimerie St. Joseph, 1973), 92-94.

[36] Le Mené and Santrot, 1: 750.

[37] Joseph Perroys, *Les Bénédictines de Notre Dame du Calvaire à Machecoul, 1673-1958* (Rezé [Loire-Atlantique]: Séquences, 1993), 19-26, 35-42.

[38]Le Mené and Santrot, 1: 750; Georges Minois, *Les religieux en Bretagne sous l'ancien régime* (Luçon: Éditions Ouest-France, 1989), 225-332.

[39] ADLA, L 1037. Entry of January 11, 1793.

[40]Whether Gaschingnard's appointment was related to the expulsion of the Jesuits from France is uncertain, but there is no record of the Jesuits directing the *collège*.

[41]Paré, *Quelques documents sur la paroisse*, 107.

[42]ADLA, L 616. Machecoul Municipal Administrators to Department Administrators of Loire-Inférieure, January 8, 1792.

[43]ADLA, L 607. Petition from the Machecoul Friends of the Constitution to Departmental Administrators, 11 February 1792, Perroys, 42-43. François Charruau was a notary at Machecoul between 1775 and an IX, whose records are found at ADLA, 4 E 78/15-17.

[44]Le Mené and Santrot, 1: 173.

[45]Perroys, 27.

[46]This was the case when the *recteur* of Trinité complained to authorities in Rennes that "Il serait à souhaiter qu'il y eût plus de travail et qu'on établit des manufactures. Il y aurait moins de pauvreté et plus de régularité dans les moeurs." See Aoustin, 35. Abbé Hervé zealously prized his position as "father of the poor" all the way up to the time when he was ousted from his parish. See ADLA, L 842. Extract from the Registry of the Machecoul District Directory, 21 December 1790.

[47]For a better understanding of what this *hôpital* probably was like, see Colin Jones, *The Charitable Imperative: Hospitals and Nursing in Ancien Regime and Revolutionary France* (New York: Routledge, 1989).

[48]ADLA, H 509. Letter of Confirmation of the Machecoul Hospital, July 29, 1777; Extract from Registry of Deliberations of the Hospital of Bourgneuf, November 14, 1781.

[49]ADLA, 1 Mi EC 324 R5. Registry of Trinité, Entry of June 7, 1785.

[50]Tackett, *Religion, Revolution, and Regional Culture*, 62; Berthelot du Chesnay, 172-73, 606-7.

[51]Ralph Gibson, *A Social History of French Catholicism 1789-1914* (New York: Routledge, 1989), 22-23. John McManners explains that the bishop

of Nantes turned over control of the seminary to the Sulpicians in 1778, much to the consternation of the Breton *parlement* and many *recteurs*. See McManners, 2: 670-71.

[52]To understand the important role that clerical assemblies had in other parts of France, see Tackett, *Priest and Parish in Eighteenth-Century France.* John McManners notes that there were no low clergy synods called in the diocese of Nantes during the eighteenth century, ostensibly indicative of episcopal and papal authority going relatively unchallenged. See McManners, 1: 279-83.

[53]ADLA, 1 Mi EC 324 R5 Registry of Trinité, Entry of September 14, 1777. On the feast day of the exultation of the Holy Cross, the obtainment of a piece of the true cross by Roland Hervé de la Bauche was officially celebrated at the Church of Trinité. One should note that this was no ordinary liturgy. The registry notes that the celebration was attended by "the *recteurs* of Sainte-Croix and of other neighboring parishes, of the clergy of [Trinité] parish, of the holy Capuchin fathers from this town, the honorable judge, prosecuting attorneys, other officers in the Duchy of Retz jurisdiction, and the great throng of people."

[54]Berthelot du Chesnay, 219, 226, 233-34.

[55]A. Bachelier, *Le jansénisme à Nantes* (Paris: Nizet and Bastard, 1934), 324; McManners, *Church and Society in Eighteenth-Century France,* 1: 213.

[56] Berthelot du Chesnay, 138; McManners, *Church and Society in Eighteenth-Century France,* 2: 385-88.

[57] See B. Robert Kreiser, *Miracles, Convulsions, and Ecclesiastical Politics in Early Eighteenth-Century Paris* (Princeton: Princeton University Press, 1978).

[58] Durand, 141. This incident undoubtedly was related to the January 5, 1757 assassination attempt on Louis XV by Robert-François Damiens, a mentally deranged drifter who ostensibly was influenced by propaganda critical of the monarchy from the *parlement* of Paris, which clearly was pro-Jansenist. See Van Kley, *The Damiens Affair.*

[59]Durand, 139-42. 60 Mille, 2: 107.

[61]In addition to their social and cultural implications, the Sunday services often had a political dimension as well. During the grand mass, following the recitation of the Credo, a Breton sermon usually started with parishioners reciting the "Our Father" and the "Hail Mary" for the intentions of the royal family and the local nobility. Following the reception of communion, the priest announced any royal declarations, orders from the Breton *parlement,* along with the *monitoires,* notifications compelling parishioners to testify about a crime. See François Roudaut, "Le message politique des sermons en breton à la fin de l'ancien régime," *Annales de Bretagne* 89 (1982): 144.

[62]Le Mené and Santrot, 180.

[63]*Catéchismes (premier et second) du diocèse de Nantes, imprimé par ordre de Monseigneur Jean Augustin de Frétat de Sarra, évêque de Nantes*, 1st ed. (Nantes: Bourgeois, 1781), "fêtes de précepte dans le diocèse de Nantes." This catechism is available at ADLA.

[64]The popularity of this procession may have been somewhat attributable to the time of the year when it was made. During the Rogation Days of May, rural Catholics prayed for good weather for the crops just planted. See Launay, *Le diocèse de Nantes sous le second empire*, 2: 548.

[65]Victor Boucard, *Saint Honoré patron des boulangers: Son culte à Machecoul et dans le Pays de Retz* (Nantes: Imprimerie Saint-Clement, 1938), 1-9.

[66]Roudaut, "Le message politique," 143-52.

[67]François Lebrun, *Parole de Dieu et révolution: Les sermons d'un curé angevin avant et pendant la guerre de Vendée* (Toulouse: Privat, 1979), 22-24.

[68]Marius Faugeras, *Le diocèse de Nantes sous la monarchie censitaire (1813-1822-1849)*, 2 vols. (Fontenay-le-Comte: Imprimerie Lussaud Frères, 1964) 2: 224-25; Launay, 2: 539.

[69]Durand, 162-68.

[70]*Catéchisme du diocèse de Nantes*, "table des leçons," 97.

[71]Although many pastoral visits took place in the diocese of Nantes during the late Old Regime, unfortunately not all the records for these visits have survived. The parishes of Sainte-Croix and Trinité at Machecoul are two of the parishes for which no pastoral visit records for the late Old Regime exists. See *Répetoire des visites pastorales de la France*, première série: *Anciens diocèses (Jusqu'en 1790)*, 4 vols. (Paris: Éditions du Centre nationale de la recherche scientifique, 1983), 3: 245-59.

[72]For a comprehensive examination of parish missions, see Louis Châtellier, *The Religion of the Poor: Rural Missions in Europe and the Formation of Modern Catholicism, c. 1500-c. 1800*, trans. Brian Pearce (New York: Cambridge University Press, 1997); McManners, *Church and Society in Eighteenth-Century France*, 2: 83-93.

[73]Durand, *Le diocèse de Nantes*, 136-39.

[74]Launay, 1: 179-80.

[75]Louis Pérouas, "La piété populaire au travail sur la mémoire d'un saint, Grignion de Montfort," *Actes du 99e congrès national des sociétés savantes, Besançon* (Paris, 1976), 259. Grignion de Montfort has been called father of the War of Vendée because his zone of missionary activity closely corresponds with the area where the insurgency broke out. Thus many historians have tried to link Montfortian missions and the 1793 insurrection.

[76]Louis Pérouas, *Grignion de Montfort et la Vendée* (Paris: Éditions du Cerf, 1989), 51-53; Châtellier, 60, 66.

[77]Pérouas, *Grignion de Montfort*, 72-80.

[78]Aston, 46-47.

[79]Châtellier, 108-15, 226.

[80]Ibid., 119-20, 220-21.

[81]Durand, *Le diocèse de Nantes*, 138-39.

[82]For more on confraternities, see McManners, *Church and Society in Eighteenth-Century France*, 2: 156-71, 181-88.

[83]ADLA, G 59. *Brevet* of Trinité of Machecoul, June 1, 1756.

[84]Hoffman, 105-12.

[85]See Note 71.

[86]Pierre Hacquet, *Mémoire des missions des Montfortains dans l'ouest (1740-1779): Contribution à la sociologie religieuse historique*, ed. Louis Pérouas (Fontenay-le-Comte: Université de Poitiers, 1964), 98.

[87]See Aston's discussion of piety among the "middling sort," Aston, 54-56.

[88] Tilly came across several incidents in the Mauges where lords and the *curés* were in conflict, but there is little evidence of a power struggle at Machecoul; There the *recteurs* usually were quite deferential to local lords. See Tilly, *The Vendée*, 110-11.

[89]ADLA, 1 Mi EC 324 R5. Registry of Trinité, entry of July 10, 1775.

[90]For more on the Charettes in the nineteenth century, see Raymond Jonas, *France and the Cult of the Sacred Heart: An Epic Tale for Modern Times* (Berkeley: University of California Press, 2000), 120-24, 226-28, 231-34.

[91]ADLA, G 429. Extract from the Registry of Deliberations of the Parish of Trinité of Machecoul, August 1, 1779. In this extract it appears that *marguilliers* and *fabriquers* were synonymous. Tilly also wrote about the assemblies after Sunday mass in the Mauges, adding that the *curés* often took part and indeed led the church wardens on many occasions. Such was not the case, however, at Machecoul. The largely bourgeois church wardens were highly politicized and did not need (and perhaps did not want) direction from the *recteur*. See Tilly, *The Vendée*, 103-4.

[92]Ibid., Extract from the Registry of Deliberations of the Parish of Trinité of Machecoul, March 12, 1786.

[93]Aston, 41-42.

[94]For a possible explanation of why men and women had different responses to Tridentine Catholicism, see Hoffman, 144-45.

[95]Ralph Gibson wrote that Jansenist spiritual beliefs "were the ultimate expression of Tridentine Catholicism.…In many ways, Jansenism was not so much a heresy as the logical extreme of orthodox Catholicism. . . . [Jansensists]

only took to extremes the nexus of attitudes which were in milder forms typical of the mainstream Catholicism of the day." See Gibson, *A Social History of French Catholicism*, 28. For the attitude of women with regard to the Ecclesiastical Oath of 1791, see Tackett, *Religion, Revolution, and Regional Culture*, 172-77.

[96]Jean-Pierre Bazin, "Les origines géographiques et sociales du clergé nantais au XVIIIe siècle," Mémoire de maîtrise, directed by Y. Durand (Nantes: Université de Nantes, 1975), 61.

[97]Durand, 159-60, 165-69.

[98]Aston, 81-99. Aston provides a thorough examination of the Enlightenment's attack on the church and its response. For more on the church's battle against the Enlightenment, see Darrin M. McMahon, *Enemies of the Enlightenment: The French Counter-Enlightenment and the Making of Modernity* (New York: Oxford University Press, 2001).

[99]Durand, 170-71; Le Mené and Santrot, 2: 750; H. Librec, *La franc-maçonnerie dans la Loire-Inférieure, 1744-1946* (Nantes, 1946), 13, 140. Librec found that the Masonic lodge in Machecoul officially did not have a constitution until 1802, but it was functional before the Revolution. For more on Freemasonry in France, see Ran Halévi, *Les loges maçonniques dans la France d'ancien régime: aux origines de la sociabilité démocratique* (Paris: A. Colin, 1984) and Daniel Ligou, ed., *Histoire des francs-maçons en France*, 2nd ed. (Toulouse: Privat, 2000).

[100]Le Mené and Santrot, 2: 750.

[101]ADLA, 1 Mi EC 323 R3. Registry of Saint-Croix, Entry of February 14, 1784.

[102]ADLA, 1 Mi EC 324 R5. Registry of Trinité, Entry of July 28, 1779.

[103]Ibid., Entries of June 22, 1774 and July 6, 1775.

[104]Ibid., Entries of February 19, 1781 and August 11, 1784.

[105]Yves Durand, "Anticlericalisme et politique dans l'ouest de la France à la fin du XVIIIe siècle," *Histoire, économie et société* 9, no. 2 (1990), 249. Durand argues that the bourgeois elite in western France (Volney, la Revellière-Lépeaux, Colliner, Mercier du Rocher) were very active in the anticlerical movement, and thus prepared the intellectual foundation in the west for the Civil Constitution of the Clergy. To what degree the Machecoul notables were influenced by the *"profonde hostilité au catholicisme,"* however, remains unclear.

[106]As Louis Châtellier aptly explained, "Basically, the main criticism addressed to the missions concerned the constraint which some missionaries imposed on the minds of the faithful. In an age of Enlightenment, everyone wanted to go to God in his own way." See Châtellier, 211.

[107] Le Mené and Santrot, 1: 179-80.

[108] Growing scholarly opinion agrees that religion and the Enlightenment were not the polar opposites that historians have often made them out to be—least of all in the minds of the eighteenth-century educated elite, which often reconciled enlightened ideas with Christian ideals. See Jonathan Sheehan, "Enlightenment, Religion, and the Enigma of Secularization: A Review Essay," *American Historical Review* 108, no. 4 (October 2003): 1061-80.

[109] Durand, *Le diocèse de Nantes*, 138.

[110] Victor Boucard wrote that an old French proverb was "faire ses pâques avec les meuniers" since millers always were supposed to wait for the last moment during Lent before confessing their sins. That way they could pursue their sinful practices for as long as possible. See Boucard, *Les anciens moulins de Machecoul*, 100.

[111] For more on the sociability of artisans belonging to corporations, see Cynthia Truant, *The Rites of Labor: Brothers of Compagnonnage in Old and New Regime France* (Ithaca: Cornell University Press, 1994).

[112] Bazin, 55 , 58. Bazin explains that priestly recruitment was particularly high at Machecoul because the *collège* produced many students who were viable candidates for the secular priesthood.

[113] Durand, *Le diocèse de Nantes*, 161-63.

[114] Le Mené and Santrot, 1: 179. Although pastoral visitation records do not exist for Machecoul's parishes, existing records for other parishes in the diocese seem to suggest that this was likely the case.

[115] Pérouas, *Grignion de Montfort*, 116-17.

[116] Le Mené and Santrot, 1: 179.

[117] For a wider discussion of "popular religion" in eighteenth-century France, see McManners, *Church and Society in Eighteenth-Century France*, 2: 119-55, 189-93.

[118] Huet, *Recherches économiques*, 404-05.

[119] Ibid., 402.

[120] Alain Croix and François (Fanch) Roudaut, *Les bretons, la mort et dieu de 1600 à nos jours* (Paris: Messidor Temps Actuels, 1984), 53-86.

[121] Thomas Kselman, *Death and the Afterlife in Modern France* (Princeton: Princeton University Press, 1993), 49-64.

[122] Croix and Roudaut, *Les bretons, la mort et dieu* , 38-43.

[123] Ibid., 222.

[124] Kselman, *Death and the Afterlife*, 37-49.

[125] François Lebrun, *Les hommes et la mort en Anjou aux 17e et 18e siècles: Essai de démographie et de psychologie historiques* (The Hague: Mouton et Compagnie, 1971), 391-415.

[126] For more on this transition, especially during the late Old Regime, see John McManners, *Death and the Enlightenment: Changing Attitudes to Death among Christians and Unbelievers in Eighteenth-Century France* (New York: Oxford University Press, 1981).

[127] Martin, *La Vendée et la France*, 58-59; Pérouas, *Grignion de Montfort et la Vendée*, 115-19.

[128] Tackett, "The West in France in 1789," 745.

[129] Robert Muchembled, *Popular Culture and Elite Culture in France 1400-1750*, trans. Lydia Cochrane (Baton Rouge: Louisiana State University Press, 1985), 208-33; Hoffman, 139-66.

[130] In the diocese of Nantes the Third Estate parish *cahiers de doléances*, the grievance lists largely written by notables for the meeting of the Estates General in 1789, frequently mentioned that the regular clergy was rapacious, served no useful purpose, and was still drawing rents from poor tenants whom it did not even know, much less help or serve. One parish *cahier* likened Franciscans and Dominicans to "vampires who feed on the blood of the poorest people." See Le Mené and Santrot, 1: 171-72, 4: 1311-12. Resentment of the regular clergy was widespread among much of the urban elite in a territorial block extending from Nantes all the way to Paris, if the general *cahiers* are any indication. See Tackett, "The West in France in 1789," 738-40.

[131] Of particular concern to many people was that benefices sometimes went to priests whom no one, except the rich benefactor, knew. Most parishioners wanted the benefices to be awarded to their own *recteur* so that local money would stay within their community. See Le Mené and Santrot, 1: 175.

[132] The role of ritual is of particular importance here, for it often was a means of mitigating or displacing violence in early modern Europe, although it sometimes led to disorder as well. On this issue, see Edward Muir, *Ritual in Early Modern Europe* (New York: Cambridge University Press, 1997), and David Kertzer, *Ritual, Politics, and Power* (New Haven: Yale University Press, 1988).

[133] Alexis de Tocqueville, *The Old Regime and the French Revolution*, vol. 1, *The Complete Text*, ed. François Furet and François Mélonio, trans. Alan S. Kahan (Chicago: University of Chicago Press, 1998), 195-202.

3

A Higher Law

Although scholars of the French Revolution are likely to disagree on many points, most seem to be of one mind regarding the importance of the National Assembly's passage of the 1790 Civil Constitution of the Clergy and its subsequent requirement that all French clergy take the 1791 Ecclesiastical Oath. William Doyle, for example, declared the 1791 oath, if not the greatest turning point in the Revolution, then "unquestionably one of them."[1] According to Gynne Lewis, the oath of 1791 produced a "seismic fault in the political geology of the French Revolution" that remained irreparable throughout the 1790s.[2] Characterizing the 1791 oath as a "sacrament" of the Revolution, Claude Langlois saw it as the most poignant expression of the Revolution's transfer of sacrality from the Catholic Church to the French state.[3] P. M. Jones argued that when it came to political reform during the early years of the Revolution, "no other policy pursued by the National Assembly tarnished the image of a nation" more than the 1791 oath requirement.[4] But probably the foremost authority on the 1791 oath, Timothy Tackett, went even further in his assessment. Tackett called the crisis that the oath provoked "a seminal event in its own right" well apart from the Revolution—a pivotal moment in the broader schema of modern French history that defined the nation's "provincial gestalt."[5]

The salience of the Civil Constitution of the Clergy and the oath crisis was nowhere more evident than in western France, particularly in a small town like Machecoul, where, as this chapter shows, religious reforms introduced during the early stages of the Revolution led to a decisive and divisive split within the community. As in many other areas of France, the Revolution at Machecoul started off innocently enough, with most in and around the town welcoming it as an opportunity for much-needed reform. But with passage of the Civil Constitution of the Clergy and its subsequent enforcement, the Machecoulais became divided into two confrontational and irreconcilable camps. How and why did civility within the town deteriorate so quickly? As already made evident, a divergence in religious culture within the community was firmly in place well before 1789. This chapter shows that attempts on the part of revolutionary officials to reform the church, as well as the efforts of the local clergy and its supporters to derail these efforts, made existing cultural divisions all but impossible to bridge. The chapter specifically reveals how proponents and opponents of these religious reforms constructed a dialectic in and around the town—a perilous dynamic fostering not only a profound political rupture at Machecoul but, more importantly, an increasing momentum toward fratricide.

Provincial Crises and the Cahiers de doléances

Although many seeking political reform in 1789 considered religious issues a highly relevant part of their program, ecclesiastical questions were forced to take a back seat to more pressing socioeconomic and political matters in France. The popular tumult unfolding in and around Paris was no doubt critical to the coming of revolution, but so too was the upheaval in the outlying provinces, most notably Brittany. The westernmost region of the country was experiencing a particularly severe economic downturn in the second half of the eighteenth century, due in no small part to the fall in transatlantic commerce in the Nantes region. The bad harvests of the 1780s, particularly that of 1788, exacerbated this long-term economic malaise. The crisis became so severe that by 1789, 40 to 50 percent of Breton peasants were in a state of deep poverty and in need of parish assistance. The second source of trouble in the region revolved around a political fight between provincial and royal authorities. When the royal fiscal crisis came to a head in 1787 and 1788, as the Paris *parlement* refused to approve the reform initiatives of royal ministers, Brittany's political institutions all but sided with the *parlement* of Paris. The political cohesion of the *parlements*, together with the lack of support from the Assembly of Notables for these initiatives, finally forced Louis XVI to call for a meeting of the Estates General.[6]

But in spite of these acute difficulties, probably the most decisive development in Brittany involved an internal provincial struggle among the ranks of the political elite, namely between nobles and leaders of the Third Estate. In Nantes as well as in the Breton capital of Rennes, leaders of the Third Estate began agitating for extensive political reform within the province. They complained that the composition of the Estates of Brittany was strongly tilted in favor of nobles and thus was not truly representative of the province as a whole. The conflict became so intense that in January 1789 fighting broke out in the streets of Rennes between those notables who supported political reform and unyielding aristocrats. Louis XVI subsequently suspended the meetings of the Estates of Brittany for an indefinite period.[7] This provincial crisis helps explain why elite members of the Third Estate in Brittany were extraordinarily united and highly mobilized over a number of issues in 1789, including comprehensive ecclesiastical reform.

Provincial infighting accounted for the highly acrimonious political debate in Brittany as preparations were being made for the meeting of the Estates General. As in the rest of France, the noble and clerical assemblies, together with all parishes in the dioceses of Brittany, were invited to compose lists of grievances, or *cahiers de doléances*, which would serve as recommendations for the deputies heading to Versailles. The parish *cahiers* were supposed to represent "the will of the people" to those Third Estate deputies elected to subprovincial (*sénéchaussée* in Brittany) assemblies, which in turn would send representatives to the Estates General at Versailles.[8] The nobility and the upper clergy in Brittany refused all deputation to the Estates General, and so their assembly never drew up *cahiers*. But the diocese of Nantes' lower clergy and the Third Estate in virtually every parish in the diocese composed their lists of grievances in late March and early April 1789.[9] Because of the unique administrative status of the *marches communes* of Brittany and Poitou, including part of Machecoul's parish of Trinité, all three of its orders likewise were to convene and elect their deputies to the Estates General. But in a highly uncommon practice, the three orders from the *marches* agreed to meet and compose their *cahier* together, "to express the union which exists between them"—an indication of their extraordinary cohesion.[10]

Given subsequent events in western France, it may seem somewhat surprising that the *cahier* for the lower clergy in the diocese of Nantes expressed much support for political reforms advocated by the Third-Estate elite in Nantes and Rennes.[11] The clergy assented, for example, to a guarantee of individual liberty, the establishment of schools in the countryside, the creation of a new tax system characterized by simplicity and the equal distribution of tax levies among the three orders, and an end to all distinctions between the lower and upper clergy. The lower clergy also embraced elements of ecclesiastical reform, recommending that the state enforce canon laws, which forbade members of the upper clergy from owning a plurality of benefices and prohibited nonclerics from receiving them. Thus the lower-clergy assembly in the diocese recognized that social improvement, the suspension of certain privileges, and a degree of religious reform were needed. But it staunchly supported the benefice system and rejected any attempt to allow the laity access to this particular source of revenue.[12]

But the Third-Estate parish *cahiers* at Machecoul, one for Trinité and one for Sainte-Croix, had perspectives on religious reform much different from that of the clergy, due in no small part to the activism of progressive notables. Although the grievances from the parishes were supposed to express the will of the entire Third Estate, they usually reflected the influence of notables, many of whom supported comprehensive political and social reform.[13] So organized were these progressive notables that they quickly mobilized in the countryside at the time when the lists were being written. They circulated, for example, model *cahiers* intended to influence many rural parish assemblies. These notables were also well prepared to choose their own as electors who would go to subprovincial assemblies, thus enabling them to influence what would be done at the Estates General.[14]

The lists for those attending the assemblies for the two Machecoul parishes, held in late March and early April 1789, illustrate this fact. Progressive notables led the assemblies and elected themselves to the subprovincial convocation in Nantes. François-Michel Robin, a town judge, led the assembly that drew up the *cahier* for the parish of Trinité. He guided a total of forty-eight individuals who met, a disproportionate number of whom were of the urban elite. To no one's surprise, the electors sent to represent Trinité of Machecoul at the sub-provincial assembly in Nantes included Robin; Alexandre Le Meignen, a lawyer from the *parlement*; Joseph-Marie Praud, a local noble; and the principal of the *collège*, Etienne Gashignard. Less is known about the composition of the Sainte-Croix parish assembly, but it would be safe to conclude that the presence of notables at this meeting was considerable as well. Although forty-three were present and twenty-four signed the Sainte-Croix *cahier*, the mere seven who identified their profession were members of the urban elite, as was the president of the assembly, a local prosecuting attorney named Pierre-Mathurin Couédélo. The Sainte-Croix electors sent to the subprovincial assembly of Nantes were Jean Perrault, a lawyer; the surgeon Augustin Mainguet; Pierre Marie Grellier de Monic, a self-proclaimed *bourgeois*; and a merchant named Jean Salaün. Absent from both the convocations were the two *recteurs*, abbé Hervé de la Bauche and abbé Blanchard. Their absence stood in contrast to many of the region's smaller parishes, such as nearby La Marne, where *recteurs* often led the assemblies that drew up the parish *cahiers*, and in doing so had a profound influence on what was written.[15]

The two parish *cahiers* for Machecoul indicate that religious matters were of the highest importance to the Third Estate elite, especially since it viewed them as central to solving the kingdom's fiscal crisis. For the *cahier* of Trinité issues involving the status of the clergy were raised, either directly or indirectly, in eight of its seventeen articles.[16] The third article of Trinité's *cahier* represented the clearest assault on clerical rights, specifically by calling for the suppression of all the clergy's fiscal privileges so that priests and religious would have the same economic obligations as members of the Third Estate. Rather stunningly, the article also implied that the state should take control of church financing, specifically stating that all debts incurred by the clergy should be absorbed as debts of the state, after which time the state should assume fiscal responsibility for clerical revenues.[17] This proposal was, in fact, an even more radical demand than those typically found in the model *cahiers* distributed by progressive notables in the area.[18] Other religious provisions addressed the fiscal crisis confronting France as well. In another section the *cahier*'s authors demanded that many religious communities should be suppressed and, after pensions were paid to those in the defunct orders, their remaining revenues be turned over to the state.[19] By no means was Trinité's *cahier* the only one in which such demands were made. Indeed, it tended to echo those demands later made in the *cahiers* of the subprovincial assemblies of the west, controlled as they were by what one scholar has termed "religiously progressive" notables from urban areas. The urban elite of the west, it has been shown, largely anticipated reforms embodied in the 1790 Civil Constitution of Clergy much more than those who drew up *cahiers* in other areas of the nation.[20]

The complaints found in the *cahier* of Sainte-Croix were similar to those of Trinité, but the Sainte-Croix list was much more succinct and attacks against the clergy were less pronounced. One stipulation called for all taxes to be paid by all three orders, and the second article specifically requested that the clergy pay poll taxes (*fouages*), as required for the other two orders. No mention of comprehensive reform of the church, its property, or payments to the clergy was made. Certainly the list indicated a desire for political reform, but unlike the *cahier* of Trinité, the Sainte-Croix list of grievances did not necessarily view the church as a major impediment to political, social, and economic improvement.[21]

The Third Estate of the *marches communes* within the parish of Trinité wrote up a list of grievances as well, but this *cahier* was later either lost or destroyed. When the *marches* electoral assembly that met at Montaigu drew up its common *cahier*, however, it seemingly condensed requests made in all the parishes within the *marches*.[22] This assembly included two landowners from Machecoul: Jean-Baptiste Passet and Pierre Brisson, both of whom represented the Third Estate. Since the inhabitants of the *marches* lived within a politically, socially, and economically privileged jurisdiction, it is hardly surprising that the *cahier* advocated little to no reform. With regard to religion, for example, the assembly recommended that "the Catholic, Apostolic, and Roman faith be the only dominant religion in the kingdom and the only one to be celebrated in public."[23] Many of the *marches* provisions sought not to reduce the power of the local clergy—as was the case with the *cahiers* of Trinité and Sainte-Croix—but rather to augment it. Indeed, the *cahier* requested that the salaries of some pastors and all *vicaires* be increased, not curtailed. Other religious demands included a more equitable distribution of church endowments among the clergy, guaranteed pensions for all sick priests and religious, a prohibition of all fairs, markets, and other assemblies on Sundays and feast days, the prohibition of any regulation requiring recipients of benefices to make known their possessions, and the establishment of an office of charity in each parish.[24]

The demands from the *marches communes* and the parishes of Machecoul are helpful in further understanding the town's religious cultures, but only to a point. To draw conclusions about what the Machecoulais religiously and politically believed on the eve of the Revolution merely from the content of *cahiers de doléances* would be unwarranted. For not only did the *cahiers* fail to represent the populace of a parish at large, influenced as they often were by politically conscious notables, but they were also subject to outside variables like model *cahiers* and preexisting political networks.[25] Still, the *cahiers* composed and written by the Machecoulais in the various assemblies seem to verify at least one finding of the previous chapter: disparate religious cultures in the community were in place on the eve of the Revolution. Some notables and seemingly some clerics sought to maintain or even augment the power of the local clergy, while other inhabitants wanted more government control and regulation of religious personnel and institutions—one result being that the laity would be more involved in ecclesiastical matters. True, there were more pressing issues than those involving the church at Machecoul and similar small towns in the province of Brittany in the spring of 1789. Yet the *cahiers* show that the many crises occurring in the province and the nation at large were often seen as inseparable from the institutional status of the church and its clergy. The politically active Machecoulais surmised that the province's crises could not be resolved apart from seeking religious reform, thus indicating the degree to which religious culture was politically influential.

The New Regime and
the Civil Constitution of the Clergy

Although the lower clergy in the diocese of Nantes had optimistic expectations going into the Estates General, it quickly became alarmed by the initial actions taken by the newly formed National Assembly in the summer of 1789.[26] Clerical discontent over revolutionary reform became evident as early as August 4, when the abolition of privileges took away the financial entitlements and sources of revenue enjoyed by the parish clergy, including the tithe.[27] In late August, not long after passage of the Declaration of the Rights of Man and the Citizen, which recognized the freedom of religion, the four priests from the Nantes region elected to the Estates General (three for the First Estate of the diocese and one for the First Estate of the *marches*) resigned and returned home. The assembly's decision on November 2 to confiscate church property, meaning that the parish priests no longer would receive funds through their benefices, only increased clerical apprehension about the Revolution's direction.[28] Later, in January 1790, when the National Assembly drew up new jurisdictions and boundaries for the entire nation, some clerics grew even more disaffected. Nantes became the *chef-lieu* of the newly created department, the Loire-Inférieure. On January 30 department administrators officially subdivided the department into seven districts, with Machecoul itself being declared a *chef-lieu* of the district bearing its name. Among other things this meant that the *marches communes*, along with the privileges that its inhabitants had enjoyed, were summarily eliminated from the fiscal administrative map.[29]

The newly created District of Machecoul, comprising a total of 780.8 square kilometers, included a total of twenty municipalities (three were added a year later), as depicted in Figure 3.1. In keeping with the new constitutional arrangement the district's administration consisted of a general council with twelve members, four of whom became members of a permanent directory, as well as a prosecuting attorney. All members of the district directory were elected indirectly, that is, by electors chosen in turn by a relatively narrow franchise. Since the administrative acts of the district's general council could be annulled by departmental authorities, the autonomy exercised by district officials was limited. Still, district authorities were expected to be the crucial "eyes and arms" of the departmental administrations, and as such were a vital link in the new regime's chain of command. Those electors who chose district administrators as well as the district officials themselves tended to come from the urban elite—the same elite heavily represented among those who chose the electors.[30]

But as important as the formation of a district administration was to Machecoul, just as significant was the establishment of municipal administrations. The National Assembly established the offices of mayor and council members in each municipality, a jurisdiction that usually was made coterminus with Catholic parishes. Similar to district administrators, the duties of officers at the municipal level were primarily concerned with executing and enforcing decisions made on

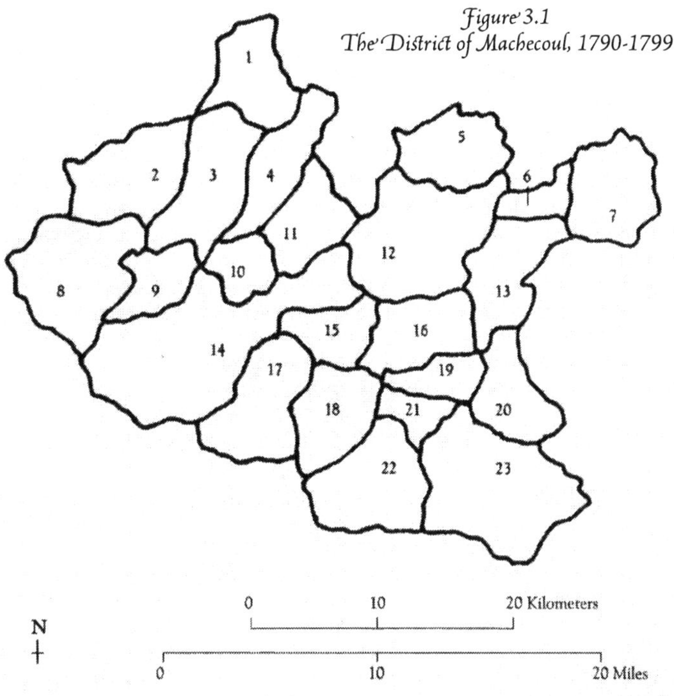

Communes by Name (corresponding to the numbers above):

1. Port-Saint-Père
2. Saint-Hilaire-de-Chaleons
3. Saint-Pazanne
4. Saint-Mars-de-Coutais
5. La Chevrolière
6. Geneston
7. Montbert
8. Bourgneuf-en-Retz
9. Fresnay
10. Saint-Même-le-Tenu
11. Saint-Lumine-de-Coutais
12. Saint-Philbert-de-Grand-Lieu
13. Saint-Columbin
14. Machecoul
15. La Marne
16. La Limousinière
17. Paulx
18. Saint-Etienne-de-Mer-Morte
19. Saint-Etienne-de-Corcoué
20. Saint-Jean-de-Corcoué
21. La Benâte
22. Touvois
23. Legé

the national and departmental tiers, not necessarily with exercising any significant degree of autonomy. Indeed, either departmental or district administrations could annul a municipal council's initiatives. Similar to the selection of district electors, a relatively narrow franchise elected the mayor and municipal council members, the number of which varied according to the size of the municipality. Only a male who could pay the municipal administration a poll tax equivalent to ten days of work could be an "active citizen" with the right to vote. That usually meant only large landowners, wealthy urban professionals, and affluent shopkeepers could cast votes, and predictably they usually elected their own.[31]

Both the creation of new local administrations and the electoral process represented a significant power shift at the local level in the early part of the Revolution, thereby creating new tensions within many municipalities of western France. This was probably no more true than among notables from the *marches communes*, who lost much power to other notables in the town who assumed positions in the district and municipal administrations. Many Breton *recteurs*, moreover, saw their political power and social prestige vanish or transferred to new public functionaries—an especially demoralizing development since many such notables were highly critical of the church. This is why elections held in 1790 often resulted in political divisions within Breton parishes between supporters of the new local administrations and those of the *recteur*. Yet by and large only a few *recteurs* in the countryside expressed overt disapproval when the elections first took place.[32] For the upper clergy, though, it was a different story. The bishop of Nantes, Monseigneur Charles Eutrope de la Laurencie, demonstrated his opposition to new municipal officials by failing to participate in the Sunday services at the cathedral with those newly elected, an act that outraged many revolutionary officials.[33]

Unsurprisingly, Machecoul's urban elite won many local elections and so came to be heavily represented in the new administrations. Two lawyers from the town were among the thirty-six elected to the departmental directory, which was given a wide range of powers over its jurisdiction by the National Assembly. Five of the fifteen elected to the district directory were also elite Machecoulais, thus ensuring that the town would be well represented at the district level. Of course the town's notables were also heavily represented in the commune's eleven-member municipal administration.[34] Some communes in the Breton departments elected their *recteurs* as mayors or municipal officers, but in Machecoul the political situation was such that neither abbé Hervé nor abbé Blanchard could amass enough political support to overtake the town notables.[35]

As alarming as the election of new local administrators was to the local clergy, legislative activity in Paris during the first half of 1790 did more to raise clerical anxiety about the Revolution. This was especially the case on February 13 when, citing the Declaration of the Rights of Man and the Citizen as a rationale, the assembly released all members of religious orders from their perpetual vows and thereby permitted them to leave their communities. Debate over the question of church financing continued in the assembly throughout the late winter and early spring, leading to a legislative confrontation on April 12. On that day Dom Gerle, largely in an effort to appease the right wing of the assembly, introduced a resolution that Catholicism be proclaimed the official state religion. His proposal backfired, for the following day the assembly's progressive wing succeeded in passing a deliberation stating the exact opposite of what Gerle had wanted.[36] To many Breton *recteurs* the rejection of Dom Gerle's resolution was the most discernible sign up to that point that the assembly, and indeed the Revolution itself, was seeking to destroy the Catholic Church. The lower clergy in the diocese of Nantes consequently condemned the new decree at an assembly held on April 19.[37]

In May and June both national and local administrators made preparations for the sale of church lands, the *biens nationaux*, that had been confiscated by earlier legislation. By July all church land was officially put up for sale in France. Some among the clergy in western France may have had misgivings about the sale of these lands, but there were no obvious protests launched by the Breton *recteurs* in the district of Machecoul or, for that matter, in the Loire-Inférieure. All members of the clergy in the region submitted to the requirements set down by government officials, probably because at that time they were still hopeful that the new settlement drawn up by the National Assembly would not result in a substantial loss of revenue.[38]

Thus, active clerical opposition to the Revolution in the Machecoul area remained relatively minor up until the middle of 1790. But that quickly changed when the National Assembly passed the Civil Constitution of the Clergy on July 12.[39] This controversial legislation stipulated that the state pay all clerical salaries, eliminated most nonepiscopal offices, rendered dioceses in France coterminus with the newly formed departments and, most controversially, required that bishops and *curés* be selected by lay assemblies, in which a Protestant or Jew could conceivably help elect a Catholic bishop. The lay election of local and departmental pastors, in effect, severed all ties between the French church and the pope, directly defying the Tridentine insistence on an unbroken chain of ecclesiastical command.[40]

Denunciation of this legislation was pervasive and prompt, among both the upper and lower clergy in the Loire-Inférieure. As tensions mounted over the implementation of the Civil Constitution during the second half of 1790, Nantes's bishop Monseigneur Eutrope was among the many bishops in France to voice his opposition to the new legislation.[41] Near the end of November a *mandement* from the bishop declared his adherence to a pastoral letter written by the bishop of Boulogne that had denounced the new legislation and recommended that the priests under his authority follow his lead.[42] The following day—the same day on which the National Assembly decreed that all priests had to swear an oath of fidelity signifying their assent to the Civil Constitution of the Clergy—department officials denounced Monseigneur Eutrope and called for the election of a new bishop for the department.[43]

Meanwhile, the lower clergy in the diocese of Nantes needed no directive from the bishop in opposing the legislation. In late October a little more than one hundred of the most vocal and influential priests, including six from Machecoul, convened to discuss the new legislation. The result of the gathering was the publication of a thirty-four-page pamphlet entitled *L'adresse à l'Assemblée Nationale*. Authorship of the text has been attributed to abbé François Chevalier, the *recteur* of a local parish within the Machecoul District and one of the priests who had resigned from the National Assembly in late August 1789.[44] Yet the first of the 104 priests to sign the protest was none other than Roland Hervé de la Bauche, the *recteur* of Trinité at Machecoul. It probably was imperative that the Machecoul *recteur* be the first to sign because the argument addressed to the National Assembly was primarily theological, and thus the signature of one of the few priests among the lower clergy holding a doctorate in theology symbolized that the protest was doctrinally sound and consistent with official church teaching.

The tract included several arguments against the new state laws. It stated that the Civil Constitution was heretical in that it compromised the function of the priestly ministry and destroyed church hierarchy through lay assemblies electing bishops and pastors.[45] This concern in particular reflected a recognition of papal authority and an emphasis on the Tridentine notion of church hierarchy to which the lower clergy in the Breton province strongly adhered. Yet another complaint was that the Civil Constitution abolished spiritual jurisdiction of the priests, a reference to the government having much more control over the church in France under the new legislation. The writer declared that "we render to Caesar that which belongs to Caesar; but we will never forget that spiritual things are not at the discretion of human will."[46] The tract's final argument was an assertion that the "true" religion was being constrained by the state's recognition of other religions. This was not so much directed at the Civil Constitution itself, but rather at the National Assembly's rejection of Dom Gerle's motion. The priests saw the toleration of other forms of religion in France as leading to an irreparable breakdown in society, most notably a decline in moral behavior.[47] The tract ended by making two requests: that an assembly of the church of France be convened in order to design, in concert with the National Assembly, a reform program regarding the church's discipline and organization; and that the National Assembly proclaim Catholicism the only official religion in France.[48]

The tract's comprehensive message was that the lower clergy in France was going to be irreversibly injured by the new legislation; a clear sense of clerical persecution was evident throughout the pamphlet. The protesters made it evident, however, that their objection to the Civil Constitution had little to do with the significant loss in their revenues. In the preface they stated that "the loss of our property and the suppression of our order does not enter in any way into the plan of our proceeding. In the school of a poor God we have learned to make some sacrifices."[49] The protesters likely realized that any reference to monetary affairs would cause those who would read the tract to dismiss their complaints all the more easily and thereby weaken their arguments. Yet it was obvious to all that the financial scheme laid out by the Civil Constitution, by which the government would provide a *traitement* of 1,200 livres to most *curés* (less than half of what the Machecoul *recteurs* were earning through their benefices), would mean a substantial loss in revenues for most *recteurs* in the diocese of Nantes.[50]

Once the tract became known, the National Assembly and departmental directory reacted swiftly and punitively toward the lower-clergy petitioners. On November 12 the Loire-Inférieure's administrators issued a decree proclaiming that those who had signed the tract were officially denounced at the National Assembly and that authorities in Paris gave departmental officials the right to take action against these "criminals of the nation." The authorities immediately denied all priests who had signed the tract their salaries and suspended them from political functions (namely those who were mayors or municipal officials). The decree itself was subsequently announced during the sermons of all parish masses in the department. After the order was promulgated, a few priests in the Machecoul District decided to retract their names from the protest.[51] But most who had signed, including the *recteur* of Machecoul's Trinité, stood firm.

The stage, therefore, was set for a decisive confrontation between the clergy and state authorities in and around the town over the Civil Constitution of the Clergy. Though it would be only one of countless political crises occurring throughout France in 1791, the conflict here quickly became more explosive than most. It has been argued—and indeed somewhat affirmed in Machecoul's case—that the extreme religious volatility in western France was attributable to a somewhat uncommon combination: a strong, Tridentine ecclesiastical structure on the one hand and a religiously progressive lay elite on the other.[52] Can it be concluded—as most revolutionary officials did at the time—that this clerical discontent over the Revolution's religious settlement was economically driven, especially since Breton *recteurs* stood to lose much revenue through the Civil Constitution? There is much here to indicate that the Breton clergy's claim that the new legislation violated their theological and spiritual principles was sincere. True to the principles of Tridentine belief, priests like abbé Hervé saw the Civil Constitution as an affront to their conception of the church and their role as local spiritual leaders. On the other hand, the same evidence suggests that the lay elite was just as genuine in its support of opposing principles; to accuse them of a simple power grab over church affairs would be just as disingenuous.

The Oath Crisis

Given the volatile situation at Machecoul near the end of 1790, true belligerence was bound to erupt. It came no sooner than the first day of 1791, when, at the high mass commemorating the Circumcision of Jesus Christ, abbé Roland Hervé de la Bauche mounted the pulpit at Trinité and reportedly addressed his parishioners in the following manner:

I commend to you most especially the very poor, for poverty is increasing. The most basic necessities are dear and resources are diminished. Deprived of what I had to assist them, I leave it to you to help. I am deprived of my revenues, and what evil have I done, my brothers? What crime have I committed? Why deprive me of my revenues? I call on you to witness the twenty years that I have been with you. Have I ever not preached the gospel, administered the sacraments, or been faithful to compassion and to religion? It was not long ago when I said to you: render to Caesar that which belongs to Caesar, and to God that which belongs to God. I gave a good example, my brothers. I paid my taxes and no one made a more considerable patriotic contribution. I am a patriot, I love my country. The object for which people paid me the tithe was assistance for the poor, and this cannot be justly deprived. People say that I do not want to give in. Give in? But my brothers, what about my duty? My religion? Have I lost it? People also say that I will be removed from my *cure*. My *cure*, my brothers, my *cure* I hold from God, I hold it from the Church, and whoever replaces me, I am not afraid to say it, will be an intruder, a thief who will not enter through the door. Do not give him your trust and do not receive the sacraments from him. I believe that is all I need to say to you. Do not worry about me, and to the poor who are trying to get aid and who will not complain, I say: submit to all, just like I myself have done.[53]

With these words the Machecoul *recteur* rejected the Civil Constitution of the Clergy by refusing to take the Ecclesiastical Oath as prescribed by law. On hearing the words, municipal officials were incensed. The following day two officers recorded the sermon to the best of their recollection in the form of an *arrêté*. Two days later it was deposed at the municipal clerk's office, which forwarded a copy of the sermon to district authorities.[54]

Abbé Hervé was far from the only cleric to reject the oath during the first few months of 1791. Of the approximately 485 priests in the Loire-Inférieure in 1791, only about 106 eventually took the oath—including those who initially swore the oath with reservations, which was in clear violation of the law. This oath-taking rate of 22 percent, according to Timothy Tackett, was among the lowest departmental rates in all of France.[55] In the Machecoul District the incidence of oath-taking was even lower than the departmental average. Of the fifty-seven priests re-

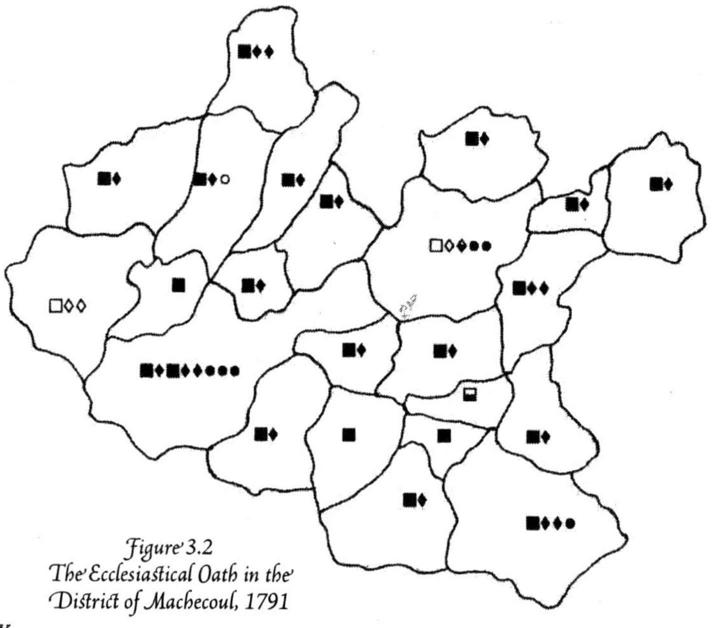

Figure 3.2
The Ecclesiastical Oath in the
District of Machecoul, 1791

Key

■ *Recteur* who refused Oath   □ *Recteur* who took Oath   ▣ *Recteur* who took Oath with restrictions
♦ *Vicaire* who refused Oath   ◊ *Vicaire* who took Oath   ◈ *Vicaire* who took Oath with restrictions
● *Aumônier, prêtre habituée, or*   ○ *Aumônier, prêtre habituée, or*
   desservant du prieuré who   *desservant du prieuré who*
   refused Oath   refused Oath

siding in the district, only eight had taken the oath by the end of March, and two of them had added restrictions. The entire Machecoul District had an oath-taking rate of 14 percent, meaning that the town was set in one of the most clerically defiant zones in the entire nation. Figure 3.2 depicts the geographic distribution of oath-taking and refusals in the district. It shows that all of the eight priests who were residing in the municipality of Machecoul (two *recteurs*, three *vicaires*, two retired priests, one chaplain) were among the majority in the district who rejected the oath.[56]

With so many clerics refusing to take the oath, district officials had little choice but to meet and promptly elect new, compliant *curés*. On March 27 district electors, together with the National Guard, a brigade of the local police, and various local officials, convened at Machecoul to elect nineteen new *curés* needed in the district.[57] The assembly first decided that the town's parish of Sainte-Croix would soon be united with that of Trinité, and so there was no need to nominate a *curé* for Sainte-Croix. Since Trinité was the most important parish in the district, the assembly started with election of the town's new *curé*.[58] The obvious choice was abbé François Villers, the pastor at Saint-Philbert-de-Grand-Lieu and later a member of the National Convention, as he was one of the few *recteurs* in the district who had taken the oath. But abbé Villers explained that he was strongly attached to the people of his parish and wanted to remain there. Two other priests were nominated to the position, but both quickly declined.

The assembly finally decided on abbé Pierre Letort, one of the *vicaires* at Saint-Philbert-de-Grand-Lieu who had followed his *recteur*'s example and taken the oath. District officials seemingly had wanted someone who was more experienced and perhaps more prestigious, but the scarcity of constitutional priests in the region necessitated the election of a relatively young and unseasoned *vicaire*.[59] Abbé Letort was about thirty-four years of age at the time of his election to the *curé* of Trinité.[60] Born in Nantes in the parish of Saint-Denis, he had become a priest in 1782. A month before he was elected as a Machecoul pastor, he had been nominated as *curé* of the parish of Saint-Sébastien in Nantes, but refused to accept the distinguished position.[61] Little else is known about this priest except that he became a faithful supporter of the Revolution at Machecoul, if indeed his subsequent membership in the National Guard detachment and the Jacobin Club is any indication.[62]

As the Civil Constitution of the Clergy began to be implemented, those refusing to take the oath stepped up their defiance and inflammatory rhetoric.[63] In early March Pope Pius VI finally reacted to developments in France by issuing a condemnation of the Civil Constitution. Armed with this proclamation, refractory bishops and *curés* denounced the new elections and proclaimed that constitutional priests were apostates. On March 28 Charles Eutrope, the deposed bishop of Nantes, issued an ordinance from the city of Ghent (Belgium) condemning the new bishop, Julien Minée, as a heretic and declaring his election null. Eutrope declared his support for all the priests who had refused to take the oath, as well as those laypeople who had declined to recognize Minée as their bishop. He also announced that all official acts performed by Minée were unauthorized, and that anyone ordained by the bishop would be excommunicated.[64] Adding insult to injury, he called everyone who abided by the Civil Constitution "intruders," "schismatics," "usurpers," and depicted them as deluded, lax, ambitious, and impious.[65]

The proclamations issued by the pope and the deposed bishop proved very beneficial to local opponents of the Civil Constitution in and around Machecoul. Yet it was the actions of the district's refractory clergy that proved most pivotal to the resistance. A case in point was an incident on the very same day that clerical elections were held in the district seat. In the midafternoon, the time at which vespers were usually held, the National Guard, the brigade of the local police, the electoral corps, the general council of the district, and the judicial tribunal proceeded to the parish church of Trinité to chant the Te Deum in thanksgiving for the well-being of Louis XVI. To the shock of everyone attending, no priest was there to perform the ceremony prescribed by law. A detachment was sent to the presbytery to ask a priest to perform the ceremony, but there was no response by any of the priests. At that point abbé Villers took the initiative to lead the singing of the Te Deum for the king.

The officials and government supporters returned to the town hall to continue the elections. A report written later that night described what followed:

> In front of the cloister wall [next to the church], a tumultuous gathering was heard, and several municipal officials went to the porch of the church where people were shouting that there was a revolt, and they found there many inhabitants of the countryside gathered. And after learning what was taking place, they knew that the gathering was initiated by *Sieur* Hervé the *recteur* who, surrounded by many people, was reading a printed letter that he said he had received from Rome, announcing that the priests who took the oath were excommunicated. After making the people of the countryside peaceful and quiet once more, municipal officials returned to the hall. They recalled that in the morning at the end of the high mass there was much clamor at the moment when *Sieur* Hervé, without warning anyone, took the Holy Sacrament and carried it to the chapel of the Calvarian monastery, accompanied by many women and some men. They said to him as they left the chapel, "What do you want us to do, *Monsieur le doyen*? Speak! We are yours." It was also recalled

> that after the *recteur* of Saint-Philbert chanted the Te Deum, *Sieur*
> Hervé said to the women, "leave, leave," and that last Friday, a feast
> day, he preached the first mass in an incendiary manner, as he had
> done at different times before. The fermentation, which appears to
> reign in the spirit of the inhabitants of the countryside particularly,
> is a result of the fanaticism that he preaches openly, just like many
> other *curés* in the district.

Abbé Hervé, the order went on to say, later chanted the Te Deum at vespers, but he did so in absence of all government officials: yet another defiant act on his part.[66] With tensions mounting, local administrators wrote to departmental officials the following day, asking that more soldiers be sent to Machecoul to ensure tranquillity. Departmental administrators agreed, and the additional troops arrived in the town at the beginning of April.[67]

As early as March 1791, therefore, popular opposition to the Revolution was considerable within the commune. The excerpt above gives some indication of those who were disaffected by the new order and lent their support to the ousted pastor. District administrators mentioned several times that many women were among the defenders of "non-juror" or refractory priests. That Hervé de la Bauche transferred the Holy Sacrament to the female monastery indicates that the women regulars also constituted a bulwark of support for these defiant priests. In any case, the political activism of women with regard to the oath crisis was by no means unique to Machecoul. Indeed, a great many women throughout France offered their support to the refractory clergy.[68]

Looking a little more closely at exactly who remained loyal to these defiant priests reveals, however, something extraordinary and unexpected. Some women who made up the monastic community undoubtedly came from the same notable families at Machecoul that also had members in the departmental, district, and municipal administrations (as names like Gigault, Lemeignen, Biclet, Reliquet indicate). In other words, these Calvarians were from the town's urban elite—the same elite that, according to most historians, comprised a bulwark of religious progressivism. This incident in the town suggests, then, that the line between those who supported the Civil Constitution of the Clergy and the Ecclesiastical Oath and those who opposed them was intricately drawn within the community, and in no way followed strict geographic or socioeconomic classifications. Notable families themselves, in fact, appear to have been divided over the Revolution's religious reform.

The description of the event also indicates that "inhabitants of the countryside," that is, peasants, also supported the refractory recteur of Machecoul. This, too, was not extraordinary in France; in many regions peasants rose up in favor of an ousted *curé*.[69] What accounts for their support in this case? Certainly there were spiritual convictions (especially among wealthy peasants) at stake in this crisis, but economic factors may have also played a part in the peasants' decision to support abbé Hervé. As difficult as peasants had it in the late Old Regime with a series of bad harvests, in many ways their lot became worse during the first few years of the Revolution. While taxes levied on behalf of the king, the church, and the seigneurs were eliminated shortly after the Revolution began, the new system of taxation actually increased the burden on many tenant farmers. Indeed, due to a series of fiscal reforms by the National Assembly, landowners—many of whom were highly represented in the local revolutionary administrations—were able to transfer more of their tax obligations unto their tenants, thereby soaking the poor.[70] For this reason, the refractory *recteur* became more or less a symbol of the Old Regime: a period when poor peasants were better able to make ends meet. Thus support for abbé Hervé among struggling peasants was an expression of their disdain and even hatred for the new regime, which they no doubt blamed for their increasingly desperate plight. But probably even more significant to this development was the disposition of relatively wealthy tenant farmers, who were often the lynchpin of rural society in this region—the leaders of the peasantry as a whole. Hoping to benefit from developments like voting and tax reform, wealthy tenant farmers grew bitterly disappointed with the new regime after initially receiving so few benefits.[71] As a key constituency within the rural society, the wealthier tenant farmers' decision to repudiate the Civil Constitution of the Clergy was a vote to reject the Revolution as a whole. To a degree those priests who had repudiated the new legislation and had refused to take the oath may have helped persuade the more affluent tenant farmers that they had gained little through the Revolution, but there is nothing to suggest that such peasants played the role of lackeys to the refractory clergy; the decision to defy the new regime was these peasants' own.[72]

The oath crisis occurred, therefore, at the critical moment when the rural community was turning against the new order, in no small part because of the dire economic distress of poor peasants as well as the Revolution's inability to confer promised benefits on relatively affluent ones. True as that may be, though, two developments occurring at the same time that the oath crisis was unfolding further cemented peasant disaffection with the Revolution. The records for the selling of the *biens nationaux* in the district of Machecoul indicate that those who acquired property either were members of the local administration or were known supporters of the Revolution, which likely gave the appearance that town notables were out to enrich themselves.[73] Even worse, the emigration of some of the most prominent landlords, who could afford to be rather lenient toward their tenants, merely compounded the economic discontent—a trend all too common in the Machecoul area. By April 1792 approximately fifteen landowners in the commune had already emigrated, and at least the same number of tenant farmers no longer were able to rely on the goodwill of these extremely affluent landlords.[74]

All in all, the oath crisis at Machecoul reveals that the episode was a defining moment for the town not only because of the large numbers of clerics who refused to take the oath and had to be removed from their posts but also because of the substantial public support that the refractory clergy went on to enjoy. Surely much of that support was indicative of political and economic discontent with the new order, especially since area peasants were suffering even more than they had been shortly before the Revolution began. But the evidence also suggests that the ties between religious culture and popular support for the refractory clergy have been too easily overlooked by historians. In Machecoul's case many notables—many women, but some men, too—lent their support to the refractory clergy, most likely because they subscribed to the Tridentine conception of the Church, together with the spirituality that informed it. The religious culture of peasants should not be easily overlooked, either, though admittedly it was quite dissimilar to that of notables. Given that area peasants were *clerical* yet not necessarily *devout* in the Tridentine sense, it is no less understandable why peasants would grow hostile at the potential loss of their pastor.[75] One can argue that for them the *recteur* was more than just a symbol of their cohesion and collectivity; his departure marked the loss of their longtime spiritual compass. It was tantamount to losing their collective soul.

Mobilization and Resistance

In response to the explosive situation in the countryside as well as to political events in Paris, many of the Revolution's supporters in the west mobilized and united through the formation of Jacobin clubs. The former province of Brittany, in fact, saw a dramatic increase in the establishment of Jacobin clubs; in March 1791 only thirteen clubs could be found in the former province, but about one year later there were forty-three. Five new clubs began in the Loire-Inférieure alone over that year, including the Friends of the Constitution at Machecoul.[76] The exact date when the Machecoul chapter began is not known, but a petition was issued by the club in November 1791, showing that thirty-two Jacobins belonged at that time.[77] The Jacobin clubs in the Loire-Inférieure were pivotal in the oath crisis, especially given their success in organizing a crackdown on refractory priests. In late May 1791 the Nantes Jacobins, about three hundred strong, composed a petition addressed to the departmental administration calling for the closing of all chapels and religious communities where refractory priests often celebrated their masses, as well as for the banishment of all refractory clergy from the Loire-Inférieure. The petitioners stated that fanatical priests were preaching insurrection, revolt, and civil war at the chapels by announcing libels, papal bulls, and *mandements* from deposed bishops.[78]

Some historians have cast the Jacobins' activities as yet more evidence that the urban elite in the west was extraordinarily hostile and vindictive toward refractory priests. A popular riot that broke out in Nantes, specifically when departmental authorities attempted to release refractory priests from confinement in 1792, confirms antirefractory sentiment among some in the urban masses as well.[79] But at the same time that Jacobins were mobilizing politically, opposition was also on the rise. Indeed, more than two thousand in Nantes, including the former mayor Daniel de Kervégan, took to the streets in 1791 to protest the departmental decision to imprison refractory priests in the first place.[80] The two incidents together demonstrate that "the crowd" in Nantes, perhaps just like the notables at Machecoul, were fundamentally divided over the oath issue, or at the very least over government policy concerning refractory priests.

In early June 1791 departmental officials partially complied with Jacobin demands by ordering the closing of all churches and chapels deemed nonessential.[81] About three weeks later, after Louis XVI's flight from the capital and his subsequent capture and return from Varennes, a special committee composed of departmental, district, and municipal officials convened in Nantes. Its first official act was to approve the arrest of twenty priests in the department, including abbé Hervé de la Bauche and one his *vicaires*, Honoré Renaudineau.[82] After receiving these orders, administrators of the Machecoul District arrested the two near the end of June.[83] From there the police conducted the priests to Nantes and detained them at the seminary.[84]

Shortly afterward departmental officials questioned abbé Hervé about his conduct during the previous months. When asked about the purpose of his arrest, the former *recteur* responded that he was unaware of any violations on his part, although someone had told him that it was by order of the department for delivering incendiary sermons. In response to a question about "fermentation" in his parish, he answered that there was none. Officials then asked him if he had spoken against the constitution from the pulpit and in the streets. The priest declared that he had preached the Gospel, the doctrine of the Church, submission to the powers established by God, and peace, and often had told his flock that God was not a God of dissension but of peace. Departmental administrators were specifically interested in the role the Machecoul *recteur* played in proclaiming and distributing papal bulls. Abbé Hervé recalled that he had received about twenty-five copies of the deposed bishop's *mandement* in Nantes and distributed them to priests in his canton. His interrogators then asked if he was specially designated to distribute them and if so by whom. He answered that he was selected by a priest in Nantes, but refused to divulge his name. When pressed on this again, he responded that he had made a confidential promise as a priest. Departmental administrators also asked him who had written the *L'adresse à l'Assemblée Nationale*, to which Hervé responded that he was not the principal author, but also that he was not able to say who was.

The interrogation likewise included an exchange over Hervé's views of the former bishop, Eutrope de la Laurencie, as well as the constitutional clergy:

> Interrogator: Do you think that Monsieur La Laurencie will always be the bishop of Nantes?
>
> Hervé: I have no knowledge that Monsieur La Laurencie is dead, or that he offered his legal and Church-accepted resignation, and so in consequence I recognize him as my bishop and that of the diocese of Nantes.
>
> Interrogator: Did you not discourage your parishioners from going to mass or confessing to constitutional priests?
>
> Hervé: I gave them advice in accord with Divine Wisdom, prudence, and my obligation.
>
> Interrogrator: Categorically answer the question.
>
> Hervé: I follow the rules of my conscience and of the Church.

The priest admitted, though, that he and his *vicaires* gave First Communion to children who were not supposed to receive it until the first day of July to preempt constitutional clerics from doing it, thereby making the sacrament "legitimate." Abbé Renaudineau was also interrogated and essentially provided similar answers.[85]

Both abbés Hervé de la Bauche and Renaudineau disavowed preaching insurrection, disobedience to the constitution, or disrespect toward the constitutional clergy. Their testimony was deceptive if not altogether false, but on the same count the questions directed at them suggest that the administrators' perception of the situation bordered on an obsession with conspiracy. Specifically officials felt that the two priests were key individuals in a plot designed by the enemies of the nation. To many revolutionaries, resistance toward the government was part of a carefully orchestrated strategy by priests, nobles, and others opposed to the Revolution to mobilize the countryside against the nation. Although a conspiracy theory obviously predated the Revolution, it quickly became more accepted among revolutionary supporters after Louis XVI's flight to Varennes in June 1791.[86] This may explain why, for example, officials asked abbé Renaudineau whether he "had knowledge of some plots by the enemies of the Constitution," and "if his refusal to take the oath was the effect of a coalition."[87] Since departmental, district, and municipal officials failed to grasp the reasons for resistance, their response to the situation—including heavy-handed interrogations—often intensified conflict.

Departmental administrators were infuriated by Hervé's responses to their questions. Regarding him as very dangerous, they officially denounced the former *recteur* and immediately incarcerated him at the prison of Bouffay in Nantes, a jail detaining the most dangerous criminals and infamous for its horrendous conditions. Joseph Hervé, Roland's brother, asked Machecoul district administrators in early July to intercede with departmental officials for the release of his brother, who at the time was sixty-five years old and purportedly in ill health. About a month later the priest himself wrote to departmental commissioners pleading that he be released and attached a letter from a Nantes doctor stating that the poor air in the prison was putting his life in danger.[88] Officials subsequently launched an inquiry at Machecoul in August to determine the extent of abbé Hervé's culpability. All thirty-five of the witnesses who testified at the inquiry were in agreement about what they had heard from Hervé on the first day of January. Their testimony, moreover, tended to contradict the responses that the former *recteur* had given during his interrogation. The district tribunal took into consideration the testimony against Hervé, as well as the fact that he was old and in poor health, and on September 7 decided to liberate the former *recteur* from the prison at Bouffay. But the release was contingent on several conditions, including that he report to police authorities every day, and that he have no other residence aside from the one in Nantes that he and his brother were to share.[89]

The judicial proceedings show that the thirty-five witnesses at Machecoul were almost evenly split between men and women. Although some witnesses were local administrators or members of their families, most seemingly were not. Many witnesses, moreover, probably were residents of the town, since they listed their professions as bakers, nail makers, merchants, and the like. Yet the witness list also included the names of Louis Giraudeau, Jean Reilleau, and Pierre Brisson, all of whom declared themselves tenant farmers.[90] Assuming that this inquiry had some semblance of integrity and witnesses came forward under little duress, the appearance of the tenant farmers at the inquiry confirms that an intensely complex split had occurred in and around Machecoul over the Civil Constitution of the Clergy and the Ecclesiastical Oath.

But neither abbé Hervé's incarceration nor his subsequent release ameliorated tensions within the town during the second half of 1791. And when an incident occurred on August 14, the eve of the Feast of the Assumption, civil conflict in the town once again came to the fore. On that day abbé Simon Blanchard, the refractory *recteur* at Machecoul's parish of Sainte-Croix, formally declared that neither he nor his *vicaire* would march in the traditional Assumption procession with the constitutional *curé*, abbé Letort. Municipal officials again were incensed, especially because the Sainte-Croix *recteur* chose the procession of the Assumption for this symbolic resistance—a feast that traditionally conferred a sacred status on the political order.

Municipal officials ordered that the two priests participate in the procession, but the following day they were conspicuously absent from the ritual. Meeting again after the procession, officials concluded that the true motive given by the *recteur* for his lack of participation was that his conscience forbade him from consorting with a constitutional priest. Officials further contended that abbé Blanchard was creating a disruption in the commune because many Machecoulais, including peasant parishioners from Trinité, were receiving the sacraments from abbé Blanchard rather than abbé Letort, the constitutional *curé*.[91] When the death of a parishioner took place, inhabitants allowed abbé Letort to conduct the rite of Christian burial in Trinité's parish church, but family members of the deceased remained outside the church doors as the ritual took place. In the form of a decree, municipal officials demanded that district or departmental officials do something about abbé Blanchard and his *vicaire*.[92]

District administrators at first deemed that abbé Blanchard was not much of a threat since he was quite ill, but they warned that if he or his *vicaire* persisted in celebrating mass at Sainte-Croix, he would be subject to the penalties marked out by the June 7 departmental decree.[93] Abbé Blanchard apparently continued to celebrate mass for another nine weeks, but on October 26 the Machecoul Jacobins insisted that district administrators make a prompt decision whether to maintain or suppress the parish of Sainte-Croix and to replace Blanchard if the parish was to be maintained. About a month later still no word came from district officials on this matter, prompting the Machecoul Jacobins to petition departmental administrators in Nantes.[94] Three days later the department decreed that Blanchard be removed from the parish of Sainte-Croix and replaced by a constitutional *curé*.[95]

The parishioners of Sainte-Croix, however, were far from ready to give up. The following Sunday all of the former *marguilliers* and other parishioners from Sainte-Croix, totaling close to one hundred men, gathered after mass to discuss the department's decision. They too composed a petition to departmental administrators protesting the decision to remove Blanchard. The parishioners argued that peace and tranquillity had reigned in the parish ever since the beginning of the Revolution, and that Blanchard himself was beyond reproach. They even included a certificate from the local commandant of the army battalion stationed in the town attesting to Blanchard's integrity. The petitioners added that the motives of the Machecoul Jacobins were, in their own words, "false and calumnious" and an affront to religion.[96]

The petition written by the parishioners of Sainte-Croix offers yet more insight into the divisions within the commune over the Civil Constitution. Many who attended the gathering were no doubt peasants from the rural sectors, which, given what we know about the situation of tenant farmers and others in the rural community, was in no way extraordinary. But the petition itself is articulate, indicating that someone relatively well educated wrote it. It also shows that the gathering was initiated by the former *marguilliers* of Sainte-Croix: a noteworthy fact since church wardens in western France during the Old Regime were usually notables.[97] Many of those assembled at Sainte-Croix, in fact, were the same ones who had gathered less than three years before to compose their parish's *cahier de doléances*.[98] That a battalion commander stepped forward and wrote to authorities in praise of a refractory priest, moreover, offers another example of a notable at odds with government policy regarding refractory priests. These and other aspects of the Sainte-Croix protest are yet more signs suggesting that the divide over the oath crisis in the town was extremely nuanced.

Several days after the Sainte-Croix petition was composed, municipal officials at Machecoul discovered what had occurred that Sunday at Sainte-Croix. They quickly denounced the petition and those who had gathered to write it, claiming that it was an attempt to employ calumny and lies against the administrative corps, and that the content of the petition was obviously contrary to the laws of the nation. They proclaimed that if all inhabitants of Sainte-Croix, and specifically the former *marguilliers*, continued to cause disorder they would be subject to the penalties established by the police to maintain civil order.[99] The Sainte-Croix petition and the denunciation by municipal officials made it all the more necessary, from the standpoint of district and departmental officials, that Blanchard be removed from his *cure*.

But by the time abbé Blanchard had been removed, the political fallout caused by the oath crisis could not be contained. In late 1791 the protest movement against the Civil Constitution of the Clergy and the removal of the refractory was already well organized and substantially supported. Many tracts, including papal briefs, pastoral letters from deposed bishops, and numerous catechisms were circulating throughout the district. In mid-December district officials exhorted all municipal officials within their jurisdiction to make a diligent search for any kind of seditious literature and to seize it immediately. They were particularly concerned about a pamphlet entitled *Catéchisme à l'usage des fidèles dans les circonstances actuelles*, which urged Catholics not to recognize the legitimacy of the Constitutional Church.[100]

By that point local administrators believed that they had no choice but to crack down on refractory priests much more stringently than administrators from other regions in France were doing. Even the so-called "law of toleration" passed in the Constituent Assembly on May 7, 1791, which in principle gave religious freedom to those who supported the refractory clergy, did not prevent administrators in the west from imposing "residence changes" (in the Loire-Inférieure, this was tantamount to house arrest) on refractory priests.[101] Although this reaction may have been somewhat attributable to the anticlerical attitudes of administrators of the west that predated the Revolution, arguably widespread popular support for the refractory clergy was an even more significant motivation. In any case, on February 8, 1792, departmental officials decreed that all refractory priests in the Loire-

Inférieure must reside exclusively in the city of Nantes. Many targeted clerics, however, refused to follow the law and in effect became fugitives. In the Machecoul District alone, two months after the departmental decree was issued, twenty-nine of the forty-eight priests known to have been in the district were considered fugitives. By that time abbés Hervé and Blanchard were in Nantes, the chaplain abbé Esseaud remained in the town, but the whereabouts of all three *vicaires* were unknown.[102] Thus on March 22 departmental authorities ordered that those priests facing prosecution would be detained at the former religious house in Nantes's parish of Saint-Clément.[103]

The March 22 decree also called on district and municipal authorities to seek out and arrest those priests in the countryside who refused to submit to authorities and take up residence in Nantes. Authorities from the Machecoul District were especially determined to go after refractory priests, and their correspondence with other districts in the Loire-Inférieure at this time reveals their zeal. In April they complained to district administrators in Chateaubriant (located on the northeast side of the department), expressing their surprise that some district authorities were not abiding by the departmental orders to arrest refractory priests.[104] About a month later the Machecoul Jacobins petitioned the Legislative Assembly, denouncing administrators in the nearby Clisson district for "protecting fanatical priests" and "giving the example of disobedience to the law."[105]

This correspondence tells us that Machecoul District administrators were especially zealous about arresting refractory priests, as well as extremely vindictive toward their fellow district administrators who lacked the same ardor. Such evidence has become the basis for some historians equating Jacobins to totalitarians of the twentieth century.[106] True, revolutionaries like those at Machecoul often equivocated on notions of political and religious freedom, but one cannot overlook that authorities in the town were truly under siege, and that the refractory priests were at the center of the quickly escalating incivility. Indeed, they saw the situation as so volatile that they called on army regulars as well as National Guard soldiers to maintain the peace. In January 1792 the Machecoul municipal corps reported that

> For ten months . . . public peace and tranquillity would have con
> tinually been troubled at Machecoul without the presence of the
> line troops that are stationed here. The peasants of the countryside,
> and even those in the town, completely devoted to the Old Regime
> and not wanting to recognize the new Constitution, apparently are
> only waiting until the moment troops depart to manifest their bad
> intentions and perhaps strike some hard blows that they would not
> have done previously . . . . The nomination of a constitutional priest
> to the *cure* of Trinité and the expulsion of the refractory pastor of
> Sainte-Croix have strongly animated the people of the countryside and
> other people who are won over and deluded by the unconstitutional
> priests, and so there is everything to fear if the detachment of line
> troops leaves Machecoul without being first replaced.[107]

Troops were needed, not just because of numerous confrontations involving local government officials and constitutional *curés* in the district in 1791 and 1792 but also because of public support for the refractory clergy was still quite palpable, particularly among former nobles.[108] Although many of these had left the area by 1792, some who had land in the district moved from the cities of Nantes or Rennes and returned to their châteaux, where they created "countersocieties" consisting of their families, notable neighbors, peasants, clients, and fugitive refractory priests.[109] Increasingly army and National Guard units, including the Machecoul detachment, went into the countryside and arrested those suspected of calling for insurrection. In the middle of August 1792 district officials took control of all firearms and gunpowder within their jurisdiction, increased patrols and surveillance throughout the region, and set an evening curfew at the local *cabarets* and *auberges*.[110] Within the town itself, police authorities sought out seditious literature and firearms, going so far as to search the houses of two well-known citizens.[111]

In view of all these developments, departmental authorities saw little choice but to order the incarceration of all refractory clergy at Saint-Clément in Nantes near the beginning of June 1792. Initially the directive resulted in the confinement of about one hundred priests, but another two hundred priests residing in the *chef-lieu* left the city or went into hiding.[112] On August 26 the Legislative Assembly passed the law requiring the deportation of all refractory priests under the age of sixty. Of the 163 refractories detained at that time in Nantes, sixty-six preferred detention to exile, while the remaining ninety-seven agreed to leave for Spain or Portugal.[113] Abbé Blanchard, who later died in Bilbao, Spain, was among those deported, but abbé Hervé stayed at Saint-Clément since he was over sixty years old and therefore judged incapable of withstanding the voyage.[114] On September 10 five ships carrying the priests and about eighty other emigrants left the department for the Iberian peninsula.[115]

The deportation of these priests was perhaps the most dramatic manifestation of two diametrically opposed movements active in and around Machecoul in the second half of 1791 and 1792: Jacobin mobilization and refractory resistance. Arguably the two movements gained their momentum from one other, thereby mutually reinforcing each other's belligerence, insecurity, even paranoia.[116] When one camp intensified its attack on the enemy, the other side not only answered in kind but frequently went one step further. Together, the two movements provide a microhistorical example of the way revolution and counterrevolution spiraled toward both popular and state-sponsored violence. Although Chapter Two revealed that the ideological underpinnings for both sides were somewhat in place before the Revolution began, it seems likely that the unfolding of the oath crisis in 1791 and 1792 was even more responsible for the town's acute polarization.[117]

While it is true that rural inhabitants were more likely to support refractory priests, just as urban inhabitants were more inclined to side with local administrators, a close look at the divide here suggests that there never were any clear geographic or social boundaries between the two sides. In Machecoul's case the disparity was geographically and socially variegated—appearing in both town and the surrounding countryside, among rich and poor alike. So why should such variations matter? First, they are an indication that more than social or economic factors motivated the Machecoulais in the taking of sides over the oath, to say nothing of the Revolution itself; ideology, including that highly informed by religious belief, was clearly at work as well—above all among notables. Second, the social and economic divergence may be an indication that networks based on family, marriage, and perhaps some economic clientage may also have played a role in the taking of sides. The existence of these networks becomes much more apparent on the microhistorical level, which is perhaps why they often have been overlooked by scholars considering the origins of revolution and counterrevolution in western France.[118] And finally, these geographic and social deviations call attention to one of the primary reasons why the conflict between these revolutionary and counterrevolutionary factions became so acute; members of the two opposing sides could not help but encounter one another, both within the town and immediately beyond it, during the course of daily life.

The New Church and the Old Believers

Despite the mass deportation of refractory priests, clerical resistance remained strong since many rebellious priests remained hidden in Nantes as well as in the countryside. Still, local administrators moved forward with the church reforms that they felt were needed in their parishes.[119] In 1791 they were immediately confronted with the problem of not having enough constitutional priests to take over most of the *cures* that were vacated by the numerous refractory *recteurs*. For this reason Monseigneur Julien Minée left the department for Paris in September 1791 for the express purpose of recruiting constitutional priests to fill all the vacated positions in the Loire-Inférieure.[120] By November 1791 only ten parishes in the Machecoul District had constitutional *curés*, meaning that the other thirteen parishes had none.[121] One of the *cures* not occupied in the district was that of Sainte-Croix of Machecoul. After all the troubles that had occurred there in November and December 1791, and in light of the severe deficiency of constitutional priests, district officials finally decided to unite the parish of Sainte-Croix with that of Trinité. In March 1792 the district declared the two parishes officially combined.[122] The shortage of constitutional priests was no doubt a formidable problem for district officials, but, as before, the most imposing difficulty in establishing the Constitutional Church in many communes was the opposition raised by those who saw the new priests as *intrus*, intruders into their communities. In April 1792 Machecoul district officials decided that two of the constitutional bishop's assistants, abbés Andreux and Grémion, would serve as circuit-rider ministers by celebrating mass and administering other sacraments at those *cures* in their jurisdiction without constitutional priests. But virtually every parish within the district affected by this decision held an assembly, at which overwhelming majorities voiced their opposition to the two priests.[123]

In the parishes of the Machecoul District where constitutional *curés* had been installed over the course of 1791 and early 1792, serious incidents and confrontations subsequently abounded.[124] The most notable strife occurred in the commune of Saint-Lumine-de-Coutais, where in July 1791 sixty members of the National Guard were needed to protect the constitutional *curé*, abbé Guidon, as he began his ministry at the parish.[125] One month later the district ordered twenty men from an army regiment be stationed in the commune to look after Guidon, who frequently was the object of assassination attempts by gunfire.[126] At the commune of Montbert the municipal corps declared that they did not want the constitutional *curé* because "those who support him are the primary cause of all the trouble that is taking place and thefts that are increasing everywhere."[127]

One incident, though not as serious, also involved Machecoul's constitutional *curé*, abbé Letort. In late January 1792, while the *curé* was conducting a burial in the cemetery in the early evening, a young woman named Claire Adelaide Dubois came into town on a horse that was toting baskets and ran into Letort during the procession to the cemetery. The *curé* and others in the town did not consider it an accident because immediately before the incident Dubois allegedly had said to her *domestique*, in reference to the funeral procession, "We're going to stop them." Letort, together with the district president, Etienne Gashignard, publicly denounced Dubois and initiated criminal proceedings against her. Approximately twenty-four people, not counting the three members of the local government, testified against the young woman.[128]

But Félix Dubois, who was also a member of the Machecoul District directory, intervened on his daughter's behalf and testified several days later that it was Letort who struck his daughter's horse and publicly insulted his daughter by saying, "someone arrest this slut."[129] Still, the town's justice of the peace found merit in the complaint and made a judgement in favor of Letort, Gaschignard, and the others who filed the complaint against the young woman. He sentenced Claire Dubois to three months in prison and fined her four hundred livres.[130] On account of an appeal made by Félix Dubois, however, the justice of the peace later dismissed the charges against Demoiselle Dubois on a technicality.[131] The incident and the judicial proceedings, in and of themselves, were of minor consequence, yet they yield more subtle information regarding the town's cultural and political intricacies during the Revolution. For one, that twenty-four individuals, most of whom appear to have lived in the town, testified against Claire Dubois indicates that social tensions must have been very high in the commune, for incidents like these forced many to incriminate fellow townspeople. Second, the incident shows that although the district administrators were adamant supporters of the Revolution, they were not always united and completely in accord with each other. On another level, the court case involved a confrontation between Félix Dubois, the vice president of the district directory, and the president, Etienne Gaschignard.

The defense of abbé Letort on behalf of local administrators also reveals that the Machecoul patriots were highly involved in ecclesiastical affairs at Trinité. What is perhaps the only surviving document from the Constitutional Church at Machecoul, a 1791-1792 *compte' de' recettes* indicating the expenses and receipts of the parish, further validates this observation. The record of receipts reflects that the Constitutional Church at Machecoul was quite active throughout 1791 and 1792. The document reveals, among other things, that members of the parish sought to maintain and renovate the church structure. In May 1791 a mason was paid for work he did on the church, as was a glassworker in February 1792 and a carpenter in May 1792. In other respects it appears that the church functioned rather normally. The linen for altars was washed, bread was purchased for communion, and the parish even allocated funds for repairing a cross on the island of Bouin in the department of the Vendée.[132]

The Machecoul account also shows that laypeople played an integral role in day-to-day parish affairs, much more so than had been the case during the Old Regime. In March 1792, for example, municipal officials named two lay sacristans to take care of many essential duties around the church and offered them a salary of 450 livres a year.[133] Increased lay involvement was partially due to necessity, for the absence of *vicaires* meant that laypeople often had to assist abbé Letort in his duties. But it may also reflect an ecclesiastical philosophy contending that lay people were as much entitled to leading the church as priests. This sense of egalitarianism may have derived from the principles of the Revolution, but it also was a Jansenist notion to which the Machecoul patriots probably had subscribed for a considerable period of time.[134]

Whether religious activity at the Constitutional Church at Machecoul was fundamentally distinct from what it had been before the Revolution is uncertain. District administrators, though, sought to suppress some of the festivals and practices that they considered superstitious—a pursuit likely inspired more by the Enlightenment than by Tridentine reform.[135] In place of these, federative and civic festivals became the focus of communal activity.[136] On July 14, 1792, district and municipal officials of Machecoul, together with various National Guard detachments stationed in the district, gathered to commemorate the fall of the Bastille. The district directory described the gathering as giving "the image of a large family, which came to bind closer its alliance in swearing its eternal devotion to the mother-country." The description of the festival indicates that the constitutional priests played a central role in the ritual:

> At 11 o'clock M. Letort, the constitutional *curé* of Machecoul, dressed honorably, proceeded to the altar, accompanied by the other constitutional *curés* of Bourgneuf, Saint-Lumine, Montbert, Port-Saint-Père, Saint-Pazanne, and La Chevrolière. The bells rang, the drums were struck, the political civil corps were placed in the center, the National Guardsmen formed in double ranks, the high arms and flags decorated the outskirts of the square, one of whose areas facing the altar was enclosed by the horse brigades of the *gendarmeries* of Machecoul and Port-Saint-Père.

It is not known exactly how many Machecoulais took part in the celebration, but the festival's *procès-verbal* suggests that participation was substantial though clearly not unanimous:

> The inhabitants of Machecoul celebrated into the night. The disputes they had with their brothers in arms were, to a certain degree, forgotten. The meals were without great preparation, but there reigned the most pure satisfaction, the walks were pleasant, and dances and the civic songs capped off this day. . . . Their antagonists remained hidden in the somber recesses of their homes, which were closed

from the outside; making people say that they were in mourning or uninhabited.[137]

In this description there is yet another indication of complex divisions in and around Machecoul over religious culture and the Revolution. That the "antagonists" were town inhabitants, possibly wealthy enough to own their homes (the correspondence employs the term *leurs maisons*), is further indication that some of the most affluent citizens by this time had withdrawn their support of the new regime.

Yet another civic rite occurred on March 3, 1793, when the Machecoul patriots honored Michel Le Pelletier, a member of the National Convention who had been assassinated. As opposed to the federative festival held the previous July, participation in this ritual appears to have been largely confined to the administrative and judicial corps, the armed forces, and the Jacobin club. Moreover, unlike the federative festival, the celebration for Le Pelletier was devoid of any Christian symbolism or association with the Constitutional Church. The event took place at the town's tree of liberty, and at the end of the service the "Marseillaise" was sung. It seems unlikely, however, that this one celebration was reflective of de-Christianization or the introduction of revolutionary cultic practice, for the popular cult of the martyrs of liberty did not begin in Paris until July 1793, and the cults of Reason and the Supreme Being followed thereafter.[138] The commemoration of Le Pelletier's "martyrdom" at Machecoul was no doubt a civic celebration and it did have some religious overtones, but there is no evidence to suggest that it was meant to be a replacement for the Constitutional Church's practices and teachings.

Religious ritual at Machecoul was touched by national events in another way as well. In September 1792 the town's Jacobins petitioned district administrators requesting that all the church bells in the district, except for the one at Trinité, be collected and donated to the war effort. They asserted that the bells should be melted down so that the metal could be forged into cannons. Even before this request was made, approximately ten bells had already been obtained from suppressed religious houses in the district.[139] For Machecoul patriots, every bell was necessary to help wage war "against the despots who want to enslave us." District officials were hesitant to take this action, though, for fear that it would inflame those in the countryside who already were consumed by the spirit of counterrevolution. Given their more pragmatic approach to the situation than perhaps that of the town's Jacobin Club, administrators consequently delayed a decision on whether to confiscate the church bells until the district received a report from each of the communes regarding possible popular reaction toward the expropriation.[140]

In addition to revising the churches and religious services, local administrators sought to reform social institutions under church auspices. The push for reform began as early as 1790, but it was temporarily halted in wake of the oath crisis. On September 17, 1790, Machecoul District officials composed a plan of action to be carried out in the following months. Their plan called for an inventory of all charitable establishments and all those who needed aid, the maintenance of educational institutions and an establishment for the poor in the district, and the composition of reports recording all urgent repairs needed to churches and presbyteries. District officials also planned to issue a decree that suspended the rents of church pews paid by the local lords, landowners, and those residing in town. They contended that these rents were often a source of conflict between town inhabitants and those of the countryside. For this reason they called for each parish to hold an assembly of all active citizens to vote whether chairs or pews were to be used in the church.[141]

The administrators' actions toward the Monastery of Our Lady of Calvary at Machecoul was another example of their push for institutional reform. In March 1790 the Calvarians submitted to the government's requirement that they declare their ownership of property and their sources of revenue. Later in the year administrators proceeded with the inventory and sale of much of the Calvarian property, as required by law, but they did not intervene in the community's way of life.[142] In February 1791 municipal officials asked each of the nineteen nuns if they preferred to stay in the monastery or leave, to which all responded that they wanted to stay. Again exhibiting a degree of pragmatism if not compromise, administrators accepted their decision and allowed the religious community to continue to live as it had, in spite of the fact that as contemplatives they were deemed "useless" and officially suppressed.[143] Throughout 1791, 1792, and the first part of 1793 district officials partially reimbursed the Calvarians for the loss of their revenues, as stipulated by law.[144]

Municipal and district officials apparently tolerated the Calvarian chaplain, abbé Joseph Esseaud, in spite of his refusal to take the oath in early 1791. They allowed him to celebrate mass and administer the sacraments to the Calvarians throughout 1791, probably because he was not outspoken in his defiance against the government. But because of the March 22, 1792, departmental *arrêté*, authorities forced abbé Esseaud to leave the monastery. The Calvarian nuns appealed the decision, but the department was unwilling to risk the chance of the priest inciting the peasants, and so the appeal was rejected.[145] What exactly happened to abbé Esseaud after he left the monastery in early April is not fully known; there is no record of his arrest or deportation.[146] The departure of the chaplain, however, failed to mark the immediate end for the community. In fact, district officials were willing to allow the Calvarians to stay together on the condition that they recognize the authority of constitutional priests. But in April 1792 the Calvarians told municipal officials that they would not attend any masses conducted by priests who had taken the oath, prompting municipal officials to proceed with the sale of all belongings within the monastery.[147] Yet in spite of this order, municipal officials dragged their feet, whether out of a spirit of pragmatism and compromise or whether some administrators or their close associates may have had family members belonging to the community. In any case, municipal officers finally went to the monastery in September and told the nuns that they must disperse; all nineteen Calvarians left the grounds without incident.[148]

What became of the former regulars is not entirely known. It can be confirmed, though, that eight Calvarians went to live in the nearby commune of Saint-Même-le-Tenu, where they attempted to maintain the community under the patronage of the Charette family. Authorities subsequently arrested these eight women in February 1793 and transferred them to a prison in Nantes. Others went to live with their families in Machecoul or in some of the other *bourgs* in the region. Many Calvarians were in and out of prison over the course of the next few years for being implicated in counterrevolutionary activities. Marie Biron and her sister Renée (a novice), for example, were charged with participating in the 1793 insurrection and were sentenced to death, but both later escaped while being transferred to Bouffay prison in Nantes.[149]

Although municipal and district authorities were unable to reform the monastery, they remained resolved to reform the schools within the commune, though they lacked sufficient funds to finance the institutions. Since the *écoles* and the *collège* were considered church property, they were funded by an endowment later taken over by the government. Local administrators thought that the Capuchin convent, which was abandoned in 1791, would serve as the perfect building for the *collège* as well as an *école* (that is, once the troops occupying the building were able to leave), but they still needed more money to maintain the institutions.[150] District administrators asked the department directory to intercede on their behalf to obtain money from the National Assembly for a school in Machecoul. They explained that the *collège* would be good not only for the town, but also for the nearby department of Vendée, since "superstition would not be so abundant there if educational institutions were not so rare." Administrators exhorted the department to allow them to "propagate the *lumières*," by which they would "destroy error," and added that the *collège* was led by Etienne Gaschignard, who was "a *laïc* and father of a large family," as opposed to a priest.[151]

The institutional decisions of district and municipal officials indicate, then, that by no means did supporters of the Revolution at Machecoul ignore, destroy, or belittle religion. On the contrary, Christianity was an integral part of the patriotic belief system, for otherwise they would have not been so intent on reforming Catholic practices and institutions in the district. Many of Machecoul's revolutionary supporters probably adhered to a syncretic combination of political ideals and religious beliefs that Michel Lagrée has termed "Blue Christianity." According to Lagrée, the main component of the Blue Christian ideology was the spirit of independence vis-à-vis both the nobility and the clergy. This notion of independence manifested itself in such ideas as an expansion of the laity's role in the life of the church and state control over church institutions.[152] Many elements of Blue or republican Christianity were obviously rooted in Gallicanism and Jansenism, but principles adopted from Enlightenment thinkers also informed it. In this ideology believers viewed Jesus as the propagator of fraternal love, human progress, and divine justice who sought to banish ignorance, superstition, and inequality.[153]

The institutionalizing of Blue Christianity, in addition to the other events at Machecoul recounted here, illustrate why the French Revolution cannot be understood mostly as a clash of ideologies; events on the ground mattered as much as, if not more than, the thinking that first set them into motion. In other words, concrete confrontations over matters like the oath crisis, more than the thinking of the likes of Rousseau, prevented opposing sides from moderating or backing down from their positions; that is how the vast majority of both revolutionaries and counterrevolutionaries became polarized, if not radicalized, during the Revolution. In Machecoul's case the defiance of the 1791 oath on the part of abbés Hervé and Blanchard, as well as their *vicaires*, alarmed government authorities and made them take vindictive actions toward such priests. Yet considerable popular support for these refractory priests, especially on behalf of some area notables, did the most to foster an uncompromisingly repressive policy among revolutionary officials, which in turn greatly diminished civility within the town.

But as this chapter shows, the unfolding of this revolutionary-counterrevolutionary dialectic at Machecoul defies an easy explanation or description. For while there certainly is ample evidence that some making up the town's urban elite who became revolutionaries were religiously progressive if not hostile toward the church, by no means did this entire group conform to that characterization; many notables seemingly supported the refractory clergy and withdrew their support of the Revolution as a result. And though from a larger perspective divisions over the oath seemed to follow a dichotomy between "urban" and "rural," the divide in and around this small town bisected the geographic origins of actors, to say nothing of their social categories. These divisions imply that the taking of sides over the 1791 oath was a deeply complex matter, likely involving a variety of motives on behalf of the Machecoulais.

Another seeming complexity found in the dialectic at Machecoul is that from 1791 to early 1793 local officials made a sincere attempt to reform and redesign religious practices, institutions, and beliefs; they were not the cold and heartless atheists that conservative and revisionist historians have sometimes made them out to be.[154] Admittedly they did this first by moving against refractory priests swiftly and harshly, motivated as they were by the increasingly explosive situation. They also sought to install the constitutional *curés* into the district parishes, as problematic as this became. But their reform of religious practices and institutions suggests that not only did they seek to reform religion according to their own vision; they also saw such reform as integral to the Revolution itself. Such a finding makes all the more sense in light of the notables' role in the political and religious struggles of the Old Regime, as Chapter Two made clear.

So what accounts for these extremely complicated divisions over the oath and ultimately the Revolution itself? Although social and economic factors such as clientage and familial alliances were certainly at work in dividing western France in 1791 and 1792, one factor that has been largely ignored is local religious culture.[155] The disparate religious beliefs held by certain segments of the population may be the best explanation why a community like Machecoul became so finely splintered over the Revolution's initial religious reforms. Indeed, the cultural divide explains why local administrators were so intent on becoming revolutionaries in both a political and a religious sense, as well as why their opponents grew so vociferous in their opposition. True, much of this divide's ideological underpinning was nothing new; previous battles over Jansenism, Gallicanism, and Tridentine reform had already created a split and in no small way guided notable and clerical reaction to the Civil Constitution of the Clergy and the 1791 oath.

Still, the Revolution and its religious reforms brought an unprecedented immediacy to this cultural conflict, without which the revolutionary-counterrevolutionary dialectic that arose in and around the town would not have been possible. In any case, what seemed to make this dialectic extraordinarily pointed at Machecoul was that much more than political power was at stake; both the opponents and proponents of the Civil Constitution of the Clergy seemingly viewed the moment as one of supreme spiritual decision. They held that the taking of one side over the other was tantamount to the separation of sheep from goats in the final judgment.[156] Both sides believed that their actions were fulfilling a higher law, though the two sides understood that law in dramatically different ways. The conflict, therefore, was no less than a dialectical battle over the meaning of Christianity. For this very reason it soon became a struggle expressed in murder and martyrdom.

Notes

[1]Doyle, *The Oxford History*, 144.

[2]Gwynne Lewis, *The French Revolution: Rethinking the Debate* (London: Routledge, 1993), 212.

[3]Claude Langlois, "La rupture entre l'Eglise catholique et la Révolution," in François Furet and Mona Ozouf, eds., *The French Revolution and the Creation of Modern Political Culture*, vol. 3, *The Transformation of Political Culture, 1789-1848* (Oxford: Pergamon Press, 1987), 375-90.

[4]P. M. Jones, *Reform and Revolution in France: The Politics of Transition, 1774-1791* (New York: Cambridge University Press, 1995), 212.

[5]Tackett, *Religion, Revolution, and Regional Culture*, 299-300.

[6]Le Mené and Santrot, 1: 23-26.

[7]Roger Dupuy, *De la Révolution à la Chouannerie: Paysans en Bretagne, 1788-1794* (Paris: Flammarion, 1988), 22-23.

[8]Le Mené and Santrot, 1: 32-34; Dupuy, 43-56.

[9]Le Mené and Santrot, 1: 31.

[10]Ibid., 4: 1518-23.

[11]To see how this compared to other clerical *cahiers*, see Aston, 114-18.

[12]Alfred Lallié, *Le diocèse de Nantes pendant la Révolution*, 2 vols. (Nantes: B. Cier, 1893), 1: 15. The *cahier* for the clergy apparently was lost sometime after Lallié had examined it. See also Le Mené and Santrot, 1: 31.

[13]For more on the progressivism in the west, see Tackett, "The West in France in 1789," 740-45.

[14]Le Mené and Santrot, 1: 32-34.

[15]Ibid., 2: 749, 761.

[16]Ibid., 2: 752. This article also includes the statement that "les citoyens des trois ordres soient admis dans toutes les places indistinctement,…soit enfin dans les grands bénéfices du Clergé, sans que dans aucun cas la roture puisse être un obstacle à l'avancement des citoyens du Tiers État."

[17]This section reads as such: "Et qu'au moyen de cette suppression du gouvernement particulier du Clergé et de son imposition dans chaque province, les dettes qu'il a contractées jusqu'à présent, pour satisfaire aux impôts levés sur lui, soient réputées dettes de l'État, pour être acquittées par la Nation et le Clergé en demeurer déchargé." A footnote by the commentator (Philippe Bossis) after this clause states, "Article qui aboutit à mettre entièrement le clergé 'dans la main' de l'État."

[18]Further discussion of these model *cahiers* can be found in Le Mené and Santrot, 1: 35-74.

[19]Ibid., 2: 752-54.

[20]Tackett, *Religion, Revolution, and Regional Culture,* 251-71; Tackett, "The West in France," 338-41. To cite just one example, the *cahier* for the *sénéchaussées* of Nantes and Guérande (after the *sénéchaussée* assemblies were held, on April 6 for Nantes and April 1 for Guérande, the leaders of the two apparently came together to compose a *cahier* representing the Nantes *comté* on April 16, 1789) states that "Les dîmes ecclésiastiques seront supprimés. Il sera pourvu à la donation des curés et vicaires, qui à ce moyen ne recevront plus de rétributions casuelles pour l'exercice de leurs functions. Le revenu des curés et vicaires sera déterminé par les États généraux." See Le Mené and Santrot, 4: 1569-71.

[21]Le Mené and Santrot, 2: 762-64.

[22]For more on the degrees of conflict and consensus among different social segments drawing up the *cahiers,* see Shapiro and Markoff, 280-324.

[23]Le Mené and Santrot, 4: 1515-23.

[24]As suggested in the previous chapter, the *portion congrue* was an important source of revenue for Poitou *curés,* but usually not for Breton *recteurs.*

[25]For more on the difficulties of content analyses of the *cahiers de doléances,* see Shapiro and Markoff, 17-32.

[26]For a broader perspective on clerical reaction to events at the Estates General, see Timothy Tackett, *Becoming a Revolutionary: The Deputies of the French National Assembly and the Emergence of a Revolutionary Culture (1789-1790)* (Princeton: Princeton University Press, 1996).

[27]To gain some context involving the clergy on the national level, see Aston, 122-39, and Michael P. Fitzsimmons, *The Night the Old Regime Ended: August 4, 1789 and the French Revolution* (University Park: Penn State University Press, 2003).

[28]Durand, 174.

[29]Anne de Baynast, "La vente des biens nationaux du première origine dans le district de Machecoul, 1790-1793," Mémoire de maîtrise, directed by P. Bossis (Nantes: Université de Nantes, 1988), 9-13, 23.

[30]Jacques Godechot, *Les institutions de la France sous la Révolution et l'Empire,* 2nd ed. (Paris: Presses Universitaires de France, 1968), 105-107.

[31]Ibid., 108-112.

[32]Dupuy, *De la Révolution,* 129-30.

[33]Lallié, *Le diocèse de Nantes pendant la Révolution,* 1: 26.

[34]Alfred Lallié, *Le district de Machecoul, 1788-1799: Études sur les origines des débuts de l'insurrection vendéene dans le pays de Retz* (Nantes: Vincent Forest et Émile Grimaud, 1869), 62-84.

[35]Dupuy, *De la Révolution*, 127-29.

[36]Tackett, *Religion, Revolution, and Regional Culture*, 19.

[37]Dupuy, *De la Révolution*, 142.

[38]Baynast, 54-55, 228.

[39]For more on the political maneuvering over the Civil Constitution of the Clergy in the National Assembly, see Aston, 140-62.

[40]Tackett, *Religion, Revolution, and Regional Culture*, 11-16.

[41]Lallié, *Le district de Machecoul*, 106.

[42]ADLA, 658. *Mandement* of the bishop of Nantes, containing the adoption of the pastoral instruction of the bishop of Boulogne, on the spiritual authority of the church, October 24, 1790; Durand, *Le diocèse de Nantes*, 174.

[43]Lallié, *Le district de Machecoul*, 110.

[44]Ibid., 103-04.

[45]*Adresse à l'Assemblée Nationale* (Nantes: Gigougeux, 1790), 10. A copy of this tract is found at ADLA, L 1399.

[46]Ibid., 17-18.

[47]Ibid., 25.

[48]Ibid., 29-30.

[49]Ibid., 5.

[50]Tackett, *Religion, Revolution, and Regional Culture*, 14. Departmental administrators believed that opposition to the Civil Constitution was primarily based on financial motives. See Lallié, *Le diocèse de Nantes*, 1: 52.

[51]Lallié, *Le district de Machecoul*, 108.

[52]Tackett, "The West in France," 341-45; Tackett, *Religion, Revolution, and Regional Culture*, 251-71.

[53]ADLA, L 1399. Testimony to the Judicial Tribunal of the Machecoul District, September 17, 1791.

[54]Ibid., Machecoul Municipal *Arrêté*, January 2, 1791.

[55]According to Tackett, only the departments of the Finistère, Ille-et-Villaine, êozère, Morbihan, Pas-de-Calais, and Tarn had lower rates of oath-taking than the Loire-Inférieure. See Tackett, *Religion, Revolution and Regional Culture*, 336, 364-66; Lallié, *Le diocèse de Nantes pendant la Révolution*, 1: 128.

[56]ADLA, L 815 (2 Mi 246). State of Ecclesiastical Public Functionaries, March 30, 1791.

[57]ADLA, L 722. Machecoul Municipal *Arrêté*, March 27, 1791.

[58]It should be noted that with the implementation of the Civil Constitution of the Clergy, the Breton term of *recteur* was discarded; the term, *curé*, took its place.

[59]ADLA, L 659. *Procès-verbal* of the election of constitutional priests, Machecoul District, March 27-29, 1791.

[60]ADLA, L 600. National Guard for the Machecoul Municipality, March 7, 1792. Letort, a member of the guard, is listed as being thirty-five years of age.

[61]Lallié, *Le diocèse de Nantes*, 2: 242.

[62]See ADLA, L 600. National Guard for the municipality of Machecoul, March 7,1792; L 722. Petition of the Machecoul Friends of the Constitution, November 20, 1791.

[63]Aston, 170-72.

[64]Charles Eutrope de la Laurencie, *Ordonnance de Monseigneur l'Évêque de Nantes, au sujet de l'election faite par les Electeurs du Département, du Sieur Julien Minée, pour Évêque du Département de la Loire-Inférieure* (Ghent: Imprimerie de Crapart, 1791), 8-12. A copy of the ordinance is available at ADLA, L 658.

[65]Ibid., 4.

[66]ADLA, L 722. Machecoul Municipal *Arrêté* of March 27, 1791.

[67]Lallié, *Le district de Machecoul*, 162.

[68]Tackett, *Religion, Revolution, and Regional Culture*, 176. Tackett also found that in one town in the Gard, women rioted against authorities on account of their opposition toward "mauvais catholiques." See his "Women and Men in Sommières [Gard] and the Ecclesiastical Oath of 1791," in Plongeron, ed., *Pratiques religieuses dans l'Europe révolutionnaire*, 351-58.

[69]Tackett, *Religion, Revolution, and Regional Culture*, 166-67.

[70]Claude Petitfrère, "The Origins of Civil War in the Vendée," in Jones, ed., *The French Revolution in Social and Political Perspective*, 350-55.

[71]T. J. A. LeGoff and D. M. G. Sutherland, "Religion and Rural Revolt in the French Revolution: An Overview," in János M. Bak and Gerhard Benecke, eds., *Religion and Rural Revolt* (Manchester: Manchester University Press, 1984), 142.

[72]Dupuy, 324.

[73]ADLA, Q 169. Registry of October 16, 1790 to March 1, 1793. Lallié found that Baré and Gry were among those who were killed in the fighting during April 1793. See Lallié, *Le district de Machecoul*, 431-38.

[74]ADLA, Q 173. Machecoul municipal officials to Machecoul District Directory, April 5, 1792.

[75]This is to say that most peasants consistently went to church and were very deferential to their pastors. But as Chapter Two indicated, they did not necessarily subscribe to Tridentine belief.

[76]Dupuy, *De la Révolution*, 191-92. Dupuy suggests that the oath crisis facilitated the growth of the Jacobin movement in the west. In the first half of 1791, however, there was a split among Jacobins in Paris, with the more moderate Feuillants forming a splinter club. The original and more radical Jacobins returned to prominence during the second half of 1791, as 500 clubs in Brittany rallied to the original club, while 100 Breton clubs favored the Feuillants. See Furet and Ozouf, 704-16. For the activities and ideology of Jacobin and other revolutionary clubs, see Emmet Kennedy, *A Cultural History of the French Revolution* (New Haven: Yale University Press, 1989), 365-73; Michael L. Kennedy, *The Jacobin Clubs in the French Revolution: The First Years* (Princeton: Princeton University Press, 1982).

[77]ADLA, L. 722. Petition of the Machecoul Friends of the Constitution, November 20, 1791.

[78]Jarnoux, 56-57.

[79]Tackett, *Religion, Revolution, and Regional Culture*, 281.

[80]Durand, *Le diocèse de Nantes*, 176.

[81]Ibid., 175.

[82]Jarnoux, 57.

[83]ADLA, L 722. Extract from the Registry of Deliberations of the Machecoul District Directory, June 29, 1791.

[84]Jarnoux, 57.

[85]ADLA, L. 1399. Extract from the Minutes of the Departmental Administration, July 1-2, 1791.

[86]Timothy Tackett, "Conspiracy Obsession in a Time of Revolution: French Elites and the Origins of the Terror, 1789-92," *American Historical Review* 105, no. 3 (June 2000), 690-713. See also Tackett, *When the King Took Flight* (Cambridge, Mass: Harvard University Press. 2003).

[87]ADLA, L 660. *Procès-verbal* of the Machecoul District Judicial Tribunal, September 7, 1791.

[88]Jarnoux, 160-61; ADLA, L 1399. *Procès-verbal* of the Machecoul District Judicial Tribunal, September 7, 1791.

[89]Ibid., *Procès-verbal* of the Machecoul District Judicial Tribunal, September 7, 1791; Jarnoux, 161.

[90]ADLA, L 1399. *Demand et accusateur* against Roland Hervé de la Bauche, August 17, 1791.

91 As Nigel Aston made clear, having two churches—one constitutional, one refractory—was not necessarily uncommon in France in 1791. See Aston, 165-66, 196-208, 220-28.

92 ADLA, L 722. Machecoul Municipal *Arrêté* of August 14-15, 1791

93 Ibid., Extract of the registers of the Directory of the Machecoul District Directory, August 19, 1791.

94 Ibid., Petition from Machecoul Friends of the Constitution to Departmental Administrators, November 20, 1791.

95 Ibid, Extract from the Registry of the Machecoul District Directory, November 23, 1791.

96 Ibid., Deliberations of the Parish of Sainte-Croix of Machecoul, December 4, 1791.

97 Le Mené and Santrot, 4: 1649.

98 Ibid., 2: 761. Approximately twenty-three of the thirty-nine who had gathered to write the *cahier de doléance* for Sainte-Croix approved the petition.

99 ADLA, L 722. Machecoul Municipal *Arrêté*, December 6, 1791.

100 ADLA, L 658. Machecoul District *Arrêté*, December 16, 1791.

101 Tackett, *Religion, Revolution, and Regional Culture*, 274-80.

102 ADLA, L 815. Table of Refractory Priests in the District of Machecoul, April 4, 1792.

103 Durand, *Le diocèse de Nantes*, 176.

104 ADLA, L 953. Letter from the Administrators of Machecoul, April 1, 1792.

105 ADLA, 1338 [2 Mi 227]. Petition of the Machecoul Friends of the Constitution, May 5, 1792.

106 See, for example, Vovelle, "1789-1917: The Game of Analogies," in Baker, ed., *The French Revolution and the Creation of Modern Political Culture*, 4: 349-78 .

107 Lallié, *Le District de Machecoul*, 241.

108 Martin, *Révolution et contre-révolution*, 32-34.

109 Dupuy, *De la Révolution*, 325-26.

110 Martin, *Révolution et contre-révolution*, 35.

111 ADLA, L 284. Reports of the Dubois and Batard searches, August 22, 1792.

112 Durand, *Le diocèse de Nantes*, 176.

113 Ibid., 176-77.

114 ADLA, L 665. List of *ecclesiastiques* of the Department of the Loire-Inférieure Subject to Deportation or Confinement, in virtue of the Law of August 26, 1792; Jarnoux, 161.

115 Durand, *Le diocèse de Nantes*, 177.

[116]Tackett, "Conspiracy Obsession," 712-13.

[117]This point is made by Arno J. Mayer in *The Furies*, especially when he discusses "the vicious circle of vengeance and re-vengeance" in France in Chapter Seven. For more discussion of Mayer's book by prominent historians of France and Russia, see the Forum, "Comparing Revolutions" in *French Historical Studies* 24, no. 4 (Fall 2001), 549-600.

[118]In his very thorough analysis of those who made up the "Whites" (insurgents) and the "Blues" (republicans) in the civil war in Anjou, for example, Claude Petitfrère found that over 20 percent of the Blues came from the agricultural category. He also discovered that a little less than the same percentage of the Whites consisted of artisans and small shopkeepers. Although he admits that ideology may have played a role, he does not provide a full explanation for why these segments of the Blues and Whites failed to conform to the typical "urban-rural" split. See Petitfrère, "The Origins of the Civil War," in Jones, *The French Revolution in Social and Political Perspective*, 346-50. Perhaps Roger Dupuy explained the situation best when he wrote, "les paysans pauvres, le gros laboureurs, le clergé paroissial ne constituent pas toute la société rurale, il y a notamment la catégorie composite de ceux qui, vivant à la campagne, ne sont pas des paysans: artisans, commerçants et rentiers, mais aussi les petits robins seigneuriaux, les tabellions de village, et, au-dessous encore, les maîtres d'école et les anciens soldats. Autant d'intermédiaires culturels, autant de leaders locaux potentiels. En fait, certains vont rallier le nouveau pouvoir, surtout dans les bocages 'bleus,' ailleurs il se déterminent en fonction des places disponibles et du jeu subtil des clientèles et parentèles." See Dupuy, 326.

[119]For more on the Constitutional Church on the national level, see Aston, 196-219.

[120]Durand, *Le diocèse de Nantes*, 167.

[121]ADLA, L 815. State of constitutional *curés* under the jurisdiction of the Machecoul District, November 7, 1791.

[122]ADLA, L 722. Extract from the Registry of the Machecoul District Directory, March 31, 1792.

[123]ADLA, L 660. Constitutional Clergy of the District of Machecoul. Refusals to accept Andreux and Abbé Grémion, *vicaires épiscopales*, 1792.

[124]This was true, not just in the Machecoul District, but in other areas of western France as well. See Tilly, *The Vendée*, 248-52.

[125]Martin, *Révolution et contre-révolution*, 34.

[126]ADLA, L 766. Extract from the Registry of the Machecoul District Directory, August 17, 1791.

[127]Martin, *Révolution et contre-révolution*, 34.

[128]ADLA, L 1399. Denunciation by Sieurs Etienne Gaschignard, Philippe Vincent Gry and Julien Renou, January 25, 1792.

[129]Lallié, *Le diocèse de Nantes*, 2: 242. At the time Félix Dubois was a member of the District Directory. See Lallié, *Le District de Machecoul*, 144.

[130]ADLA, L 1399. The Dubois Judgment, February 17, 1792.

[131]Ibid., Repeal of the Judgement against Dubois, February 20, 1792.

[132]ADLA, Q 508. Account of Trinité of Machecoul, 1791-92.

[133]ADLA, L 1039 [2 Mi 278]. Extract from the Register of Deliberations of the Machecoul Municipality, March 25, 1792.

[134]This theological view represented an assault, among other things, on the efficacy of clerical celibacy. See Bernard Plongeron, *Théologie et politique au siècle des lumières (1770-1820)* (Geneva: Librairie Droz, 1973), 191-207.

[135]This was the case at Saint-Lumine-de-Coutais, where a game called *Cheval Merlet (Mallet)* was played on the day of Pentecost. It was a secular tradition, yet given that it was played on a feast day, it did have some religious overtones. See Martin, *Révolution et contre-révolution*, 34.

[136]For a full discussion of the federative and civic festivals and their meanings, see Mona Ozouf, *Festivals and the French Revolution*, trans. Alan Sheridan (Cambridge, Mass.: Harvard University Press, 1988).

[137]ADLA, L 600. *Procès-verbal* of the Federative Festival, July 14, 1792.

[138]Albert Soboul, *Understanding the French Revolution*, trans. April Anne Knutson (New York: International Publishers, 1988), 131-44.

[139]ADLA, Q 503. Bells of Suppressed Churches in the District of Machecoul, December 30, 1791.

[140]ADLA, Q 173. Extract from the Registry of the Machecoul District Directory, September 14, 1792.

[141]ADLA, L 1031. Plan of Action, September 16, 1790.

[142]Perroys, 46.

[143]ADLA, L 801. Execution of Article 15 of the Law of October 14, 1789, February 5, 1791.

[144]ADLA, L 1037. Book of Finances, November 1, 1790-January 18, 1793.

[145]ADLA, L 47. Entry of March 29, 1792.

[146]Perroys, 47-48.

[147]ADLA, Q 173. Extract from the Registry of the Machecoul District Directory, April 9, 1792.

[148]ADLA, L 801. Departmental *Arrêté* of September 12, 1792.

[149]Perroys, 48-51.

[150]It should be noted that in 1791 or early 1792 either municipal or district administrators took control of the Capuchin library and alphabetized all

of the books according to title. Exactly what they were going to do with the books is unclear. See ADLA, L 623.

[151]ADLA, L 616. Machecoul District administrators to the Department Directory, January 3, 1792.

[152]Michel Lagrée, *Mentalités, Religion, et Histoire en Haute-Bretagne au XIXe siècle: Le diocèse de Rennes, 1815-1848* (Paris: Librairie C. Klincksieck, 1977), 79-91; Tackett, *Religion, Revolution, and Regional Culture,* 67-73; Aston, 196-97.

[153]Plongeron, *Théologie et politique,* 149-150.

[154]As Aston emphasizes, the Constitutional Church was probably the preference of the French majority in 1791, and its clerical corps, to say the least, was strongly devoted. See Aston, 197.

[155]See note 117.

[156]As Nigel Aston observed, millenarian beliefs were quite common in the Constitutional Church, especially the notion that a "New Jerusalem" was being built through the Revolution. See Aston, 203.

4

Two Stories

In the summer of 1794—just as the Terror was reaching its denouement—Louis-Marie Turreau approached the bar in the National Convention and submitted a proposal that priests in France be excluded from every municipal council and all public functions. Although by that point many Catholic clerics had been deported, were in hiding, or had renounced their vows and gone on to marry, Turreau argued that they remained a threat to the republic. "Their empire is destroyed," he announced to his colleagues, "but their passions still survive; in secret they nourish the desire for vengeance, so dear to their heart." Voicing his unqualified support for the initiative, another legislator then rose from his seat and offered one more reason why priests were not to be trusted:

> Do you want new proof of the ferocity of these priests? At Machecoul, eight hundred patriots were slaughtered, and this is the funeral that they gave them: they buried only part of the body, in such a way so that the head and arms remained exposed to the elements and to the voraciousness of carnivorous animals. The next day they found many of these cadavers still quivering: ah well, these were priests who ordained such infamy!
>
> They said to the brigands: "Strike the patriots in the heart, for that is there where they sinned." ... This age is not the only one when priests caused the world's misfortunes; France in particular still recalls with horror the *dragonades* of Cévennes, the St. Bartholomew's Day [Massacre], and the massacres of Cabrières.[1]

As startling as the allegation was, it was merely one of many about the Machecoul massacres circulating in Paris during 1793 and 1794. Indeed, similar references to atrocities allegedly committed in the small town are periodically sprinkled throughout the records of the National

Convention during those tumultuous years—once more underscoring the multifarious repercussions arising from this singular episode.

Though replete with extraneous melodrama, the legislator's words reveal several key aspects of the revolutionary-counterrevolutionary dynamic in France. They confirm, for example, republican perceptions of the Machecoul massacres, specifically that the event was motivated and inspired by a religious fanaticism first made evident in the region's pervasive resistance to the 1791 oath. The rhetoric also underscores the critical role that representations of atrocity and corporal suffering played in republican discourse on counterrevolutionary violence. Here the graphic emphasis on the victims' suffering was seemingly meant not only to confirm the incivility of the insurgents but also to bolster republican resolve against it.[2] But perhaps most important, the accusation demonstrates how a little over a year after the Machecoul massacres took place, the republican "memory" of the event was already starting to congeal.

But was the allegation true? And even more central to this story, did religion motivate the massacres? These questions may seem innocuous enough, but among historians they have been extremely divisive, perennially dividing scholars into contesting camps. While scholars generally sympathetic to the Revolution have held refractory priests and their supporters responsible for the massacres, to say nothing of the crimes accompanying them, those quick to castigate the republic have contended that a repressive regime, through disregarding the religious sensibilities of western inhabitants, all but invited an atrocity to occur.[3] By no means will this chapter provide a definitive answer to the question of motive, much less verify whether some Machecoulais were indeed buried alive. Still, what follows shows why most queries about this episode defy simple answers. Microhistories are often helpful because they clarify certain processes or activities, often by analyzing them on a smaller scale so that they can be better understood. But on occasion a more acute focus on historical events only complicates attempts at illumination. This chapter shows that the Machecoul massacres are an excellent example of this paradox. The following examination of these small-town murders and their immediate aftermath suggests that one of the reasons that there has been no consensus among scholars regarding *why* the massacres happened is that there has been little agreement over *what* happened during the massacres themselves.

The Massacres

To be sure, no one disagrees about conditions in and around Machecoul just before violence erupted. The previous chapter illustrated that tensions began to mount at the approximate time when refractory priests had been expelled from district parishes in 1791. This bitterness reached a crescendo, however, in March 1793, when civil war exploded in several areas of western France.[4] Many scholars have long held that the immediate crisis unfolded in late February, when the National Convention ordered that lots be drawn for the conscription of three hundred thousand men into the military. True though this may be, popular anger and resentment had been mounting in the west for some time. The draft merely constituted the proverbial last straw for peasants in the region, most of whom were not about to sacrifice their lives for a regime that exacerbated their oppression.

Organized acts of violence sharply escalated in number in Machecoul's district less than two weeks after the drawing of lots was announced. On the night of March 6 a municipal officer at La Chevrolière was threatened with death by bands of young men who refused to participate in the drawing of lots. Armed with large poles, resisters then marched to neighboring Saint-Etienne-de-Mer-Morte and later to Saint-Même, where they announced their intention to behead municipal officers. Similar incidents began to break out in a vast area comprising the southern and western Loire-Inférieure, the southern Maine-et-Loire, the northern and central Vendée, and the northern Deux-Sèvres: seemingly a confirmation that popular revolt was both spontaneous and sporadic. On March 10 one district administrator from Machecoul barely escaped death while on his way to Saint-Etienne-de-Corcoué. That same day at Saint-Philbert-de-Grand-Lieu a contingent of about six thousand men, armed with poles and firearms, imprisoned all the municipal officers and intercepted all communication between Nantes and Machecoul. Later in the evening the large rebel contingent from Saint-Philbert proceeded to the district seat, apparently approaching the town from the east as morning broke. They reached the hamlet of

Sainte-Croix, known to be a hot spot of resistance ever since its pastor was ousted and its parish closed.[5]

It is at this point of the story when historical reality becomes nebulous, for what emerged almost in concert with the events themselves was not one rendition of what happened but arguably two: a story created by the republicans at Machecoul and their partisans, and a quite different narrative constructed among the insurgents and their subsequent sympathizers. The two competing stories, which are integral to the larger phenomenon of contested memory, have more or less persisted up to the present, thereby reflecting the ongoing dialectic of revolution and counterrevolution in France.[6] How and why did these two narratives emerge? Suffice it to say that the dialectic that produced the event in the first place dictated a rapid and irreparable blurring of lines between individual memory and the polemical, to such a degree that even the most accomplished scholar has found it difficult to differentiate understatement from exaggeration in the various accounts, let alone fact from mnemonic fabrication.

To start, both the republican and insurgent narratives agree that local officials from Machecoul went out to meet the rebels at Sainte-Croix on the morning of March 11 in a gesture of conciliation, but that the rebels could not be appeased. Both concede that the mere one hundred or so National Guardsmen protecting Machecoul that morning, while armed, were unable to fend off the approximately 1,500 insurgents and were easily overwhelmed. But an inconsistency appears in how the shooting began. The republican narrative claims that on reaching the town the rebels immediately slaughtered those public officials seeking to mollify them, after which they savagely attacked the townspeople. According to the insurgent narrative, however, the National Guard troops fired the first shots, thus provoking the wrath of the rebels, and that what followed resembled more of a pitched battle.[7]

While there is agreement in the two narratives that some killing took place that morning as well as the following day, there is a dispute as to how many perished; the numbers in the narratives range from ten in an insurgent account to hundreds in republican counterparts.[8] Still, the various narratives agree that among the first to be killed at Machecoul were Etienne Gaschignard, the principal of the *collège* and onetime president of the district administration, and abbé Pierre Letort, Trinité's constitutional *curé*. But even in the killing of these town notables there is disagreement. According to the republican narrative the murder of abbé Letort was one of the most heinous acts of the invasion. One version claimed that he was killed by bayonet stabs to the face, after which a woman ripped away his genitals, and that he was intentionally kept alive for ten minutes in order that he suffer.[9] Another republican version—a most dubious one at that—claimed that the priest was put on a spit and paraded around the town, subsequently mutilated, and while, still alive, nailed to the town's tree of liberty.[10] But such discrepancies in the republican narrative have suggested to insurgent sympathizers that these atrocities were fabricated, particularly by vengeful republicans or even insurgents who, at the time of trial, sought to save their own necks by telling republican officials what they wanted to hear.[11]

The character of the invasion is also a source of contention in the two narratives. Among the claims made by republicans was that some insurgents hunted down the Machecoulais like animals, even using a hunting horn and making traditional hunting cries once the prey was seized. François Villers (a former constitutional *curé* of Saint-Philbert-de-Grand-Lieu) and Joseph Fouché (later the minister of police for Napoleon), charged with investigating the events for the National Convention, stated in their report that the elderly, women, and children among rebels were especially cruel—apparently in an attempt to underscore the barbarity of insurgents. Some women purportedly chanted "Kill, Kill," while other rebels cried victory. Meanwhile, according to the republican narrative, the victims themselves reportedly acted heroically, crying "Long live the nation" as they were being slaughtered.[12] Those supporting the insurgent story have countered these charges by stating that the specific witnesses interviewed by Villers and Fouché were never fully cited and thus the claims cannot be verified.[13]

There is some harmony in the two competing stories regarding what happened after the town was taken. The insurgents imprisoned most Machecoul "patriots" at the former women's monastery, while their relatives fled to Nantes and other area towns, whereupon the rebels ransacked their property.[14] Yet the two narratives diverge again over what happened in the town during the six-week occupation by insurgents. The republican narrative depicts the occupation of the town as a theater of horrors. Some republican witnesses claimed that assailants hacked one man to pieces in front of his wife and children and threw his body parts into the moat of an old château.[15] Another alleges that some rebels dragged abbé Marchesse, the constitutional *curé* at Bourgneuf, by a horse and later crushed his skull by placing it between the door and wall of the prison.[16]

In response to these allegations the insurgent narrative makes several rejoinders. First, insurgent sympathizers point to the discrepancies in the various accounts as a basis for not believing them.[17] But even when the insurgent narrative reluctantly agrees that such acts did occur, it emphasizes that these atrocities pale in comparison to the revolutionary violence that took place throughout France and for which republicans were responsible, including the 1792 September massacres in Paris and above all the Terror.[18] Rather recently, insurgent narrators have alleged that the sporadic violence at Machecoul was a far cry from what the republican response to these atrocities was: a full-scale genocide.[19] The insurgent narrative argues, moreover, that such rage among the rebels was understandable, if not somewhat justifiable, considering the oppression that the perpetrators faced at the hands of the republican minority.[20] Finally, insurgent sympathizers insist that if indeed such cruelty did occur in the town, it was largely the result of the personal initiative of a reckless few and thus in no way was systematically implemented by rebel leaders.[21]

But just who were leaders of the insurgency at Machecoul? Again there is both agreement and disagreement in competing accounts. One point of consensus concerns an early leader of the insurrection, René Souchu, a town lawyer and small property owner who organized the rebel leadership shortly after the town was taken. Who exactly joined up with him and when they united with him are unclear. Both versions confirm that Souchu invited local notables to join him, most notably a former nobleman and retired naval officer named François-Athanase Charette de la Contrie. Some republicans testified that among the foremost leaders was Joseph Praud de la Nicollière, the first president of the Machecoul District administration who later resigned in protest. There is disagreement, however, regarding when or even if the influence of these men was felt on the insurgents occupying the town.[22]

Several accounts contend, moreover, that many commoners from communes adjoining Machecoul were in positions of power. The merchants Louis-Joseph Guérin and François Pageot are often mentioned in both insurgent and republican narratives, as is the salt maker Vrignault.[23] But many of the insurgent leaders are thought to have come from Machecoul itself, including Plantier, the Berthaud brothers, and Léger, all of whom were tenant farmers. The three Eriaud brothers, *cultivateurs* living in the former parish of Sainte-Croix, were cited as insurgent leaders as well. Both narratives seem to agree that refractory priests assumed prominent leadership roles as well: the tonsured cleric Archambaud; six refractory priests, including Poitier, Rousseau, Guillou (the former *vicaire* from Fresnay), Pierrot (a priest from Angers), Massonnet (the ousted *curé* from Saint-Même), and a former *vicaire* from the town's parish of Trinité named François Priour (sometimes referred to as Prioul or Priou).[24]

Both narratives concede that the day after the taking of the town, Souchu and other ringleaders sent a petition to administrators at Paimboeuf demanding that all refractory priests be freed and be granted the right to move about as they wished, that all mayors and district officials be removed from their positions, and that the drawing of lots for the conscription of three hundred thousand troops be abandoned. The stories agree, moreover, that revolutionary officials at Paimboeuf and Nantes rejected any compromise with the insurgent leaders, which in turn provoked another attack by the insurgents on March 23, this time at the town of Pornic. There also is little doubt that rebels initially captured Pornic, but shortly thereafter republican forces surprised the insurgents by counterattacking and retaking the town. Either in the course of the counterattack or shortly afterward, republican forces inflicted heavy losses on the rebel side. Republican versions claim, though, that as few as fifty insurgents were killed, whereas insurgent versions allege that two or three hundred not only lost their lives but were massacred only after being taken prisoner.[25]

In either case, the insurgent leaders at Machecoul perceived that their comrades had been unjustly murdered at Pornic, and thus they quickly resolved to even the score by sentencing the imprisoned Machecoul patriots to death. Who ordered the executions? Again there is a discrepancy. The insurgent version claims that Souchu was almost solely responsible, while republicans like to spread the blame and include the likes of more prominent Vendéen leaders like Charette de la Contrie.[26]

Still, there is little question that some prisoners were released but also that most were condemned to death. The executions began on March 27, when the insurgents conducted many of the prisoners to a field near the former Calvarian monastery and shot them.

Naturally the republican and insurgent narratives differ dramatically regarding the death toll. Among republican versions one finds numbers ranging between 150 and 800.[27] The lower number appears in what may have been the episode's first report in Paris, which is found in the official newspaper for the National Convention in late April 1793. According to this account 150 patriot prisoners were "slaughtered or burned."[28] But less than a week later the same source reported that "at Machecoul 550 patriots, municipal officers, judges, administrators were slaughtered; one day later, their wives, their children, underwent the same fate."[29] In June 1794 town administrators themselves reported to the National Convention that "not all the republicans at Machecoul are dead, those who remained have promised to live free or to die, and that 557 of their brothers who were slaughtered by the brigands, were willing to sacrifice their lives because the salvation of the fatherland required it."[30] The insurgent narrative tends to avoid ascribing precise numbers to the massacre, though in the late nineteenth century a royalist sympathizer fixed the number at one hundred.[31]

For those 160 or so who can be authentically confirmed as killed in the massacres, the most recent research on their social backgrounds demonstrates that not just public functionaries like municipal and district officials were victimized. The substantiated dead at Machecoul include artisans and shopkeepers, such as grocers, a coppersmith, a salt merchant, a cooper, and a woodworker. Even some day laborers and tenant farmers, like Honoré Plaintive, became the target of the insurgents' rage.[32] The social backgrounds of the victims, not to mention those of the insurgent leaders, verify the complexity of internal divisions that closely paralleled those involving the oath crisis in the town, thus suggesting that many were killed because of the religious and political positions that they took. While there was a general tendency for an urban-rural division between insurgents and republicans, the dissimilarity in the victims' social backgrounds suggests that, as was the case in the oath crisis, clear-cut social and economic correlations among those killed cannot be made.

Although the massacres at Machecoul ended by the middle of April, the wider War of Vendée was still in its infancy. By early May General Charette de la Contrie had emerged as the foremost rebel leader in the northwestern sector of the insurgency zone (namely in or near the *marais*). Republican forces successfully regained Machecoul on April 22, yet the town changed hands a number of times during the following two months.[33] Vendéen rebels knew, however, that the uprising could not be sustained merely by controlling small towns and the countryside, which is why they attacked the larger city of Nantes near the end of June—albeit unsuccessfully. Republican armies then went on the offensive, forcing Charette and his forces to retreat into the *marais* near Machecoul. The fighting continued until the end of 1793, by which point Machecoul and many parts of its district had been lost and regained by both republican and rebel forces several times over.[34] Although the insurgency continued into 1794, by the early part of that year much of the fighting in and around the town was over. Yet for this reason the republican reprisals for the massacres were just getting under way.

These two conflicting stories about the Machecoul massacres illustrate why scholars have been unable to determine what actually happened in the town in March and April 1793. To be sure, the accusations of atrocity are many, but scholarly verification of such acts has proved highly problematic. So what should be substantively concluded on the basis of such scant and conflicting evidence? On the one hand, some of the atrocities seem quite plausible, especially since they are consistent with a highly divisive civil war in which bitter partisans not only knew each other but lived side by side in the same community. On the other hand, though, the exaggeration of atrocities is also a compelling characteristic of civil war, especially a struggle in which republicans sought to dehumanize insurgents. An effective means of accomplishing that goal, of course, was to emphasize the barbarism of the rebels, as well as to underscore the human suffering of innocent republican victims. In all likelihood some insurgents did perpetrate grisly violence against townspeople, but probably nowhere near the extent to which republicans subsequently claimed.

Retribution and Republican Justice

Momentous as the massacres were, they made up only one aspect of the civil war—an emphatic point made in the insurgent narrative. In January 1794, in accord with a decree that in effect called for republican troops to lay waste to the area where the Vendéen insurrection began, the republican General Turreau unleashed his "infernal columns" in areas of insurgency. He called on his troops to seek retribution against those who rose up against the republic. One of Turreau's underlings ordered his soldiers to "burn water mills and wind mills . . . knock down chimneys. . . . If you find some peasants, some women in the communes where our columns recently passed, shoot them, there are so many partisans of our enemies, there are so many spies." The troops ostensibly made no distinctions among those crossing their paths. The destruction often served no military purpose. Though the columns did not penetrate Machecoul per se, one *cultivateur*, Honoré Plaintin, a self-proclaimed patriot whose father was killed in the Machecoul massacres, saw three of his brothers and a sister-in-law cut down when the infernal columns unleashed their wrath. In a subsequent sweep by the columns, his only remaining brother, sister-in-law, and their fifteen-year-old niece were killed. The troops slaughtered all of his cattle and destroyed all furnishings as well. Plaintin's own life was spared only because of his imprisonment.[35]

While republicans troops were ravaging the countryside during 1794 and early 1795, Charette's forces had little choice but to hide in the *marais* and mount small and sporadic attacks on local targets in the Machecoul region. Following the execution of Robespierre in July 1794, General Lazare Hoche took control of republican forces in the west. With the approval of authorities in Paris, Hoche attempted to bring peace to the area by negotiating with insurgent leaders. On February 17, 1795, at La Jaunaye, Hoche and Charette agreed to peace terms, which included an amnesty for insurgents and a guarantee of freedom of religion.[36] But the treaty merely proved to be a brief respite from the bloodshed. Taking up arms again in the summer of the same year, Charette sought to rekindle the insurrection with the assistance of the British, who tried to supply the insurgents with arms from ships off the west coast. Ultimately, though, it was to no avail.[37] Charette's final attack, near Legé in October 1795, amounted to a miserable failure. Finally, republican forces apprehended Charette in March 1796 and executed him in Nantes. His execution, together with that of General Stofflet, brought the War of Vendée to a definitive end.[38]

Although Vendéen leaders like Charette were the foremost target of republican retribution, government authorities were out to punish all who revolted, as again the insurgent narrative makes abundantly clear. Even while the war was still raging, local officials responded with fury to those who had been part of the insurgency at Machecoul through judicial and extra-judicial proceedings. Held throughout 1793 and 1794, the tribunals heard the testimony of numerous Machecoulais and sentenced to death many local residents implicated in the massacres. The records for these judicial and military tribunals indicate that, as was the case with the victims of the Machecoul massacres, there was little socioeconomic similitude among those accused of committing the atrocities. Among those condemned to die for their alleged participation in the massacres were the justice of the peace from Saint-Lumine-de-Coutais, merchants from Legé and Port-Saint-Père respectively, a boat worker, and a *farinier*. An eighteen-year-old *domestique* named Pierre Vilaine boasted that he had killed abbé Letort, but for some reason the tribunal judges refused to believe him.[39] Louis Chiffoneau, a Machecoul woodworker, was not so lucky. He was denounced as one of the leaders of the brigands by a former municipal official who survived the massacre, and paid with his life.[40]

If there is a pattern regarding those who purportedly committed the massacres, it falls more along the lines of gender, not socioeconomic origin; the judicial proceedings resulted in a significant number of women from the Machecoul area being implicated in the massacres. It was women in and around the town who, according to the commandant of the National Guard, were guilty of the "indecencies so terrible so as to be unspeakable." Some Machecoulais accused a widow of recommending that the town's imprisoned patriots be poisoned, and alleged that a linen maid, Marie Chevet, committed a great many crimes, including persuading peasants to join in the rebellion and applauding the massacres. Judges sentenced the wife of a shoemaker to death for committing "great cruelties to the bodies of patriots" and for purportedly parading around the town with a patriot's severed head.[41]

A tribunal found validity in the accusations that Marie Heriau Bornigal, who lived in the neighboring commune of Paulx, struck "the corpses of those assassinated by the brigands with a stick, including that of Letort," as well as cried "Long live the king" after a rebel victory.[42] A tribunal even imposed capital punishment on an eighty-year-old woman, Rose Troishenry Despérières, the wife of a onetime prosecuting attorney. She purportedly had announced that those who voted to have the king killed would perish, on top of persuading insurgents to shoot their prisoners. A great many other women in the area were accused of similar kinds of crimes, and most were ordered confined to prison.[43]

No doubt republican conceptions of gender played a role in the prosecution of these women. As Olwen Hufton found, most if not all revolutionary officials were latently antifeminist, in part because so many women had refused to accept the Constitutional Church and its clergy. That many women rejected the Civil Constitution of the Clergy merely reinforced revolutionary officials' ideas about feminine ignorance, gullibility, and proclivity toward emotion and sentimentality over reason and logic.[44] Clearly such notions are implicit in the republican prosecution of these women for the massacres. The documentation suggests that although prosecutors held the inculpated totally responsible for their own actions, they also viewed the women as easily deluded by the insurgency's leaders (including priests), or on occasion seemingly descending into a hysteria. Yet in equal measure, republican concepts of gender also dictated how officials dealt with these women. Republicans may have accused the female Machecoulais to a greater extent because they had egregiously transgressed gender boundaries—often a common fear arising during a community crisis. In committing alleged atrocities like striking corpses and removing body parts, these women had violated republican expectations of gentle and nourishing mothers who were to remain within the domestic sphere and thus aloof from political matters; they were acting too much like men—and imitating barbarous male insurgents made them all the more insidious.[45] Prosecuting these women, therefore, was a way of reinforcing republican gender roles and restoring sexual differentiation. Republicans achieved such a goal by underscoring the ghastly transgressions that female insurgents had committed against the natural order.

As important as these notions of gender were, however, the primary reason why women were prosecuted was because of their concrete support of refractory priests. Republicans both at Machecoul and beyond were quick to conclude that the insurgency was caused by rebellious priests in league with local notables, both of whom were believed to have coordinated a carefully planned plot. And since many women in the town championed those priests who had refused the oath, it followed in the minds of republicans that these women were in no small part responsible for the massacres. The existence of this conspiracy theory certainly predated the massacres themselves, as seen in Chapter Three.[46] By 1793, however, it had informed the outlook of republicans on virtually every level. Villers and Fouché claimed in their report that the insurgents were battling for the faith, especially since refractory priests purportedly encouraged them by saying that fighting would guarantee them entry into heaven and that bullets could not hurt them if they possessed faith. Among the more outrageous claims by Villers and Fouché is that the killings at Machecoul by insurgents were considered part of a celebration traditionally held at mid-Lent called *mi-carême*: as if the massacre of Machecoulais was religiously condoned since temporarily breaking Lenten vows was permissible.[47] An accusation in a similar vein—and one still leveled by the most partisan republicans—is that the prisoners were conducted to the place of execution with a rope that purposely made them resemble beads on a rosary, hence the infamous term "les chapelets de Machecoul."[48]

Local republicans seemed especially taken with the conspiracy. One finds the evidence in the testimony against accused women, such as the twenty-five-year-old linen maid, Chevet:

> Considering that the Tribunal learned by the deposition of the previous witnesses and the identifications of Marie Chevet that since the month of September 1792, she traversed the countryside of Machecoul to incite its inhabitants to rise up in order to seize by force the named la Bauche, refractory priest, former *curé Doyen* of Machecoul, who had just been taken before the constituted authorities; that since the insurrection on March 10 she propagated catechisms and other incendiary writings in the Machecoul area in order to maintain and fuel the fanaticism of the inhabitants of the countryside;…that when the brigands entered Machecoul on March 11, 1793, she appeared at

their head, designating to them the houses of patriots, and told the brigands to make them cry, long live the king; that she walked arm in arm with them in the streets; that she made white *cocardes* and [Sacred] Hearts which she distributed to the brigands; . . . that she applauded the horrible massacres of the Machecoul patriots which the brigands committed by saying that they got what they deserved, and that their assassinations were well-done; . . . that she attended a mass said for the benediction of the flags, cannons, firearms, and munitions, and celebrated on an altar placed in the same spot where the day before the brigands sacrificed patriots and their blood was spilled; . . . that when the brigands united to march toward Nantes and attack on June 29, she accompanied them with a bludgeon in hand; . . . and that she wanted to be the first to enter [Nantes] so that she could, above all, release from prison the former *curé doyen* of Machecoul.[49]

Regardless of the validity of these accusations (many of which seem rather dubious), the testimony shows that republicans were convinced that refractory priests were directly culpable for the massacre, consequently blaming their supporters, like Chevet, for the atrocities. When two other Machecoul women, Renée and Emilie Réal, were implicated for the insurrection, several of their defenders wrote to the departmental authority, stating that the Réals were "victims of denunciations created by their enemies for frequenting their parish served by an unconstitutional priest [Sainte-Croix] in preference to another served by a constitutional priest [Trinité]; that is their only crime."[50]

That military and judicial officials who tried those involved with the massacre always asked questions about the activities of refractory priests indicates that they too sought to make a correlation between the refractory clergy and the massacre. Some witnesses, perhaps in an effort to save their own lives, were quick not to disappoint officials in their accounts. Perhaps the most celebrated example of this came when witnesses discussed the alleged activity of abbé Priour:

> There arrived among the peasants, some refractory priests, named Piarre, Goguet, Massonnet, former *curé* of Saint-Même, and Priou. The latter appeared in his cassock, beginning on Wednesday the thirteenth. He had been the *vicaire* of Trinité of Machecoul; they invited him to say mass there; he responded that the church was

polluted, that it had not been blessed since the constitutional priest said mass there. So he chose another place more consecrated. He prepared an altar, at the crossroads of the prison, and said mass in the area where the constitutional *curé* had been massacred, along with thirty patriots; the monster had his feet in blood, the bottom of his alb was stained.[51]

In such testimony was the republican narrative reinforced. For Fouché and Villers, gems like this one became the centerpiece of their report to the National Convention.[52] Sympathizers for the insurgents, however, have always been quick to point out that such testimony lacks corroboration and thus is highly doubtful.[53]

At the risk of appearing to prefer one narrative to the other, an interjection must be made; to dismiss all republican testimony is unwarranted. The claim by insurgent sympathizers that somehow all of the accounts given by witnesses were fabricated is just as incredible as the republican notion that priests and nobles coordinated a plot. A case in point are accusations regarding abbé Priour during the insurgents' occupation of the town. Several witnesses agreed that abbé Priour said an open-air mass on April 21 (but not on March 13, as claimed by Villers and Fouché) and later blessed the arms used by the insurgents in the battle that shortly followed. As already shown, the service also figured in the testimony against Marie Chevet, who allegedly attended the mass. In addition, Julien Archambaud, a *farinier* from the parish of Sainte-Croix, swore that he attended this mass, as well as "the benediction of the cannons, pikes, poles, guns and generally all the arms that they were able to have, this benediction being made by one of the three priests." Louis Rousseau, another accused insurgent, also claimed that Priour said mass and blessed the insurgents' poles.[54]

The allegation that refractory priests were responsible for the massacres was also prevalent among officials of the department of the Loire-Inférieure in Nantes. The fate of the approximately one hundred refractory priests who were detained in Nantes at the former convent for Carmelites, including abbé Roland Hervé de la Bauche, had yet to be decided when the insurrection started. After the Vendéen insurgents mounted their unsuccessful attack on Nantes in June 1793, local officials transported the priests to a boat anchored in the Loire River, and later to the religious house known as the Little Capuchins.[55] The precarious situation in the west prompted the National Convention to send one of its own to Nantes near the end of September, largely for the purpose of reorganizing the army and directing military operations. The Convention decided on Jean-Baptiste Carrier, an outspoken radical even by Montagnard standards. But even before Carrier came to Nantes the city's sans-culottes were more than ready to support the representative on his mission. When he arrived, Carrier set up a revolutionary committee composed of the most dedicated sans-culottes and invested it with much authority. One of the most formidable problems for Carrier and the committee was that all of the city's prisons were filled to overflowing, and many of the incarcerated were suffering from disease and malnutrition.[56] One short-term solution arrived at by the committee was to transfer eighty-six refractory priests from the house of the Little Capuchins to another boat on the Loire River called the *Gloire*.[57]

Once again, a discrepancy opens up between competing narratives. The republican version tends to blame Carrier for what followed, while the insurgent version tends to spread blame among many republicans both on the local and national levels.[58] Regardless, a radical idea was conceived: what Carrier reportedly styled "vertical deportations," meaning the execution of prisoners by drowning in the Loire River.[59] On the night of November 16, 1793, the committee moved forward with its plan when it transferred eighty-four of the priests from the *Gloire* to a leaky barge (it is not clear whether the victims were bound), which was then set adrift on the river to sink shortly thereafter. Abbé Hervé de la Bauche and a *prêtre-habituée* from Machecoul, François Mulon, were among the victims drowned in the incident. Four weeks later a second round of *noyades* or drownings took place, when fifty-eight priests from Anjou met their deaths. In all—of course depending on whose narrative it is—about seven to thirteen *noyades* took place in late 1793 and early 1794, with anywhere from 2,000 to 4,800 victims being drowned.[60] As ghastly as the *noyades* were, however, probably twice that number were killed by Carrier's firing squads. Systematic repression continued in and around Nantes until Carrier departed in February 1794, after which time the political terror slowly subsided. Although Nantes had become the center of terror in western France, it was far from the only place where retribution unfolded. Vengeful republicans located in other towns in the west followed Carrier's lead by performing "patriotic baptisms." *Noyades* similar to Carrier's took place in Ancenis, Angers, Saint-Florent-le-Vieil, and at the Bay of Bourgneuf, which was located very close to Machecoul.[61]

Ironically the *noyades* seemed to strengthen insurgent resolve rather than diminish it. In the minds of many who had rejected the Constitutional Church, their cause was justified by the *noyades*, for the victims were marked with the ultimate sign of Christ-like emulation, namely martyrdom. Almost immediately after the Terror, the contextualization of the *noyades* amid the persecutions of early Christians, as well as the Vendéens among the Maccabee dynasty in the Hebrew Scriptures, was under way.[62] The *noyades*, in effect, were an affirmation of the long-held belief among refractory priests and their supporters that republicanism was intrinsically evil and that the Revolution had satanic origins.

Thus, by the end of 1793, two stories about the Machecoul massacres and, more generally, the troubles in western France, were well in place. Both tended to see religion as central to the events that had take place in the town. The testimony given by various Machecoulais helped form the republican narrative that the refractory clergy and its supporters—especially gender-transgressing women—were culpable for the civil war, including the town's massacres, most notably through their participation in a conspiratorial plot.[63] Yet at the same time the insurgents had constructed a counternarrative that debunked any plot but that still exalted the role of religion in the insurgency. Elements of the insurgent narrative, moreover, seemed to justify the rebellion, in part by casting it as a divinely sanctioned crusade.[64]

Explaining the Inexplicable

Stepping back from the two narratives for a moment allows for a reengagement with this chapter's central question: What role did religion play in this episode at Machecoul? The claims by both the republican and insurgent narratives that religion was closely tied to what occurred in the town were not made without reason. The presence of abbé Priour and the other refractory priests in the town during the insurgency, their participation with Souchu, and the probable liturgies that took place while rebels held Machecoul indicate that the insurgency indeed had a religious dimension. The grisly killings of abbés Letort and Marchesse, if believed, were ritualistic murders—as if the priests who had sworn the oath merited special suffering at the hands of the insurgents, who may have taken it on themselves to personify divine wrath. The evidence from other episodes in the War of Vendée confirms the presence, albeit superficial at times, of religious phenomena. The insurgents themselves called their own force the "armée catholique et royale," and many insurgents wore a symbol of the Sacred Heart when they engaged in the fighting.[65] Clandestine priests celebrated mass with the insurgents, usually at night, and also kept registries recording all baptisms, marriages, and burials of those who supported insurgency.[66]

In spite of such phenomena, it would be absurd to discount the relevance of social, political, and economic rivalries underscored in the studies of counterrevolution by Tilly, Bois, Faucheux, Sutherland, Petitfrère, and Martin, all of which have purposely looked beyond the conventional narratives described here. Just because contemporaries were not able to grasp the magnitude of social, economic, and political factors in the instigation of civil war does not mean that these were of no consequence. Of special import is the insight of Martin, who, though not necessarily disagreeing with Tilly, Bois, and others favoring a socioeconomic explanation, has emphasized that at its inception the War of Vendée looked analogous to popular insurgencies that had exploded throughout Europe during the early modern era. Many of these popular revolts were generated by social and economic grievances but similarly took on a religious hue and claimed divine justification.[67] This is why Martin, in his specific examination of the Machecoul massacres, observed that "the explosion of March 10 and 11 had thus allied the form of a *jacquerie* well known in the countryside to a primarily political agitation founded upon religious division."[68]

Jacqueries were unextraordinary events during the early modern era. Between 1590 and 1715 alone more than 450 rebellions took place in just one region of France. Although peasants made up the majority of those who revolted, such rebellions were more than purely peasant uprisings based only on economic grievances. Indeed, a Christian, millenarian message often accompanied such revolts, as participants frequently became convinced that God was on their side and that they were carrying out divine will; many rebels believed that they were paving the way for the final judgment.[69] Another key characteristic of these rebellions was that they were usually led, not by peasants, but by discontented members of the elite. George Huppert explained that "peasants were led by village notables who could read and write, who hired lawyers to represent them and who formed alliances with urban radicals. [Peasants] did not hit out blindly."[70] Given the pivotal role of notables in a *jacquerie* as well as the notion among rebels that it was divinely ordained, the religious culture of a local elite is highly relevant here—especially since the political divide among notables at Machecoul was largely based on the oath crisis.

The salient role of notables in a *jacquerie* is just one of the reasons why it can be argued that while political and socioeconomic variables contributed to the massacres, local religious culture was just as critical, especially if its role in the revolt is clarified and qualified. When the traditional narratives cite religion as the basis for revolt, they usually mean that religion acted as a *motivation* for the insurgents. Studies emphasizing the social and economic dimensions of the insurgency tend to dismiss such a notion out of hand, but some historians now seem to be rethinking the issue.[71] As seen in the oath crisis, notable women were among the most ardent supporters of the refractory clergy, and as such they may have truly believed that armed insurrection (and perhaps killing constitutional priests) was the only means of restoring the one Roman and Apostolic Church. This is not to say, as Michelet did, that women were "duped" by priests in the confessional; rather, it is to suggest that women tenaciously adhered to Tridentine teachings, and thus could not support the Constitutional Church or ultimately the Revolution itself. The same was perhaps true of some male notables at Machecoul, such as the Sainte-Croix *marguilliers*.

One form of evidence at Machecoul cited for religion being a motivation for the insurgency is the chronology of unrest. Narratives on both sides point out that tension in the town was not appreciable up until the refractory pastors were removed from their offices and replaced with a constitutional priest. But that is not all. A predominant theme in this chapter, as well as the previous one, is that the divisions that emerged in and around Machecoul during the Revolution and counterrevolution transcended social status, economic backgrounds, and professional categories: the implication being that there was much more to the conflict than social and economic animosity. Certainly political and religious ideologies were at play, and as scholars who have studied Jansenism show, the political and the religious often remained one and the same even as the Revolution was unfolding. In this vein, more than a few historians have remarked that the French Revolution resembled not so much a war *against* religions but rather a war *between* religions—a notion that seems especially applicable at the local level in western France.[72] If the Revolution is cast in this light, that elite insurgents would revolt against the republic based on firmly held ideologies involving both political and religious beliefs does not seem incredible at all.

The most compelling evidence for religious culture serving as motivation in the republican narrative concerns the massacres themselves. Republicans made much of the mutilation of corpses, mostly in an effort to demonize the insurgents, but the allegation may also be helpful for untangling the "logic" of violence. Although we may never know for sure whether bodies were mutilated, the accusation is certainly in keeping with a pattern of popular violence going at least as far back as the French Wars of Religion in the sixteenth century—events renowned for the rituals of bodily mutilation. Of special significance here was the way in which corpses at Machecoul were reportedly disfigured, particularly that of the constitutional *curé*, abbé Letort.[73] Natalie Zemon Davis and Denis Crouzet showed that Catholics in France during the sixteenth-century civil war often cut away the genitalia of their Protestant victims, in large part because the perpetrators perceived them as sexually aberrant.[74] The logic, according to Davis, was that removing the offending part of the victim's body constituted a symbolic purging of the dreaded source of pollution among the body social.[75] For Crouzet, such mutilation constituted a ritualistic confirmation among Catholics of the impending retribution that Protestants would face in hell.[76] Although such acts of ritual killing were two centuries removed from the Machecoul massacres, arguably the lexicon of murder remained remarkably intact among those untouched by Enlightenment ideas, as Alain Corbin demonstrated.[77] Arguably, the mutilation of abbé Letort's body was a declaration by the insurgents that the constitutional *curé* was not only a heretic but also that he feigned his clerical celibacy. The smashing of skulls and reported decapitations are also significant in this light. Since false doctrine was purportedly being issued from the mouths of the constitutional priests and their supporters, the ritualistic prescription would call for the desecration of the head.

Yet no matter whether religious messages were being sent through such acts, it must be acknowledged that the majority of insurgents showed no signs of claiming divine inspiration, and thus the motivational explanation falls short of explaining all. For those not spiritually inclined, religious culture—especially as it concerned the oath crisis—may have served as a *catalyst* for the revolt. In other words, religious culture may not have been directly responsible for generating long-standing animosity within the Machecoul community, but it certainly accentuated and intensified the strife. The implementation of the Civil Constitution of the Clergy and the oath crisis likely activated dissatisfaction that was political, social, and economic in nature—some of which predated the Revolution—to such a degree that this discontent exploded into violence in March 1793. Thus, much like a catalyst used in chemical experiments, religious culture provoked a reaction while not necessarily being the primary cause for such an effect. What makes this argument especially applicable to Machecoul is that although peasants in and around the town who made up the bulk of the insurgent contingent attended church rites on a regular basis, they were not known for their strong devotion to Tridentine Catholicism. To be sure, peasants had little idea of the theological implications of the Civil Constitution of the Clergy, yet they could easily identify the expulsion of abbé Hervé and abbé Blanchard as the most concrete manifestation of their oppression.

It can be further argued that leaders of the insurrection utilized religious culture as *fuel* for the revolt. Vendéen leaders saw in that culture a means of adding energy and support to their cause. By turning the struggle into a crusade, they sought to inflame the emotions of their followers and garner more support for a cause that nevertheless was inspired by nonreligious developments and oriented toward a predominantly nonreligious end.[78] True, this notion of the Vendée as a crusade was much more popular after the war, and in many cases was retroactively applied to insurgency. As for 1793, though, the incorporation of religious culture was perhaps rooted in a political maneuver on behalf of Souchu and other Vendéen leaders to sustain and maintain the revolt. In the case of Machecoul, this may be why refractory priests, including one who was a lowly *vicaire* before the Revolution, may have assumed roles of leadership among the insurgents. Abbé Priour's presence may have been meant to rally those whose religious culture served as the primary basis for participation in the revolt.

In keeping with the notion that religious culture had a functional capacity in the insurgency, one can also see that religious culture became a *vocabulary* of the insurgency. Such an argument is drawn from Claude Lévi-Strauss's idea of *bricolage*, in which preexisting cultural elements are reconfigured to generate a new cultural expression.[79] This is to suggest, then, that religious culture (namely that of Tridentine Catholicism) had been around for a prolonged period, but it took on a new guise in the insurgency. It must be recalled that Tridentine spirituality emerged at a time when the Catholic Church was at war with the Protestant Reformation, and therefore it was highly imbued with militancy. This cultural lexicon was easily adaptable to the insurgents' need to interpret themselves and their cause, especially since religious rituals constituted a symbolic system well known to virtually everyone involved in the revolt. The symbol of the Sacred Heart of Jesus was perhaps the most salient expression of this insurgent vocabulary. Popularized by the French mystic Marguerite-Marie Alacoque in the seventeenth century, this devotion was especially appropriate for counterrevolution because it suggested that France was destined to greatness by God, but only if it submitted to divine authority and corporal self-denial.[80] The Sacred Heart thus suggested that suffering and death in the struggle against the republic and in defense of the monarchy had salvific value, and it served as a fitting metaphor for the social and political hierarchies that the Revolution supposedly was dismantling.

But perhaps the most fundamental role that religious culture assumed in the revolt was that of *cohesion*. Emile Durkheim and other scholars have long contended that religion, especially in terms of its ritual, often is a source of *cohesion* in a community. While it is also true—as in the case of Machecoul—that religious culture can just as easily divide a community, its cohesive capacity becomes all the more pivotal in times of crisis. In comparing counterrevolution in western France with other manifestations of rural revolt, the scholars János Bak and Gerhard Benecke concluded that "religion may be seen less as a supplier of scriptural legitimation and justification, but rather as the unifying force of a village and regional community." In other words, religious culture was frequently the means by which participants in a rural revolt (especially since they came from different social segments within a rural community) were able to unite and become a coherent force. But the cohesive capacity of religion was due to much more than just the regular sociability that peasants enjoyed at mass on Sundays and religious holidays. Bak, Benecke, and others argue that the key to rebel unity was not only the social contact made in and through religion but also the mythology to which they all subscribed and the very rituals and activities in which they engaged.[81] When seen in this context, one can better understand why abbé Priour held a liturgy at which he blessed the pikes, firearms, and munitions used in the fight against republican forces. The act may have served as some kind of inspiration, but more significantly it coalesced the rebels, confirmed their solidarity, and gave them the sense of being unified by one purpose and one cause as they went into battle.

Thus the role that religious culture played in the insurgency at Machecoul was, in all likelihood, multifaceted: a complex combination of *motivation, catalyst, fuel, vocabulary,* and *cohesion.* If religious culture's affiliation to insurgency is seen as such, it fails to negate the relevance of political, social, and economic rebellion, yet it also proposes that popular religious practice and belief were indeed decisive to these events. At any rate, the multifarious connections between religious culture and revolt are still more indications of how complex this revolt was. It also seemingly explains why the search for a thorough explanation for what happened in western France, as well as why it happened, is far from over.

Contested Memory and Pacification

A year after the massacres, republicans at Machecoul reportedly held a solemn commemoration "in honor of the martyrs of liberty sacrificed by the brigands of the Vendée," as the records of the National Convention put it. A detailed description of the ritual is found in the convention's minutes, complete with an address purportedly given by the president of Machecoul's Jacobin Club in which the horrors of one year earlier were recalled:

A child of sixteen years, assassinated and left among the number of dead, was revived after several hours; [the brigands] saw him: the assassins ran to the priest's home; the monster came, hastily delivered a pretended absolution, and coldly ordained what they would do to him.

The cortege was then taken to the wall of the former Calvarian monastery, among the ashes of three hundred other patriots slaughtered at that time. . . . he responded to his torturers, who promised him his life if he cried, "Long live the king," and joined them: "No, monsters, no I swear to live free! I abhor your phantom king; I abhor the fanatics, the imposters and their vile followers. I am faithful to my oath; you may dispose my body, but my soul is independent; Long live the Republic!"

Here were the fathers of families, their tender wives, virtuous magistrates in which the love of liberty was always inseparable from the philanthropy that inspired it. Their entire life having been consecrated to the fatherland, their last wish was for the triumph of the republic. Covered with cruel wounds, Garreau-Cormier, Fleuri, and others cried, at the same time the brigands crushed their bones with massive blows, after having torn up their bodies with pike stabs. . . . [The wounded said,] "Strike us on our heads and finally deliver us from the torment you see."

Cavisez, sick and already mutilated, said to the assassins with a voice that underscored and reinforced patriotism: "Tyrants, in your false pride you delight in victory, you are deluded. . . . Dread the terrible day of vengeance that is approaching. You will soon have to pay the price: the entire republic is armed against you and will punish the most horrible of insurgencies."[82]

If this rite took place (which is no certainty), it was one of the first manifestations of republican memory of the event. But even if the rite was fabricated, it reveals a republican mythology about the massacres that began to emerge as early as the spring of 1794, which then became the basis for how future republican generations would remember the episode.

Most striking about the report is how republicans appropriated Christian vocabulary in creating their own spiritual universe; the term, "martyrs," stands out above all, but more generally the account of a sixteen-year-old boy defying his assassins is a typical scenario found among the stories of Catholic saints.[83] Indeed, the mention of a young boy was formulaic, being not only reminiscent of Christian martyrology but also remarkably similar to the revolutionary cult of Joseph Bara, a fourteen-year-old boy who heroically died at the hands of insurgents outside Cholet in December 1793. Like the alleged young Machecoulais described here, Bara allegedly was asked to say, "Long live the king," but instead cried "Long live the Republic," and was killed for doing so.[84] Also remarkable is the length to which republicans went in describing the corporal and mental suffering experienced by the victims: the butchering of victims, the crushing of their bones, the mutilation of their bodies. Such graphic illustration seems to suggest, as Antoine de Baecque found, a republican preoccupation with the body, if not human suffering and death as well. More specifically, discourse on the Machecoul massacres reveals how the human body became a metaphor for the republican ideals of fidelity, sacrifice, and regeneration. Yet this, too, was an appropriation of Catholicism, especially its long-standing notion that the blood of martyrs sustained the life of the Church.[85] Thus even when republicans were trying to create a mythology completely devoid of Christian belief, they could not help but build it on a foundation of Catholic culture.

Such appropriation may suggest to some scholars that the town's republicans were quick to abandon the most fundamental tenets of Catholicism to conform to Montagnard de-Christianization, thus indicating that Machecoul's republicans had simply paid lip service to Catholic belief. But caution is required when reaching this conclusion for several reasons. For one, the records of the National Convention also include a report about the town from October 1793 (before massive de-Christianization began) in which district administrators attended a mass at nearby La Chevrolière, where a republican priest "donned sacerdotal garb, celebrated mass, which was said and heard with the greatest pomp." At the end of mass not only did the *curé* sing "Domine salvam fac legem, Domine salvam fac gentem," but administrators then repeated the chant three times. Following the mass came a ceremony in which a tree of liberty was planted, led once again by the *curé*. At a separate site, moreover, republicans purportedly took a royalist white flag, "threw it down with furor, tore it into pieces, lit a pyre, threw it in, and with pleasure gazed at its burning while cursing this fatal sign of tyranny, of federalism, as well as vowing the extermination of tyrants, kings, and federalists."[86]

The very rhetoric included in this report to the National Convention offers another rationale for why caution is merited. For such reports to enter the convention's minutes, they had to be passed through numerous governmental channels, which offered many opportunities to modify or alter them so that they conformed to the party line. Thus, whether or not Machecoul's republicans truly equated federalism with royal tyranny may never be fully known, but the report—at least as it appeared in the convention's records—undoubtedly served Montagnard political purposes at that precise moment. For similar reasons, the sentiment found in a report to the National Convention from the town's administrators in the spring of 1794, in which they revealed that all the communes in their district "sent their [ecclesiastical] silverware, linen, and ornaments that formerly fooled the people" remains somewhat suspect, especially since it was submitted at the height of the de-Christianization campaign.[87] In other words, more than anything these reports to the National Convention reveal that Machecoul republicans who had survived the massacres became the political poster children for Montagnards in Paris during 1793 and 1794; the town had become the personification of republican fidelity, sacrifice, and regeneration.[88]

What the level of Catholic belief was among republican survivors, therefore, remains unclear. After the killing of abbé Letort and several other *curés*, most of the other constitutional priests in the countryside abandoned their parishes and took refuge in Nantes. The de-Christianization campaign, which brought about the suppression of the seminary in Nantes and the resignation of Julien Minée as bishop of the Loire-Inférieure, made any effort to revive the Church at Machecoul moot. As for the insurgents, after the 1795 treaty of La Jaunaye those refractory priests who had been in hiding reappeared, and some of those who had been deported returned to the region.[89] In the summer of 1795—at about the same time that hostilities between Charette and the Hoche resumed—the National Convention resolved to grant amnesty to all refractory priests.[90] General Hoche complied with this policy and tried to restrain his troops from hunting down refractory priests and to allow Vendéens to practice their religion freely.[91]

Still, what little political and religious peace there was in the west proved short-lived. Hoche's policy and the wishes of the post-Thermidor convention stood in direct opposition to the sentiments of embittered patriots in the Loire-Inférieure. Many republicans in the department strongly opposed the appeasement policy pursued by Hoche and authorities in Paris, as exhibited in the departmental officials' refusal to recognize the amnesty of refractory priests. In August 1795 departmental authorities ordered that any priest not able to present a certificate verifying his obedience to the nation would be arrested.[92] They subsequently moved quickly against priests whom they deemed insidious. Yet another priest connected to Machecoul became the target. In mid-September a former *vicaire* of Trinité, Honoré Renaudineau, was arrested at Palis and immediately executed.[93]

Republican indignation at Hoche's liberal policy was especially strong among the surviving republicans at Machecoul. In late September the commissioner of the Machecoul canton wrote to departmental authorities and vehemently complained about abbé Priour, the priest who had been implicated in the massacre.[94] Republican memory of the episode remained unequivocal:

> You did not take heed of the letter of last 20 Fructidor where I denounced the mobs caused by *Priou*, the priest and head of the Machecoul slaughters, exercising his ministry at Quinquenevant in this commune. Have you any doubt that he and the other monsters, male and female, who support this black devil were the rogues who had been there? I informed you many times that these people had cut throats or beat to death the patriots of the countryside. Why have the generals authorized them to practice their religion without submission to the laws? I tell you again that if no one arrests these priest-leaders and the religious who cause all kind of harm, we will see, unfortunately, our poor countryside rise up once more. It is with sadness that I say I asked you many times for their confinement, as well for all those who wear the religious habit. It is only with prompt measures that we will save the peace.[95]

The author of the plea, Guillaume Gigault, was one of the Machecoul patriots who had witnessed the massacres and remained deeply angered by Hoche's appeasement. He sought to underscore the barbarity of the rebels, in part by emphasizing that the perpetrators were both "male and female," which again reflected republican assumptions about gender transgressions. When the Directory came to power in late October 1795, it no doubt was to the satisfaction of Gigault and many other republicans in the Loire-Inférieure, mostly since laws passed against refractory priests were reinstituted. This in turn caused such priests in the department to return to their clandestine lifestyle.

But only about one year later yet another political shift in Paris likely disheartened Machecoul republicans. As part of a dramatic shift to the right, in November 1796 the Directory abrogated all laws imposed against refractory priests.[96] In spite of this change in policy at the national level, the town's patriots persisted in their hostility for refractory priests. In a cantonal surveillance report to departmental authorities that year, Gigault again complained about abbé Priour and asserted that he was one of the first instigators of the insurrection and perhaps the "author" of the Machecoul massacres, since those who committed the massacres went to him for confession. The canton commissioner added that "his presence in the Vendée [war] will never cease to be a subject of discord and objections."[97] Gigault and his colleagues probably applauded the coup d'état of September 1797, for with it came a new round of refractory-priest persecutions. Thereafter all priests were required to swear their hatred of royalty and anarchy, and any cleric who stood against the government ran the risk of being deported to Guiana.[98] The coup did not come a moment too soon for Machecoul patriots, for two days after the new government came to power, Gigault wrote to departmental authorities again, this time claiming that refractory priests in his canton were stirring up trouble—not so much by preaching incendiary sermons but allegedly through their counsel given during confession (how he would know of what was said in confession remains unclear).[99]

The Directory's repression of refractory priests continued throughout 1798 and 1799, as did the formation of republican memory of the massacres. In the Loire-Inférieure the government arrested approximately twenty-three priests, fourteen of whom were deported, with five of those eventually dying in Guiana.[100] Still, authorities were either unwilling or unable to apprehend the three or so refractory priests in the Machecoul canton, and the presence and active ministry of these priests continued to be of great concern to republican Machecoulais. Although the War of Vendée had all but ended when Charette was executed in March 1796, instances of *chouannerie*, characterized by sporadic guerilla attacks, broke out in many parts of the west between 1796 and 1800. Over this time republicans residing in small towns like Machecoul lived in a state of perennial fear because of the potential for hostilities breaking out again.[101] In light of this constant menace, the Machecoul canton commissioner advocated that both priests and former members of religious orders in his canton be detained. He explained that

> if we had had the money to pay [spies], we would find some, and in this way we would soon be able defang these monsters, both male and female. Without this we are not able to free ourselves. If the minister would like to delegate some funds for these operations, let that be secret. Without this we will not be able to succeed in anything.[102]

Hiring spies and defanging monsters (who were, significantly, "both male and female") further suggested that although Vendéen hostilities had ended in 1796, the memory among town republicans regarding the massacres was guiding their politics.

Frustrations among the town's republicans were probably exacerbated by the prospect of rebuilding an entire community. Since much of the town was razed to the ground during the successive invasions by both sides, public functionaries sought to reorganize and reconstruct most of their institutions, including those that formerly belonged to the church. This task began shortly after the insurgency subsided in the Machecoul area but did not get under way in earnest until the Directory period. Not long after the massacres, one Machecoul official asked departmental authorities that those redeemable books owned by prominent insurgents be turned over to the "bon patriots" so that a new reading room could be established in the town.[103] But other problems were even more pressing, many of which required a fiscal solution. Most requests for government financial support, however, fell on deaf ears. The reason was obvious; with a war still being fought against the major powers of Europe, not to mention ongoing guerilla attacks in their own backyard, state officials had few funds to spare. In July 1796 Machecoul canton administrators requested both material and financial aid from the department so that they could reopen the town's *hôpital*. The building itself had not been destroyed, but the *hôpital* was in dire need of new beds and clean linen.[104] A year and a half passed before departmental and national officials responded. The minister of war finally accorded the institution twenty complete beds, yet when the *hôpital* commission attempted to procure the beds, the local military concierge refused to give them out. By the beginning of 1798 the Machecoul *hôpital* still did not have the beds needed to become fully operational.[105]

The primary schools in Machecoul were likewise in need of government assistance immediately after civil war. The acute shortage of books for students prompted local officials to request funding from departmental administrators for new books that stressed republican ideals. Other problems plagued the town's educational institutions as well. Machecoul had a sufficient number of instructors, all of whom were reported to be good republicans, but ironically there was a shortage of students. Very few children were attending the schools because the harsh economic difficulties arising from the war meant that their families needed them to work in the fields. When it came to the very few students who did attend, instructors faced yet another political and cultural dilemma:

> The fathers and mothers, for the most part, are not disposed to adopting republican institutions . . . . some [students] have left school because [the instructor] gave the children leave on [republican] days of rest and lessons on the feast days of the old calendar. Some others also stopped taking lessons from him because he proposed that students come to school on republican feast days.[106]

The report deftly revealed that patriots had no easier time of propagating republicanism after the civil war than they had had before it. Indeed, the animosity generated by the insurgency and the Terror made the republicans' task of establishing their institutional base infinitely more difficult.

Republicans faced an uphill battle, therefore, in institutionalizing their memory of the massacres, especially since at the same time the rebels and their supporters were busy cementing their own memory, yet perhaps in a more effective manner. Indeed, for the insurgents, religious ritual became the most viable avenue for perpetuating their memory. The Mauges priest abbé Yves-Michel Marchais, for example, delivered sermons in which he underscored the atrocities committed by the infernal columns, calling republicans "barbaric persecutors" who killed children just as Pharaoh and Herod had done in the scriptures. He encouraged his flock to pray for the return of the monarchy and to resist republican propositions for amnesty. He implied that the scourge of republicanism was linked to the people's sins of drunkenness, material vanity, and sexual impurity.[107] Other refractory priests openly told their followers not to vote for republican candidates, provoked conflicts with local administrators by ringing church bells, conducted processions during which they were escorted by armed insurgents, and declared marriages and first communions performed by constitutional priests invalid.[108] All of this suggested that the insurgent memory was being institutionally solidified, augmented, if not subtly altered in accord with a clerical agenda.

Refractory priests were also somewhat responsible for adding a religious justification to the massacres, which then became part of the insurgent memory. Abbé François Chevalier, a refractory priest and former pastor of Saint-Lumine-de-Coutais, wrote in his account—based on his personal observations at Machecoul—that the altar at the Calvarian monastery had been desecrated by republicans. He concluded that "one is able to say that this evil Revolution was the time of the infamous substitution of paganism for Catholic principles. . . . Thus is it all that striking that God finally avenged his cause and delivered these criminals, who knew no limits, into the vengeful arms of an angry populace?"[109]

In light of all that had happened to inhabitants in the region, the apocalyptic diatribes of Chevalier, Marchais, and other refractory priests delivered in the wake of the Civil Constitution of the Clergy seemed to have come true, which is perhaps why the rebellious clergy gained a great deal of credibility among the former insurgents. Following the war, peasants generally were more inclined to heed the exhortations of the refractory clergy on both religious and political matters. They tended to hold rebellious priests and their counsel in very high regard, moreover, because the insurgency and the Terror had diminished much of the social distance between these priests and their rural parishioners. When refractory priests were being hunted down and persecuted by civil authorities, they were completely dependent on their rural supporters and had little choice but to participate in rural life. Peasants and clandestine priests experienced the trauma of republican wrath together, and this common experience may very well have strengthened the bond between them. Peasants, as a result, seemingly grew to value their religious identity more. In spite of the imposition of the new republican calendar, the rural populace in the Machecoul area continued to live according to the church calendar by observing old feast days and abiding by the Catholic interdiction of marriage during Advent and Lent.[110]

Refractory priests were winning over peasants especially through their pronouncements on popular insurgency. By invoking the memory of the *noyades* and the infernal columns, calling for the return of Old Regime, comparing the War of Vendée to the early Christian persecutions or massacres mentioned in the Bible, provoking conflicts with local authorities, and by popularly canonizing victims of republican brutality, the refractory clergy was not just furthering the insurgent memory of the Revolution; it was also shaping the new character of Catholic belief in the region. The remarkable revival of Catholic practice that occurred not long after the civil war owed its success, at least in part, to a clerical forging of insurgent memory. In 1797 one canton administrator in the Loire-Inférieure reported that his communes were littered with crosses and that insurgents were reuniting in order to attend mass together.[111]

So formidable was the priests' mnemonic influence that it may have contributed to a renewal of armed conflict in the Machecoul area in 1799. In late January a severe earthquake struck the region, causing a considerable amount of damage to buildings but no loss of life. In keeping with their own memory, republican officials claimed that refractory priests were interpreting the quake as proof of God's anger and telling peasants that unless they partook in the new revolt God would condemn them to eternal damnation. Whether true or not, guerilla warfare returned to the region in 1799, particularly when the Council of Five Hundred ordered another round of military conscription in the west. The formation of rebel armies followed, and several small but intense battles between insurgents and republican troops were fought in the region in August, September, and October. But given the devastation resulting from the War of Vendée and *chouannerie*, the insurgents had no hope of holding out. At the same time, moreover, Napoleon Bonaparte had no desire to fight a civil war shortly after he took power. In December 1799 he proposed generous peace terms to the insurgents: pardon and amnesty for all Vendéen combatants as well as a guarantee of their religious freedom.[112]

Although Machecoul canton officials may have felt otherwise, they had little choice but to comply with Napoleon. Two days after Bonaparte announced his terms, canton officials wrote to abbé Baudet, the ex-*vicaire* of Sainte-Croix apparently well known and respected by many insurgents. They told the priest that the inhabitants of Machecoul were ready to welcome him back, that he would be free to perform his ministry, and that his protection would be assured by civil authorities. But they also wrote that his safety was only possible if insurgents ceased fighting. They warned that if the rebel activity did not stop, "forces well capable of destroying them will march against them, and the vengeance will be terrible." Overall, though, the message was conciliatory:

> We are persuaded that you always preached peace. We invite you to redouble your zeal in order to restrain those who would dream of joining the insurgents and to recall or help recall those who are among them. . . . You will save these blinded men. You will keep husbands with their wives, fathers with their children, and children with their fathers and mothers. We already have lost too many people in such a deplorable manner. In preaching peace you will fulfill the first obligation of your ministry.

The canton officials' words were a far cry from their previous rhetoric regarding abbé Priour and other refractory priests. The appeasing content of the letter seemingly represented a willingness among Machecoul republicans to relinquish or maybe alter their memory of the massacres. Or did it? The reality was that the sentiments expressed in the letter were imposed from above. "We give you this assurance," canton administrators wrote further, "according to the orders of Batier, commandant of cantonal republican forces of Machecoul, received from the General."[113] In any case, about one month later Vendéen leaders accepted Napoleon's terms and hostilities officially ended. Some guerilla warfare continued after the peace accord was signed, but Bonaparte was largely successful in pacifying the region.[114]

The perpetuation of the massacres' memory during the Directory period suggests, therefore, that the revolutionary-counterrevolutionary dialectic in and around the town was just as pronounced in 1800 as it had been in the spring of 1793. Local officials persisted in their adamant belligerence toward refractory priests, as evidenced in the ever-present contention of such priests being responsible for the insurgency and, in the case of abbé Priour, for the massacres at Machecoul. Shifts in religious policy at the national level over this period did little to modify their memory. For their part, refractory priests and former insurgents consolidated their own memory during the same period. Thanks to the refractory clergy, a Christian mythology became not only the basis for insurgent memory but also a potent cultural force in the region. Thus, as early as 1800, revolution and counterrevolution had become a holy war—or at least so said both sides of the massacres' contested memory.

But was the Vendéen insurgency truly a holy war? Was it indeed caused by religion? The answer given here—as *mal posée* as answers about "causes" in history now seem—fails to conform to those implicit in either of the two stories described in this chapter. For while there can be no doubt that religious culture had its imprint all over the insurgency, it was not always for the reasons stated in the two competing narratives about the Machecoul massacres. Some insurgents were quite likely inspired by religious culture, whether it was in their decision to revolt or in the logic of their destructive behavior, as the republican story claimed, but by no means was every rebel, and certainly few if any did so on the counsel of the refractory clergy. To an extent, the insurgency resembled a crusade dedicated to the preservation of religion, as the insurgent narrative suggested, but certainly more pressing and immediate concerns inspired most rebels, not the least of which was a desire to avenge perceived economic and political repression. But in any case, to what degree religious culture was tied to the events at Machecoul will remain something of a mystery, largely because what happened in and around the town during those bloody days of March and April 1793 will never be fully known. The early emergence of two irreconcilable stories of the massacres, not to mention the larger schema of contested memory of which these stories were a part, all but guaranteed it.

Still, while the historical "facts" have proved elusive in this chapter, a larger truth has not: what *really* happened in the past often becomes less important than what was *believed* to have happened. Thus the two stories of the Machecoul massacres are relevant, not so much because an underlying reality about religious culture and its affiliation to revolution and counterrevolution can be taken from them, but because they subsequently provided the Machecoulais with an understanding of themselves, their community, the trauma that they experienced, as well as the wider world in which they lived. Arguably the greater value of the two narratives was the beliefs on which they were built, to say nothing of the lessons that they were believed to impart. For this reason the contested memory of the massacres was destined to become much more than political cannon fodder among partisans. One side of that memory, in fact, went on to shape the town's identity in the century that followed.

Notes

[1] *AP*, 92: 53, 9 Messidor an II (June 27, 1794).

[2] Baecque, 136.

[3] See, for example, François Lebrun, "Religion et Révolution dans l'Ouest, publications scientifiques et luttes historiographiques," in Jean Clément Martin, ed., *Religion et révolution: Colloque de Saint-Florent-le-Vieil 13-14-15 mai 1993* (Paris: Anthropos, 1994), 43-55.

[4] The review of the war itself here is quite limited, with the exception of the Machecoul massacres. For a more detailed military account, see Yves Gras, *La guerre de Vendée* (Paris: Economica, 1994).

[5] Martin, *Révolution et contre-révolution*, 36.

[6] Admittedly to divide what was said to have happened at Machecoul into two narratives is somewhat oversimplistic; the various accounts cited are more nuanced than this schema implies. Still, during the Revolution and counterrevolution, as well as over 150 years thereafter, the political climate in France often necessitated sole allegiance to one of these two perspectives.

[7] For the republican story of the Machecoul massacres, see Germain Bethuis, *Les massacres de Machecoul et considérations générales sur la guerre de la Vendée* (Nantes: Imprimerie Mangin et Giraud, 1873), 6-7. Bethuis was born in Machecoul, witnessed the insurgency at the age of six, and later was a judge in Nantes. His father, a Machecoul notary, was among the republicans killed during the massacres. See also Charles-Louis Chassin, *La préparation de la guerre de Vendée 1789-1793*, 3 vols. (Paris: Imprimerie Paul Dupont, 1892),

3: 335-39. Chassin drew from Bethuis, but he himself also reproached the insurgent narrative, as one can see in 3: 346. For the insurgent side, see the account of abbé Francois Chevalier, as recorded in Chassin, 3: 332-33, as well as Alfred Lallié, *Le district de Machecoul*. Chevalier was a refractory priest from the region and Lallié was a committed Orleanist and an unabashed critic of the republican narrative.

[8] Alain Gérard, *La Vendée 1789-1793* (Seyssel: Champ Vallon, 1992), 127-28. Gérard's take on the massacres constitutes an updated version of the insurgent narrative. Jean-Clément Martin, a historian who has tried to remain above the polemical fray (and with much success), has recently concluded about a dozen administrators were killed the first day and about the same number the following day. See Martin, *Révolution et contre-révolution*, 36-37.

[9] According to Boullemer, a local republican official who was one of the first to be interviewed about these events, "Le curé constitutionnel Letort fut assommé à coups de fourche et de baïonnettes dans la tête, et, pour comble d'horreur, *une femme* lui ôta sa qualité d'homme; son supplice dura environ dix minutes; encore un de ces monstres disait-il, quand il fut mort: 'Ce b..... de prêtre n'a cependant pas vécu longtemps.'" See Lallié, *Le district de Machecoul*, 302.

[10] Jean-Baptiste Carrier, while later testifying in his defense at the National Convention tribunal, claimed that "Le curé constitutionnel fut embroché et promené dans les rues de Machecoul, après qu'on lui eut mutilé les parties les plus sensibles de son corps; il fut cloué, encore vivant, à l'arbe de la liberté." See Lallié, *Le district de Machecoul*, 302.

[11] Alfred Lallié purposely inserted these two accounts of Letort's killing in order to illustrate the discrepancy. Alain Gérard has recently argued that Boullemer had switched from insurgent to patriot in the midst of events, thereby making his testimony somewhat suspect. He has also pointed out that by the judge's own admission Boullemer had remained hidden under the roof beams of his house during many of the events that he describes, thus calling his claims into question. See Gérard, 128-29.

[12] Chassin, 3: 341.

[13] See, for example, Gérard, who explains, "Dans la mesure où Villers n'était pas témoin direct ces événments, il faut cependant retrouver et vérifier ses sources. . . . Mais il ne les cite pas et aucune des sources connues n'accrédite sa relation." See Gérard, 128.

[14] See, for example, the testimony of Alexandre Lemeignen, who was imprisoned by the insurgents and whose house was pillaged, in ADLA, L 349. Lemeignen to the Citizen Representing the People at Nantes, no date.

[15] Martin, *Révolution et contre-révolution*, 40-41.

[16]Chassin, 3: 351-52.

[17]Gérard, for example, claims that the various problems with eyewitness accounts suggest that the accusations are more a product of republican phobias and individual obsessions than the facts themselves. See Gérard, 129.

[18]See Chevalier's account in Chassin, 3: 335. See also Gérard, 132, especially when he argues that the killing at Machecoul "rapelle d'ailleurs la violence à laquelle les sans-culottes parisiens ont recours pour se libérer de l'oppression. Mais seules les brutalités commises par ceux qui sont dans la ligne révolutionnaire sont légitimes, d'après le groupe qui détient le pouvoir ou en tire les ficelles. Ainsi est justifiée la dictature des idéologues."

[19]See Secher, *La genocide franco-français*.

[20]Again, Gérard's explanation serves as a good example. Before discussing what happened at Machecoul, he demonstrates how the town's officials berated peasants, the nobility, the refractory clergy, and the monarchy after it fell. The purpose, of course, is to show how the republican minority was completely out of step with the hopes and wishes of the region's majority. He later adds, ". . . les revolutionaires qui, pour minoritaires qu'ils soient, n'ont pas moins par leur présence et surtout par leur radicalité exacerbé les passions." See Gérard, 129-31.

[21]This is what Gérard is suggesting when he says that the insurgents from the Machecoul area "sont également considérés comme difficiles à commander, ce qui paraît déjà vrai dès les premières heures de la révolte." See Gérard, 135.

[22]Chassin, 3: 331-32, 345-47. Most insurgent sympathizers claim that Charette did not join the committee until several days after the town was taken. See Lionel Dumarcet, *François-Athanase Charette de La Contrie: Une histoire véritable* (Paris: Éditions Les 3 Orangers, 1997), 154-55.

[23]For more on the likes of Guérin, Pageot, and Vrignault, especially from the insurgent perspective, see Frédéric Augris, *Vendéens et républicains dans la guerre de Vendée 1793-1796*, 2 vols. (Cholet: Éditions du Choletais, 1993).

[24]According to testimony given at the military commission held after republican forces temporarily regained control of Machecoul, several other Machecoulais may have been on the committee, including Guilloteau, the Berthauds, Chenaux of Trinité, the two Reigeards, and Fouchet. See Lallié, *Le district de Machecoul*, 334-37. See also Chassin, 3: 346-51.

[25]Dumarcet, 157-64.

[26]Bethuis unequivocally claims that Charette was complicit in the massacres. See Bethuis, 8-14. Insurgent sympathizers argue that Souchu acted alone. See Dumarcet, 179-85.

²⁷Villers and Fouché claimed that the number killed was 542. See Chassin, 3: 343-44; Dumarcet, 179-80.

²⁸*MU*, April 29, 1793.

²⁹*MU*, May 5, 1793.

³⁰ *AP*, 92: 16, 1 Messidor an II (June 19, 1794).

³¹ Lallié, *Le district de Machecoul*, 295. For his part, Jean-Clément Martin has confirmed through careful documentation the death of about 150 to 160 Machecoulais. See Martin, *Révolution et contre-révolution*, 41, 47-50.

³² Martin, *Révolution et contre-révolution*, 41.

³³Latteux, 129.

³⁴The retreat is known as the "Virée de Galerne." See Jean-Clément Martin, *La Vendée et la France*, 167-72.

³⁵Ibid., 226-33. Of course the infernal columns take up substantially more room in the insurgent narrative than in the republican one.

³⁶Latteux, 130.

³⁷Samuel F. Scott and Barry Rothaus, eds., *Historical Dictionary of the French Revolution*, 2 vols. (Westport, Conn.: Greenwood Press, 1985), 1002-03.

³⁸Latteux, 130.

³⁹Martin, *Révolution et contre-révolution*, 42-43.

⁴⁰ADLA, L 1490. Testimony of Baudry, 6 Brumaire an II (October 27, 1793).

⁴¹Martin, *Révolution et contre-révolution*, 42-43.

⁴²ADLA, L 1436. Director of the District of Nantes, Jury of Accusation, 15 Brumaire an III (November 5, 1793).

⁴³See, for example, ADLA, L 1499 [2 Mi 285]. Inculpated from the Machecoul District, an II (1793-1794). Approximately twenty-two women and twenty-four children from the Machecoul District were detained.

⁴⁴Hufton, "Counter-revolutionary Women," 283-307.

⁴⁵Hunt, *The Family Romance*, 89-123. Hunt's notion of Marie-Antoinette being the bad mother applies to prosecutorial perceptions of women accused of the massacres. For more on republican notions of gender roles, see also Lynn Hunt, "The Many Bodies of Marie Antoinette: Political Pornography and the Problem of the Feminine in the French Revolution" in Hunt, ed., *Eroticism and the Body Politic* (Baltimore: The Johns Hopkins University Press, 1991), 108-30.

⁴⁶Again, for the growth of conspiracy theory among the political elites in France during the Revolution, see Tackett, "Conspiracy Obsession," 691-713.

⁴⁷Chassin 3: 344.

48The "chapelets de Machecoul" are mentioned in several accounts. See Chassin, 3: 343, 350, 355. To assess the staying power of this part of the republican narrative, see Oury, *Les chapelets de Machecoul.*

49ADLA, L 1502 [2 Mi 287]. Judgment against Marie Chevet, 9 Floréal an II (April 28, 1794).

50ADLA, L 271. Julienne and Louis Praud to the Citizen Representing the People, 17 Messidor an II (July 5, 1794).

51Lallié, *Le district de Machecoul,* 338.

52Martin, *Révolution et contre-révolution,* 45.

53Lallié, *Le district de Machecoul,* 339.

54ADLA, L 1508 [2 Mi 265]. Interrogation of Archambaud, April 25, 1793.

55Durand, *Le diocèse de Nantes,* 177-78.

56Jean-Joël Brégeon, *Carrier et la terreur nantais* (Paris: Librairie Académique Perrin, 1987), 95-123.

57Durand, *Le diocèse de Nantes,* 178.

58It is a somewhat parallel phenomenon to what the competing narratives say about Souchu. And similar to the infernal columns, the *noyades* figure much larger in the insurgent narrative than in its republican counterpart. Compare the account of Brégeon with that of Alphonse Jarnoux in *La Loire servit de linceul.*

59Martin, *La Vendée et la France,* 218-20.

60Durand, *Le diocèse de Nantes,* 178; Jarnoux, 161, 176.

61Martin, *La Vendée et la France,* 221-25.

62Jean-Clément Martin, "Les martyrs de la foi, histoire et sacré," in Martin, ed. *Religion et Révolution,* 92. For an in-depth discussion of this popular religious phenomenon, see Michel Lagrée and Jehanne Roche, *Tombes de Mémoire: La dévotions populaire aux victimes de la Révolution dans l'Ouest* (Rennes: Apogée, 1992). Note this tendency in one of the sermons of abbé Marchais as well, as found in Lebrun, *Parole de Dieu,* 116-27.

63See Bethuis, 12.

64Jonas, 102-9.

65Ibid., 102-17.

66Louis Delhommeau, *Le Clergé vendéen face à la Révolution* (La Roche-sur-Yon: Siloë, 1992), 102-12; Patricia Lusson-Houdemon, "La vie sacramentelle des fidèles dans l'Ouest à travers les registres clandestins," in Bernard Plongeron, ed., *Pratiques religieuses, mentalités et spiritualités dans l'Europe révolutionnaire* (Turnhout: Brepols, 1988), 216-24.

67See Huppert, 80-100.

68Martin, *Révolution et contre-révolution,* 38.

⁶⁹Huppert, 81-86.

⁷⁰Ibid., 90.

⁷¹For more on how Tilly and Bois interpret the religious question in their schematic explanations of popular counterrevolution, see Timothy Tackett, "The West in France in 1789."

⁷²For more on this notion, see Van Kley, *The Religious Origins*, 369-75.

⁷³As opposed to many other accusations made by republicans, the mutilation of abbé Letort's body was not only corroborated, but done so almost immediately after the massacres, conceivably reducing the likelihood that it was a rumor spread among republicans. See ADLA, L 349. Testimony of Jean Baulu, March 13, 1793.

⁷⁴Natalie Zemon Davis, "The Rites of Violence: Religious Riot in Sixteenth-Century France," *Past and Present* 59 (May 1973): 51-91; Denis Crouzet, *Les guerriers de dieu: la violence au temps des troubles de religion (vers 1525 - vers 1610)*, 2 vols. (Seysell: Champ Vallon, 1990).

⁷⁵Davis, 57-65.

⁷⁶Crouzet, 1: 240-55.

⁷⁷Alain Corbin, *The Village of Cannibals: Rage and Murder in France, 1870*, trans. Arthur Goldhammer (Cambridge, Mass.: Harvard University Press, 1992), 87-101.

⁷⁸According to Roger Dupuy, religion "permet d'enflammer les enthousiasmes, de galvaniser les énergies et de transformer une révolte en croisade." See Dupuy, "La religion et les débuts des insurrections de l'Ouest," in Jean-Clément Martin, ed., *Religion et Revolution: Colloque de Saint-Florent-le-Vieil* (Paris: Anthropos, 1994), 76.

⁷⁹Peter Burke, *Popular Culture in Early Modern Europe*, 2nd ed. (Aldershot: Ashgate, 1994), 123.

⁸⁰Jonas, 24-33, 83-90.

⁸¹János M. Bak and Gerhard Benecke, "Religion and Revolt?" in Bak and Benecke, eds., *Religion and Rural Revolt*, 9.

⁸²*AP*, 88: 27, 21 Germinal an II (April 10, 1794).

⁸³Baecque, 134-35.

⁸⁴Société des Etudes Robespierristes, *Joseph Bara (1779-1793): Pour le deuxième centenaire de sa naissance* (La Couronne: Sopan, 1981); Hunt, *The Family Romance*, 78-79.

⁸⁵Baecque, 121-42.

⁸⁶*AP*, 76: 78, October 12, 1793.

⁸⁷*AP*, 88: 27, 21 Germinal an II (April 10, 1794).

⁸⁸Baecque, 127-40.

⁸⁹Martin, *La Vendée et la France*, 268-70.

90Durand, *Le diocèse de Nantes*, 179.

91Martin, *La Vendée et la France*, 271-83.

92Apparently, this was a reference to *certificats de civisme* that the government gave out to verify one's loyalty to the nation.

93Marie-Claude Guillerand-Champenier, "Le diocèse de Nantes et la Révolution 1794-1801," in Jean Garaud, ed., *L'église de Nantes et la Révolution* (Nantes: Université de Nantes, 1989), 21.

94During the period of the Directory some important changes were made to the structure of local government, most notably the creation of cantonal commissioners to oversee communal government. Machecoul had one of these cantonal commissioners, as indicated by most of the local government correspondence from 1795 to 1799. See Vivian A. Schmidt, *Democratizing France: The Political and Administrative History of Decentralization* (Cambridge: Cambridge University Press, 1990), 18-22.

95ADLA, L 722. Machecoul Canton Commissioner to the Executive Director of the L-I Central Administration, 4 Vendémaire an IV (September 26, 1795).

96Guillerand-Champenier, 21.

97ADLA, L 688. Administration révolutionnaire. Culte. Clergé. Affaires générales, an VI-an VIII. Machecoul Canton Commissioner to Commissioner of the Departmental Central Administration, 24 Brumaire an V (November 14, 1796).

98Guillerand-Champenier, 22.

99ADLA, L 688. Machecoul Canton Commissioner to Commissioner of the Departmental Central Administration, 20 Fructidor an V, (September 6, 1797).

100Durand, *Le diocèse de Nantes*, 180.

101Martin, *La Vendée et la France*, 326-37.

102ADLA, L 668. Machecoul Canton Commissioner to Commissioner of the Departmental Central Administration, 20 Ventose an VI (March 10, 1798).

103ADLA, L 623. Duporteau to the Departmental Library Administration, 3 Nivose an II (December 23, 1793).

104ADLA, L 833. Machecoul Canton Administrators to Departmental Central Administration, 23 Messidor an IV (July 11, 1796).

105Ibid., The Machecoul Civil *Hospice* Commission to Departmental Central Administration, 12 Nivôse an VI (January 1, 1798).

106ADLA, L 614. Machecoul Canton Report (a response to the law of 3 Brumaire an VI (October 24, 1797), no date.

[107]Lebrun, *Parole de Dieu et révolution*, 109-25; Martin, *La Vendée et la France*, 291.

[108]Martin, *La Vendée et la France*, 328.

[109]Chassin 3: 334.

[110]Martin, *La Vendée et la France*, 304-5.

[111]Ibid., 327-28.

[112]Ibid., 331-35.

[113]ADLA, L 1262. Letter to Baudet, priest, 9 Nîvose an VIII (December 27, 1799).

[114]Martin, *La Vendée et la France*, 335.

5

A Memory of Holy War

Although the counterrevolutionary violence that began with the Machecoul massacres all but ended by 1800, the struggle over how the episode would be remembered—both within the town and beyond it—continued unabated throughout the nineteenth century. On a national scale, the ever-changing political landscape in France, teamed with a persistence of the dialectic that had arisen in the 1790s, ensured that neither a republican nor an insurgent memory of the Revolution would gain full supremacy in the French mind.[1] Within Machecoul, however, the outcome was dramatically different. By 1914 the vast majority of the town's inhabitants subscribed to an insurgent memory of not only the massacres but more generally the entire revolutionary decade. Why over the long term did an insurgent memory become more accepted in the minds of the Machecoulais than a republican equivalent? No doubt multiple social, economic, and cultural developments during the nineteenth century allowed an insurgent memory to flourish, while at the same time impeding a republican counterpart.[2] In this respect, though, one factor was paramount: no institution—arguably not even the state—was more culturally influential in the town from 1800 to 1914 than the Catholic Church, due in no small part to its ability to maintain a prodigious number of institutions and to supply them with ample personnel.[3] With this influence the town's clergy was able to institutionalize an insurgent memory of revolution and counterrevolution—despite Machecoul's having been home to the most grievous insurgent excesses.

But institutional influence by itself fails to explain the Catholic Church's success in promoting an insurgent memory, let alone in convincing many townspeople to accept it. As Chapter Four showed, even while the church had virtually no institutional presence in the late 1790s, refractory priests provided sacred meaning to the War of Vendée by way of religious ritual, symbolism, and mythological narrative. Indeed, as the Revolution was drawing to a close, the local clergy, through its pastoral ministry, cast the insurgency as a holy rebellion, a divinely sanctioned resistance fought against the evil forces of republicanism. In the nineteenth century, as the Catholic Church recovered and rebuilt its institutional base, the local clergy became all the more successful at propagating this memory, but only by having more occasions to raise it within the context of religious ritual, semiotics, and storytelling. Given the many instructional opportunities available in sacramental rites, sermons, catechisms, missions, parish organizations, and pilgrimages, it comes as no surprise that most of the town grew to prefer this memory. But how can one verify such a preference, especially if it existed mostly in the mind? Evidence for the town's memory is found not only in how notions of the past were overtly expressed by the Machecoulais during the nineteenth century but also in how the townspeople interpreted their own times, to say nothing of how they behaved politically.[4]

This chapter considers how in the nineteenth century Machecoul remembered not just the town's massacres but the revolutionary and counterrevolutionary context in which they took place. It proposes that religious phenomena like sermons, catechisms, spiritual exercises, parish organizations, popular devotions, and iconography both influenced and embodied the town's collective remembrance of the 1790s—characterized here as "a memory of holy war." The chapter also shows the ways in which memory shaped the townspeople's assumptions about their own day and age, in addition to their political deportment. Merely acclaiming a memory of holy war in word and ritual, it seems, was insufficient for the town's Catholics between 1800 and 1914; they also sought to apply the lessons of that past to the present, as is evident in their numerous confrontations with state officials over religious rites, local institutions, national and international political issues, not to mention the church-state relationship itself. But whether the memory was expressed in word, symbol, ritual, or embodied in the postrevolutionary beliefs or very actions of the Machecoulais, there always was one constant: the town's religious culture remained central to the construction, maintenance, and proliferation of this memory throughout the nineteenth century. The pervasiveness of a memory of holy war within the town's religious culture, in fact, may be the primary reason why such memory was powerful enough to unite, even homogenize, what had been a diverse and divisive community recently torn asunder by a savage civil war.

The Peaceable Kingdom

In order for the Machecoulais to understand, let alone believe, a memory of holy war, it was first necessary to grasp a prologue to the war itself. Indeed, complete comprehension of the town's troubled past would be lacking unless one began with the Old Regime—a time when, according to this memory, the vast majority of people in western France was God-fearing and extremely devout. Such memory alleged that life in the west was peaceful at this time, thanks to a clearly defined social hierarchy whose trademark was charity and justice. No one was more responsible for creating this halcyon view of the Old Regime than the town's Catholic clergy. *Curés* and *vicaires* at the parish of Trinité often recalled this past through its teaching, but since priests could not make comments construed as political in nature (especially earlier in the century), they rarely expressed this memory to the people in a direct manner.[5] But as the sermons given at parish masses, vespers, and other liturgies indicate, the clergy was able to perpetuate the notion of an idyllic Old Regime through the style of pastoral ministry that it favored in the nineteenth century.

Fortunately, the parish archives of Trinité at Machecoul include numerous sermons delivered over the course of the nineteenth century. A thorough examination of these archives yielded an approximate total of 106 sermons or conferences—the latter being a series of sermons having the same theme and given during a specified period of time, such as Lent. Eighty-nine of the sermons can be divided into two distinct categories: those for certain occasions, like feasts, seasons, and special events; and those for certain subjects, like the sacraments, dogma, theology, and spirituality.[6] Different though they are in content, most sermons found at Machecoul incorporate the theology and spirituality prevalent in France during much of the Old Regime, namely Tridentine Catholicism. To reiterate, Tridentine teaching was quick to make a clear distinction between the sacred and the profane. One consequence of the distinction was a *contemptus mundi*, a scorn for the here and now, as well as an emphasis on ascetic moral behavior that inevitably invited a preoccupation with guilt and sin. Tridentine Catholicism insisted, moreover, on the clerical control of religion and lay obedience to a hierarchically structured church.[7] The preaching tied to this belief, as a result, often accentuated the harsh, dreadful, and bitter aspects of God and humanity: the need to confess sins, God's commandments, penitence, mortification, the final judgment, hell, and the suffering of the cross.[8] All of these themes found their way into the sermons held in the parish archives.

Lent was an especially poignant time for the Tridentine message since the season emphasized returning to God in a contrite manner. Thanks to a schedule written down by one of the town's nineteenth-century *curés*, abbé Jean-Baptiste Augustin Bouron, we know what kind of preaching was done for Lent in 1848:

1st Sunday	Mass:	The State of Mortal Sin
	Vespers:	The Divinity of Confession
2nd Sunday	Mass:	*Mandement* of May for the Elections
	Vespers:	The Satisfaction Derived from Confession
3rd Sunday	Mass:	Sermon on Hell
	Vespers:	Satisfaction from Confession (continued)
4th Sunday	Mass:	The Abuse of the Sacraments
	Vespers:	The Examination of Conscience
5th Sunday	Mass:	Frequent Communion: Its Qualities, Requirements, Advantages, Disadvantages

Abbé Bouron wrote down a similar schedule for the first part of Lent in 1860:

1st Sunday	Mass:	Salvation: Its Necessity
	Vespers:	Advice on How to Profit from Lent
2nd Sunday	Mass:	Death in the State of Sin
	Vespers:	The Parable of the Sower: The Correct Disposition for Instructions
3rd Sunday	Mass:	Death of the Just: Its Necessity
	Vespers:	Conference on Faith: Its Necessity, Its Motive, Its Transmission
4th Sunday	Mass:	Our Lord Asks for Our Hearts
	Vespers:	In Order to Receive the Forgiveness of Sins, It Is Necessary to Quit the Habits and the Occasions of Sin[9]

One sees in both years the predominant themes of Tridentine Catholicism: sin, death, and the need for sacramental sanctification. To be sure, the message was not all grim; the sermons were intended to help parishioners achieve ultimate happiness, namely, eternal salvation. Yet the clergy held that doing God's will on earth implicitly invited a preoccupation with death, pain, and suffering.

The sermons' contents certainly confirm this Tridentine perspective. Human life, according to these sermons, was little more than an existence steeped in misery. During the Lenten season of 1832 a priest declared to the congregation that

> For man, the sorrows, pains, and continual work will be a part of his life, because you have sinned. The land . . . will not at all respond to your work. . . . You will eat your bread with the sweat of your brow until you return to the earth from where you came. These are all the works, the pains, the death, and the miseries of the present life.

He went on to explain that the original sin committed by Adam and Eve was the primary source of human pain and suffering, but that fortunately God promised to send Jesus as a liberator. The orator added, however, that it

> was after this promise of life that [God] showed [Adam and Eve] all the pains that they would undergo so as to prepare their hearts for their return to their God. . . . All the pains of the present life thus come from the God who wants to save us and not from the God who wants to punish us.[10]

Pain, suffering, and death, therefore, were more than just the results of original sin; according to the clergy, they acted to deter humans from sinning and enabled them to fight against evil.

But the clergy not only perceived the present life as full of pain and sorrow; it saw the afterlife too, as being full of misery and distress. Even those Christians fortunate to be saved were subject to the purifying flames of purgatory. Again, in an accusatory tone, one cleric characterized parishioners who failed to put their faith into practice as "hardened and insensible Christians to whom I want to prove that the pains of the souls in purgatory are extreme, and that for their sad fate they must be pitied." He went on to describe purgatory, although one would think he was discussing hell:

> Disabuse yourselves, Christians: the rigors of this netherworld are excessive; the torments of purgatory are extreme; for the faults that one expiates there inflame the anger of God; and who is able to understand how far it goes? Who renews the power of your anger? Open up, horrible chasms, somber dungeons, open up, and reveal to our eyes these captive souls whom you detain! Oh! What ravenous flames envelop and penetrate them! Flames ignited by divine love and maintained by the anger of the all-powerful.[11]

If God reserved such pain for the saved, one can hardly comprehend how much more suffering was arranged for the damned. Portraying purgatory as a mini-hell was typical of Tridentine spirituality in the seventeenth and eighteenth centuries.[12]

One can also see in the sermons how Tridentine Catholicism insisted on putting the clergy on a plateau high above the laity; the clergy was prone to talk down to parishioners in its discourse. Indeed, priests were not above hurling atrocious insults at their audience. In one sermon entitled "Sacrilège," the orator complained that many were taking communion even though they continued to commit sins. He charged that "unworthy communion" was a frequent crime, so much so that the Machecoulais were

> making but a game out the adorable sacrament of the Eucharist. You go from mortal sin to communion without any scruples, and in an instant after, lips still colored by the blood of Jesus Christ, you fly back again toward the same passions. One must think that our Easter obligation is nothing more than a group of sacrilegious communions; a facade of religion to cover better a dissolute life. Nothing counts less in the world than a sacrilegious communion, a desecrated sacrament, and the blood of Christ wasted.[13]

In the "Respect Due to the Churches," the priest said to the congregation that "you know that this [church] is holy and solemn, you confess Jesus Christ as being present upon our altars, and yet you show up in our churches without respect for him and without veneration for his sanctuary." Yet another sermon entitled "A Discourse on the Obligation of

Children toward Their Fathers and Mothers" finds a priest openly confronting and condemning those children who despised their parents:

> Oh perverted children, you are parent-killers, you promote the death
> of your parents, who often succumb to your callousness toward
> them. Oh perverted monsters, you are not worthy to see the day
> you deserve when the earth opens up its abyss to devour you; and,
> in order to fulfill the terms of holy scripture, the day when the crows
> peck out your eyes, tear out your heart, and eat your intestines. Soon
> thereafter you will feel the curse that the Lord pronounced against
> you: Cursed is the one who does not honor his father and mother
> (Deuteronomy 27:16).[14]

Such is how fear and graphic imagery were employed to motivate
parishioners to live a resolute life—a common tactic of Tridentine
evangelization.

Though the sermons indicate that Tridentine Catholicism was ubiquitous in the town's parish during the nineteenth century, such content
says little about how widespread was the affinity for this religious culture.
At least some evidence suggests, however, that Machecoul's bent for
this "old-time religion" was more of a regional rule—not the exception.
Indeed, the catechisms used in the diocese of Nantes during the nineteenth century confirm that clerics well beyond the town also subscribed
to Tridentine practice and belief between the 1820s and 1914. During
the First Empire the bishop of Nantes, like all other bishops in France,
utilized the imperial catechism prescribed by Napoleon himself. But
during the Restoration Monseigneur Joseph Micolon de Guérines, the
bishop of Nantes from 1822 to 1838, chose to use, not a contemporary
catechism that other dioceses in France were using, but rather the old
diocesan catechism first published in 1755.[15] That edition had been
written in 1689 by the Jansenist abbé de la Noë-Mesnard, which is
why it smacked of an unapproachable rigor.[16] Monseigneur Micolon de
Guérines' immediate successors, Monseigneurs Jean-François de Hercé
and Alexandre Jaquemet, continued with the old catechism even though
it did not fully discuss all points of doctrine and, by 1850, many of the
expressions used in the manual were unintelligible to the youth of the
diocese.[17] In 1870 Monseigneur Félix Fournier reprinted yet another
edition of the very same catechism, as did Monseigneur Jules-François

Le Coq in 1888.[18] Thus as late as 1892 (and perhaps up to 1914), the clergy in the diocese was utilizing a catechism first conceived and written near the end of the seventeenth century.

That each successive edition was reviewed and authorized by the bishop of Nantes resulted in few if any changes in the primer. A comparison between the indexes of the 1826 and the 1888 editions, for example, finds that they were remarkably similar; both embody Tridentine Catholic rigor and belief. This does not necessarily mean, however, that the bishops of Nantes, like the flock they guided, adhered to the old pastoral approach throughout the nineteenth century. A more likely explanation for the use of the same old catechism is that since the diocese's priests and the laity preferred Tridentine Catholicism well up to 1900, the bishops saw no need to rock the boat, especially since religious belief and practice in the diocese remained so vibrant at that time.[19]

Regardless of the reason, such pronouncements and teachings were, according to some historians, peculiar for a French parish during the nineteenth century, especially as 1900 drew closer. Over the past twenty years many scholars have argued that a "feminization" of French Catholicism took place during this time, meaning that the image of God was increasingly transformed by the growing influence of women in religious orders.[20] An additional catalyst was a kinder and more temperate Ligourian theology, which, on account of papal centralization, was increasingly expanding beyond Italy. As a result, the argument claims, the old Tridentine *pastorale de la peur* was displaced by a new pastoral approach that portrayed God as more loving and compassionate.[21] True as this may be, however, the sermons in Trinité's archives along with the diocese's catechism suggest that Tridentine Catholicism remained in place in this part of France much longer than average. Thus the feminization thesis cannot be applied to each and every parish, let alone to some regions: a testament, in and of itself, to the great variations of religious culture within the nineteenth-century French church.[22]

So why did a feminized Catholicism elude Machecoul, if not much of the diocese of Nantes, during the nineteenth century? Many may find a rationale for the disparity in the lack of communication, transportation, and education in the undeveloped *bocage*, the implication being that geography kept the town and its region from national integration.

But the isolation of the *bocage* has been exaggerated, particularly as it pertains to the nineteenth century.[23] It seems more likely that Tridentine Catholicism became commonplace at Machecoul in the 1800s not so much by circumstance but by choice. The town's clergy and the laity, to say nothing of those from similar communities in the region, clung to Tridentine belief not because of any social or economic backwardness but because of their deep belief in its validity and efficacy.

That the Machecoul clergy *chose* Tridentine Catholicism over a newer pastoral perspective, however, does little to resolve the apparent historical anomaly. Yet here is where the chapter's principal theme, the memory shared by Machecoul's Catholics during the nineteenth century, merits attention. Since the memory held that the Old Regime was a golden age for western France, its purveyors deemed that this era's culture was worthy of imitation in the nineteenth century, especially in the sphere of religious belief and practice. Still another implication of a memory of holy war was that Vendéen insurgents were able to recognize the Revolution for the evil that it was, consequently compelling them to take up arms against the republic. The memory thus suggested that their proper response was due to the effective pastoral efforts during the Old Regime. Tridentine evangelization, in other words, had successfully prepared devout rebels for their heroic course of action. It was only logical, from the perspective of those upholding the memory, that the best way to train the new troops to fight against the lingering revolutionary evil in the nineteenth century was to prepare them in the same way. Thus for those who subscribed to a memory of holy war, the insurgency itself suggested Tridentine Catholicism's success. They saw no need to abandon it.

Still, the official teachings pronounced from the pulpit and in the catechisms were just that: official. Little of what we have seen thus far tells us about the kind of piety prevalent among the people in the pews. In some respects, though, the distinction made between "popular piety" and "official piety" seems ill-suited to the Machecoulais, to say nothing of many other Catholics in western France during the nineteenth century.[24] Though parish priests in this region often tried to stay aloof from their flocks, the reality was that they identified very closely with them, in part because most of them originated from the very rural communities that they shepherded.[25] Pastoral visit reports from the town's parish in the nineteenth century seem to confirm this unanimity, for no mention is made of parishioners believing or engaging in pre-Christian, animistic rites such as those associated with sorcery.[26] Many conventional and long-standing stereotypes about peasants of the west have been found to be false, but at least one seems legitimate: there *did* seem to be a profound respect for the clergy among the laity in nineteenth-century Machecoul. Clerical deference became, as André Siegfried suggested, a cornerstone of regional identity.

The lack of distinction between popular and clerical piety is apparent, for example, in a popular religious festival resurrected in the town after the civil war. The Feast of Saint Honoré, observed on or around May 16 for much of the nineteenth century, shows how the line between popular and clerical religiosity was often blurred.[27] Parish records give very little indication of when the celebration recommenced after the Revolution, but it is certain that by the 1840s the Saint Honoré commemoration had become a prominent ritual in the town. In preparation for the festival of 1839 the *curé* abbé Alexandre Tolle was able to secure the bishop's approval for the procession and for a votive mass in Saint Honoré's name.[28] Seven years later the bishop of Nantes helped the parish acquire new relics of Saint Honoré from the diocese of Amiens.[29] In 1854 abbé Bouron received permission from the bishop to transfer the procession of Saint Honoré to another day (in case it fell on a Sunday)—an indication of how popular the festival had become.[30]

That the bishop of Nantes often attended the festival is also indicative of its popularity. According to parish and diocesan records, the bishop went to Machecoul for the celebration (in conjunction with conducting a pastoral visit and administering the sacrament of confirmation) eight times between 1846 and 1898.[31] If the bishop were unable to go, he frequently sent a vicar general or some other high-ranking cleric to the town to represent him at the festival.[32] No exact numbers of how many people usually attended the celebration can be determined, but in 1850 the parish clergy reported that about ten parishes were represented in the festival's procession, and approximately sixty priests from the dioceses of Nantes and Luçon were present as well.[33] The procession probably ceased in 1903, when the departmental administration of the Loire-Inférieure forbade any religious ritual on public streets.[34] The availability of rail travel and increasing popularity of national pilgrimages to Lourdes, Paray-le-Monial, and the Basilica of the Sacred Heart at Montmartre may have contributed to the end of the festival as well.[35]

The highlight for the festival of Saint Honoré in the nineteenth century was, as before the Revolution, the town's public procession. Following the mass, which included a *panégyrique* or a formal address of praise to the saint, individuals from Trinité and the surrounding parishes gathered for the procession.[36] Garlands, ribbons, and flowers decorated many of the town streets through which the procession advanced. While making its way through the town, the procession passed under arches of triumph made by various trade groups (carpenters, woodworkers, blacksmiths, coopers) and decorated with the tools of their trades. But the day truly belonged to the corporation of bakers, which carried the statue of Saint Honoré in the procession. As the cavalcade moved forward, the bakers sang a canticle in honor of the town's patron. The lyrics sung in 1894 included verses that, in keeping with a memory of holy war, saw the period before the Revolution as a golden age:

> Inspired by holy zeal,
> Bakers, near his altar,
> Ask for the true bread of life,
> Which nourishes the soul for heaven.
>
> *Laboureurs*, plough with patience,
> Your furrows, like your ancestors,
> And reap, in abundance,
> The golden grain while searching the heavens.
>
> Disregarding all hollow wisdom,
> In peace look for prosperity,
> Workers, show the heroism
> Of the faithful Christian to the Lord.

At the end of the procession the bishop delivered a short address to all those who participated or came to see it.[37] During most years, moreover, a town inn served a lunch for all of the participants immediately after the procession.[38]

As with the parish's Tridentine Catholic teaching, many may see in the festival an anachronism in a region that remained relatively untouched by modernization. If seen within the context of the memory shared by Catholics at Machecoul in the nineteenth century, though, the festival reveals much more than an antiquated regionalism. The procession itself, the lyrics of the Saint Honoré canticle, the corporate structure of the festival, indeed the very veneration of the patron saint of bakers—all of this called to mind the insurgent contention that a peaceable kingdom had existed in France before the advent of evil in 1789. The festival did this by praising the virtues of a corporative, hierarchical, and seigneurial society supposedly widespread before the Revolution.

This is also why, as noted in Chapter Two, Monseigneur Alexandre Jaquemet asked his flock to prepare for Lent in 1867 by trying to recover old religious edifices and rebuilding old calvaires that had been erected during the Old Regime.[39] Such buildings and monuments served as local *lieux de mémoire*, reminders of a mythic past before the advent of Enlightenment and revolution.[40] But even so, recalling the virtues of the Old Regime was only a means to a greater end; the supposed greatness of the Old Regime was purposely juxtaposed with the 1790s to emphasize the destructive and irreligious nature of the Revolution, as well as to show why violent resistance against the new regime was not only justified but worthy of admiration.

Revolutionary Persecution

The second segment of a memory of holy war comprised the Revolution itself. This part alleged that in spite of the peace and stability prevalent during the Old Regime, the satanically inspired Enlightenment, replete with its blasphemous and heretical ideas, destroyed all that was good in France. The *lumières*, in concert with Protestants, Freethinkers, and Freemasons, helped bring about the French Revolution in an effort to divorce God from his people and obliterate the age-old benevolent social order. For those who subscribed to a memory of holy war, there was no better exhibit of revolutionary evil than the repressive Terror as well as the de-Christianization campaign that accompanied it. As true as the mnemonic claims about the Terror were, however, state authorities often took issue with clerical and lay efforts to recall the episode. Since this segment of the memory of holy war was much more controversial than proclamations about the Old Regime, it was less likely to be told overtly through sermons, catechisms, or public processions.

Still, declarations about the Revolution were made, most frequently under the guise of ritual activity. Of the many rites performed at Machecoul, few reflected this memory more effectively than those enacted at parish missions, which had been legion in the diocese of Nantes during the Old Regime but became even more numerous after the Revolution. From 1849 to 1907 alone the diocese of Nantes sponsored close to 450 of these religious revivals.[41] Like many rural parishes of its size in the region, Trinité became a prime mission venue. Parish records reveal that eight missions were held in the town between 1820 and 1905.[42] Much of the missions' popularity was attributable to the demonstrative form of piety once common among Tridentine missionaries, a spiritual élan that most clerics and the rural populace found increasingly irresistible in the nineteenth century.[43]

The bold expression of piety, such as when missionaries motivated their audiences by reminding them that death was ever-present and that they would soon have to face the final judgment, often proved successful in stimulating the zeal of the faithful.[44] Parish missions lasted anywhere between five days and a month, with most typically ending on a Sunday morning with a high mass, when massive numbers of people received communion. A great procession sometimes followed the mass, during which a cross or *calvaire* was erected as a souvenir of the mission. The photographs of Figure 5.1 are examples of mission souvenirs erected in or around Machecoul during the nineteenth century. Finally, the missionaries encouraged popular cries at the souvenir sites, such as "Long live the king," "Long live religion," or "Long live Pius IX."[45]

This last act of the mission, the placement of a souvenir, offered the best opportunity to invoke a memory of holy war, particularly the notion that the French Revolution had satanic origins. At a mission held at Machecoul in 1894, for example, following the Sunday high mass, approximately 250 participants marched to the outskirts of the town to erect a cross at the site of the old parish church of Sainte-Croix. The *Semaine religieuse du diocèse de Nantes*, a nineteenth-century weekly religious newspaper, demonstrates how a memory of holy war cast the Revolution:

Figure 5.1
Machecoul's Nineteenth-Century Mission Souvenirs
(Three photographs by the author, 1994-1995)

What religious emotion in seeing this gigantic tree being raised, carrying the image of the crucified divinity where our fathers adored it
for centuries, upon the ruins of a church dedicated to the Holy Cross
in the good old days! A providential manifestation which attests,
once again, that the Cross and the Church are immortal; that they

are rising again where impiety, one hundred years ago, thought to destroy them, and that all the rage of hell will never eradicate religion and love on the earth![46]

Not only is there an allusion to the revolutionary persecution, but mention is made of the "good old days" when Tridentine Catholicism supposedly reigned supreme. The two, it seems, went hand in hand.

Other rituals connoting revolutionary persecution abounded during the nineteenth century. During the Restoration, for example, the diocese of Nantes saw many commemorative masses and expiatory services for members of the royal family and members of the clergy killed during the Revolution. Every January 21 many priests performed commemorative rites for Louis XVI, as on October 16 for Marie-Antoinette.[47] Although even the Restoration government made concerted efforts to repress the memories of revolution, or as Sheryl Kroen aptly put it, to pursue a policy of *oubli*, ritual activities that commemorated revolutionary persecution continued in western France well into the Third Republic.[48] One such act of remembrance took place at Machecoul in 1889. On the feast of Saint Honoré the bishop of Nantes, Monseigneur Jules Le Coq, recalled one of the town's own, mostly in an effort to decry the Revolution—in keeping with a memory of holy war:

> Also it is justified to render great homage to the zealous pastors who successively prepared the property that we enjoy and to look all the way back to the illustrious Hervé de la Bauche, a holy priest who inspected his parish by hand, to whom God gave the inward honor of martyr in the *noyades* of the Loire, a victim chosen to expiate the faults of the past and to give unto the children of the future the productive graces, the hope and the Christian faith well alive in our Machecoul land, which has flowed all the way up to us and well beyond.[49]

That abbé Hervé de la Bauche, the onetime *recteur* of Trinité, had been killed in the *noyades* was well known to the bishop's audience. Le Coq's pronouncement surely ingratiated him with the crowd, yet even more important it made the memory that much more relevant to the town's believers.

Even devotion to Mary found a place in this memory, particularly within the segment concerning revolutionary persecution. To be sure,

Marian devotion was ubiquitous in the nineteenth-century Catholic world. What made this parish's devotion to Mary unique, however, was its integration with the memory's emphasis on revolutionary persecution. An 1888 article in the diocese's *Semaine religieuse* concerning Machecoul brought together devotion to Mary with what supposedly happened to the town's faithful during the Revolution:

> One likes to believe that this devotion merited the deliverance of the women of Machecoul at the time of the Terror. They were imprisoned at Bouffay [Nantes] and habitually recited the Rosary together. Fortified by their confidence in the Virgin Mary, they tried to get an audience with the fierce Carrier. This favor (!) was secured by Goyé, employed at the prison, who recognized one of them, the Widow Fleury, and sought to pay her back for a previous kindness. He ordered the woman to speak on behalf of all of them. When Carrier glanced at her in front of the others, he said to her, "*Citoyenne*, what do you want?" "*Citoyen*, the widows of Machecoul are encumbering the republic. They ask to return to their homes and so that they can attend to their responsibilities." "Leave by boat," responded Carrier. "The widows of Machecoul," retorted Madame Fleury, "do not want to be drowned; they want to be shot, just like their husbands and brothers; they will perish on the ground." Carrier, struck by this fiery response, said to her, "You are a good [expletive]; perish where you want."
>
> Against all hope, they were freed. Some years after, when religious practice at the church of Trinité resumed, the women of Machecoul, in their pious thanksgiving, pledged to meet together each night to recite the Rosary together. This tradition was observed as late as 1838. The Rosary then was recited by a Miss Seigneuret (aunt of Monsieur Alexandre Dubois, treasurer of the *fabrique* of Saint-Peter in Nantes).[50]

Whether or not the account was true is beside the point. Of greater significance here is how the narrative personalized the memory and made it, in essence, Machecoul's own.

As important as consideration of the Old Regime was to a memory of holy war, therefore, the invocation of the Revolution, particularly the Terror, was equally vital. The memory portrayed the Machecoulais as victims of republican repression and cited their religious belief as the basis for such persecution. Machecoul no longer was the site of numerous atrocities done to republicans; instead, the town was a bastion of faith whose inhabitants remained loyal to the church and Christian belief despite overwhelming pressure to do otherwise. Proclaiming the Revolution as a great abomination, however, did more than condemn republicanism per se; it served another purpose as well. The part of the memory that emphasized revolutionary persecution of the faithful Machecoulais was meant to give even more justification for their participation in the Vendéen insurgency.

Holy Resistance

In its central message, a memory of holy war held that in response to the evil propagated by revolutionary authorities, the Catholic faithful in the west launched the Vendéen insurgency. Indeed, its key contention was that the insurgency was a rebellion fought for the faith and by the faithful. The memory indicated, however, that this holy struggle was more than just one episode of good versus evil in human history; it claimed that the civil war constituted an introductory skirmish in the cosmic, apocalyptic war to be fought between God and the devil at the end of history. This apocalyptic perspective was apparent in local clerical discourse almost immediately after the insurgency, as the sermons of abbé Marchais show, and such a view remained prominent throughout the nineteenth century, particularly whenever local Catholics believed that their faith was under threat.

One of the best ways to appropriate a sacred if not an apocalyptic meaning to the insurgency was to invoke a local saint who, perhaps more than any other figure, personified Vendéen virtue. As revered as Louis-Marie Grignion de Montfort was when alive, the missionary became even more popular among Catholics in western France in the nineteenth century. Many believers began to subscribe to yet another contention of this memory: the western missionary was responsible for the spiritual foundation that helped spark the insurgency in 1793. Even republican memory of revolution and counterrevolution in the nineteenth century conceded as much. As opposed to republicans, however, most Catholics saw the bond between insurgency and the missionary as a venerable one. As one nineteenth-century biographer of the missionary explained it:

> Montfort will be considered in history as the Dominic of western France, for having destroyed heresy here.... and as the Saint Bernard of his century for having made the Vendée [War] and having preached here the most heroic crusade that one ever saw. That Montfort formed the Vendée [War]—it is the testimony rendered by the clergy in all areas of the country.... It is equally the unanimous voice of all the Vendéen people.[51]

Catholics in the Machecoul area, above all the clergy, adhered to this notion about Grignion. At a pilgrimage held in his diocese in 1873, Monseigneur Félix Fournier exhorted his audience to "follow the foot-steps of [Grignion de Montfort] who did such good," and added that "if it is necessary to suffer for this faith: We will be there, We will be there, as the Vendéen hymn says."[52]

Grignion's role in a memory of holy war was most pronounced in popular pilgrimages to three centers of Montfortian spirituality located close to Machecoul: Pontchâteau (the site of a *calvaire* erected by the missionary in the Loire-Inférieure); La Garnache (the site of Grignion's tomb in the Vendée); and Saint-Laurent-sur-Sèvre (home to the male and female religious orders inspired by Grignion in the Vendée).[53] La Garnache was located just beyond the borders of Machecoul and thus became especially appealing to parishioners of Trinité.[54] Yet of the three shrines related to Grignion, the most celebrated became the one at Pontchâteau.[55] The site's popularity among Catholics throughout the diocese of Nantes during the nineteenth century was largely a result of the clergy's approbation of the shrine.[56] In 1863 the bishop of Nantes asked the missionaries of Saint-Laurent-sur-Sèvre to take over the shrine so that the pilgrimages could be better regulated (the brothers were to eliminate "profane" elements such as drinking) and the pilgrims receive sound doctrinal instruction.[57] Later, in 1890, the Montfortians expanded the shrine yet again and subsequently published a monthly bulletin, *L'ami de la croix*, in which they reported that numerous acts of miraculous healing were taking place there.[58] Pontchâteau received much publicity in local Catholic and royalist papers as well. Following a pilgrimage in 1873, for example, the *Semaine religieuse* gave a complete description of the event and included the full transcript of the bishop's address to the pilgrims.[59] The shrine also became more revered when, in 1888, the Catholic Church beatified Grignion de Montfort. The bishop of Nantes subsequently called for a pilgrimage to Pontchâteau in September, which he and the bishop of Blois attended. According to one source, about fifty thousand pilgrims from more than fifty parishes followed the bishops in a procession to the shrine.[60]

Although the entire diocese of Nantes claimed Grignion as its saint, the Catholic Machecoulais saw the missionary as uniquely their own. The *Semaine religieuse* of Nantes included such sentiment when the Vatican announced his beatification:

A tradition preserved at Machecoul reports that the blessed Père Montfort came into the town on his way to La Garnache, whereupon he preached and vibrantly urged the inhabitants to fervently embrace the devotion of the Rosary.

His austerity made a great impression. Many people were believed to have made the observation that with such fatigue from his missions, he would decide to lessen his mortification. Historians declare that he responded in these words:

"The cock crows better once his feathers have been ruffled."

From that day forward parishioners have had much zeal for reciting the Rosary.[61]

Other aspects of nineteenth-century parish life at Trinité also imply a strong reverence for Grignion. The parish's youth gymnastic club, which was started in the early twentieth century, called itself the Gilles de Retz after a medieval lord and companion of Joan of Arc whose chateau's ruins were still standing near the town.[62] Yet the club originally was called "Pater des Vendéens," a reference to Grignion de Montfort.[63] Second and more important, the iconography within the parish church reflected the popular appeal of this figure. Several documents, including those kept by the government and pastoral visit reports held by the parish, invite a comparison of the parish church's liturgical settings at three different times: 1854, 1876, and 1906. The comparison indicates that among the relatively few statues added to the church interior during the second half of the nineteenth century, one was of Grignion.[64]

Even given Grignion's role as facilitator for the 1793 crusade, those heroes who—like Christ himself—had shed their blood in accord with divine will were just as indispensable to a memory of holy war. As with other segments of the memory, ritual and symbol became the means of expressing the heroic resistance of the saintly Vendéens. As early as 1826, for example, the duchesse de Berry and the mother of the Bourbon heir apparent made a donation (albeit anonymously) of eight thousand francs to eighty parishes on the south side of the Loire River in the diocese of Nantes. The money was expressly for the foundation of a perpetual mass to be said each year for General Charette de la Contrie and his soldiers who, in keeping with the memory, fought "for the cause of religion and the monarchy."[65] Similarly, in 1828 four officers who sought to resurrect a Vendéen insurgency in 1815 (when Napoleon returned to France), gave six thousand francs to sixty-seven parishes in the southern Loire-Inférieure for the repose of the souls of Louis-Athanase Charette and Suzannet, both of whom had been their comrades and had died in the 1815 rebellion.[66] High praise for Vendéen rebels extended all the way up to the monarchy during the Restoration, as Louis XVIII, Charles X, and their ministers publicly honored Vendéen leaders. The state also granted many former insurgents military pensions and monetary relief to the wounded and widows of insurgents who had died in the rebellion.[67]

The role of the Catholic clergy was paramount in the commemoration of Vendéen heroism. Parish priests oversaw the raising of mausoleums and monuments for the war dead and statues of the Vendéen generals and Louis XVI in many parishes where the insurgency had been fought.[68] That virtually all public commemorations and memorials relating to the Vendéen insurgency involved religious services or revolved around religious themes was indicative of how much the memory had gained wide acceptance in and around Machecoul by the Restoration period. One manifestation of this success was the 1826 dedication of a commemorative chapel to Charette de la Contrie and his companions at Legé (only about ten kilometers southeast of Machecoul). On this occasion the bishop of Nantes celebrated mass at the site and remarked that it was fitting "to recall the Christian hero that we cherish, the approbation of religion, and the desires of the faithful."[69]

After the Revolution of 1830, however, government officials made a concerted effort to suppress this politically explosive part of the memory, especially by prohibiting those rituals through which the saintly virtue of the Vendéens was expressed. This is why in 1831 the prefect of the Loire-Inférieure argued to the minister of religion and public instruction that memorial masses for Charette, Suzannet, other Vendéen generals and those killed in the 1793 insurrection should be forbidden. He claimed that the ceremonies were nothing but "an appeal to passion and to the civil war of which they revive all the memories, whereas it is so important that every effort be made to suppress [the memories]."[70] Thereafter the government closely regulated Vendéen commemorations, such as masses for Louis XVI, Marie-Antoinette, and Charette. Some priests rebelled against such regulations, causing the Loire-Inférieure's prefect to deny state salaries to some priests and even imprison a few.[71]

Despite the best efforts of government officials during the July Monarchy, a memory of holy war—particularly its emphasis on the heroic and saintly actions of insurgents—took on new life after 1848. This was perhaps why the mayor of La Garnache (Vendée) observed during the Second Empire that all the religious ceremonies held in the area had for their goal "the revival of what can be called the Vendéen spirit, and to nourish the people of the countryside with the hope of seeing the white flag again."[72] When Napoleon III began to allow for more political expression in the 1860s, symbols associated with the Vendéen insurgency, such as white flags and fleurs-de-lis, started reappearing in religious processions and special services like first communion, and parish missions frequently ended with crowds holding white flags and green ribbons (a symbol of the comte de Chambord, the last French Bourbon heir).[73]

Commemorative rituals of the Vendéen insurgency became especially commonplace as the centennial of the French Revolution approached. The parish clergy and royalist politicians in the west frequently made attempts to match republican and civic celebrations by holding their own countercommemorations. In 1887, for instance, a statue of Saint Michael the Archangel was unveiled near the chapel at Legé originally dedicated to Charette de la Contrie and his comrades in 1826.[74] The *curé* of Legé declared the chapel a "noble relic" of the Vendéens "that decay did not conquer" and exhorted his audience to "show that we are worthy" like the saintly rebels. Throughout 1892 and 1893, moreover, commemorations were held in western parishes, convents, and religious houses to memorialize the refractory priests who had been exiled, killed, or persecuted during the Revolution. Accompanying these was a proliferation of historical or quasi-historical literature, often written by clerics or legitimist scholars, recounting the heroic efforts of refractory priests and Vendéen insurgents.[75]

Few rites, however, better acclaimed the heroic memory during the Third Republic than those performed at Couffé (Loire-Inférieure), the home parish to many in the Charette family, on August 27, 1896. Many gathered on that day to mark the one-hundredth anniversary of the death of Charette de la Contrie. The commemoration started in mid-morning with a service at the Couffé parish church, which was decorated with banners bearing the name of various Vendéen leaders. At the foot of the altar stood the supposed uniform of Charette, along with a red handkerchief and a saber. The bishop of Montpellier gave the oration, in which he declared that the Vendée had been a "glorious war" and called for "honor to the vanquished" Vendéen chiefs "who died for the defense of their God and their King."

When the service concluded a luncheon for 1,200 individuals was held at the château of la Contrie, during which could be heard constant cries of "Long live the king!," "Long live Charette," and "Down with the *chéquards*," the last being a reference to the "public malefactors" of the Third Republic. A speech by the General Charette who had fought for the pope in the 1860s followed the luncheon, in which he commented that he saw no difference "between the words of *ralliement* and *reniement* [repudiation], nor between the *ralliés* and the *renégats* [turncoats]."[76] As those conducting state surveillance of the event correctly observed, in such instances a memory of holy war made its presence felt in the political arena. Past rebellion thus became a guide for the then-current resistance against anticlerical republicanism, to say nothing of French Catholic moderation.[77]

That the government would maintain surveillance of such rituals or react so earnestly to certain devotions speaks both to the mnemonic power of ritual and symbol as well as the political potency of the memory itself. State reaction to such ritual, moreover, suggests that although the nineteenth century saw the rise of a new mass culture, the cultural and political potency of symbol and ritual did not appreciably diminish.[78] The rituals enacted during the centenary of the Revolution imply that a memory of holy war, particularly the part that dealt with the insurgency, had tremendous staying power; it had remained well intact for more than one hundred years. Yet in all of this there was more than simply nostalgia at work. One reason why the memory persisted was because of its perceived capability to impart valuable spiritual and political lessons that could be applied to present times.

The Impious Present

Although a memory of holy war acknowledged that most religious strife ended with the signing of the Concordat of 1801, it nonetheless implied that the malevolence of the Enlightenment and revolution was continuing to wreak havoc in France during the nineteenth century.[79] Indeed, since the memory cast revolution and counterrevolution in the 1790s as a foreshadowing of an impending, consummate battle between good and evil, those subscribing to it in the nineteenth century prepared themselves for no less than Armageddon. Although the outcome of the great battle was never in doubt, arguably the memory gave no indication of the ultimate outcome, for it was up to the Catholic faithful in western France to hasten God's victory by imitating their Vendéen ancestors in their willingness to shed blood for the holy cause. Thus, although a memory of holy war dealt with the past, the Machecoulais found that it had broader implications. The enduring value of the memory was that it showed the faithful how to do God's will in the present.[80]

In accord with the memory's contention that Enlightenment and revolution had unleashed unprecedented evil in the nineteenth century, the town's clergy seemingly assumed that delivering sermons, holding parish missions, teaching catechisms, and even holding commemorations only went so far; they were merely periodic, if not sporadic, attempts to counter sin in all of its forms. This is why, in part, the clergy was quick to establish confraternities and other parish groups in the nineteenth century. Such organizations were intended to pick up where other pastoral efforts left off in the battle against contemporary evil. As in many parishes within the diocese of Nantes, confraternities at Machecoul grew in number and size in the nineteenth century, especially between 1850 and 1914. Pastoral visit reports for the parish indicate that between 1854 and 1889 the number of confraternities doubled from three to six.[81] The clergy often founded these lay organizations when religious fervor was at a fever pitch—the best time being immediately after a parish mission.[82] Although the confraternities were created for both men and women of the parish, the latter participated in them in larger numbers and for longer periods of time.[83]

Confraternities constituted, however, only one level of lay organizations within the parish. The clergy also created other associations for different segments of the parish populace. The Enfants de Marie, begun at Trinité in 1853, was expressly for the girls in the parish, most if not all of whom attended the town's Catholic school. The Patronage de Saint-Joseph, established shortly after World War I began, drew its members from boys in the parish between the ages of nine and fifteen. Similarly, the Action Catholique de la Jeunesse Française (ACJF, or simply called the Jeunesse Catholique) chapter for Machecoul, founded in 1906 and which later included a gymnastics club, was for teenaged boys.[84] Two other organizations, the Société de Saint-Vincent-de-Paul and the Mères chrétiennes, established in 1852 and 1909 respectively, were adult associations like the confraternities, but they did not serve the same function. The Société de Saint-Vincent-de-Paul (short-lived in the department of the Loire-Inférieure because officials feared that the organization would stir up propapal sentiment during the 1860s) was intended to provide, above all, material assistance to the poor.[85] The Mères chrétiennes sought to help women become better mothers. Its self-proclaimed mission was teaching women how to "maintain the Christian life" within the confines of the home as well as to sanctify each and every member "as woman, as mother, and as mistress of the house." Another young women's group in the parish (about which there is little information) was called the Fleurs de Lys, a name replete with counterrevolutionary connotations.[86]

Establishing these organizations was seen as necessary for combating contemporary ills in a variety of ways. For one, they offered additional opportunities for the clergy to instruct the laity. In Machecoul's case this meant yet one more occasion to instill Tridentine moral guidelines, especially among the youth. At a gathering for the Enfants de Marie in 1861, for example, abbé Bouron spoke to members "about the virtues that must distinguish them: purity, humility, obedience, and charity." At another association meeting, the _curé_ discussed wedding celebrations and "recommended not to make the rounds within the town since it is not appropriate for the Children of Mary to be thus seen. For in this walk one often loses modesty, and one always gives a bad example."[87]

That the town's clergy embraced the rigor of a long-standing form of Catholicism did not always mean, though, that it ignored the fundamental social, economic, and cultural changes associated with the nineteenth century. A case can be made, in fact, that just the opposite was true.[88] In his study of Breton religion and culture from 1850 to 1950, Michel Lagrée emphasized the role that Catholic youth organizations had in transforming Brittany and helping it to undergo, for lack of a better term, modernization. As Lagrée showed, these organizations introduced elements of contemporary mass culture, such as sports and the cinema, to the Breton people.[89] Some evidence regarding Machecoul's Jeunesse Catholique supports his argument. The records for one particular meeting show how the association's members learned about modern notions of health and hygiene:

> With sound morals and proper hygiene, they say, a human will die of nothing but old age, perhaps that is saying a lot, however it is certain that good hygiene helps to maintain and conserve health. For this reason, our speaker talked to us successively about alcoholism, tobacco, personal care, physical exercise, sports, and preventive measures against tuberculosis.

> … The speaker then spoke to us about bodily care that we must do to ourselves: care for the head, nose, mouth, ears, and of bathing. On this subject he made an apt remark; we think it well to wash a horse from head to toe, but too often we forget to do the same to ourselves; for the horse perspires in the open air, but because clothes cover us, our sweat falls on ourselves, staying on our skin and forming filth. The main conclusion: it is necessary to bathe in order to have a sound body.[90]

Although weekly or monthly organizational meetings offered prime occasions for the clergy to teach the faithful, closed retreats held for organizational members became even better opportunities for instruction. Many religious retreats took place in the diocese at the house of the Jesuits in Nantes, but occasionally Machecoul was a site for them as well.[91] Such retreats were particularly effective teaching venues because they forced the participants, in the words of one Machecoulais, to "leave the world, our home, our family, all of our little affairs that habitually occupy us, our work so that we retire into the silence and meditation."[92] In 1863 the Enfants de Marie held one such retreat for four days in December, with the final day falling on the Feast of the Immaculate Conception.[93] Later, in the 1890s, retreats for military conscripts from the diocese of Nantes were held in the town before the future soldiers went off to training.[94] Typically the military retreats lasted three or four days, during which young men were given "spiritual arms" (a rosary, a crucifix, holy medals), attended conferences, recited various prayers and chanted hymns, and established friendships that perhaps could later be renewed in the military.[95] The 1896 army retreat, for example, included general communion, a renewal of baptismal promises, and a consecration of the new conscripts to "Our Lady of the Armies."[96] A high-ranking officer in the army (and obviously one sympathetic to the church) frequently gave advice to the conscripts, and a doctor instructed the men on the dangers of venereal disease.[97]

The records for these closed retreats indicate that key elements of Tridentine Catholicism were inculcated there, just as they were in sermons. When a three-day retreat was held for the Enfants de Marie, the retreat director emphasized the Tridentine themes of death, humility, the final judgment, and Christian resolutions. The clerical instructions on death were certainly reminiscent of a Catholicism from days gone by:

> He then spoke to us about death: yes, my dear sisters one day you will die, perhaps sooner than you think, so prepare yourselves here, for the thought of death is a beneficial one, if you think about death you will not sin. There is nothing so striking as death. My dear sisters will the riches, honors, pleasures, and vanities of this world remain with you at your last hour? You will take nothing of this, nothing

will remain after your death but your good works which will preserve your memory.

The priest concluded the retreat by recommending a contemplative exercise, which similarly reflected a preoccupation with death, hell, and sorrow:

> Make three stations, to heaven, to hell, and to Calvary. First at heaven, see the beautiful sky, contemplate for a while the grandeur of God and Mary. Second, in hell see the walls all on fire, the roads all on fire, all is on fire, my sisters. See the poor souls, the torments they suffer there, they are all in the flames, quiver at the sight of all of this. Third, at Calvary see Mary at the foot of the cross, consider the sorrows of Mary from the view of the crucified Jesus, and you, how many times have you crucified him by your sins. And so! Take up, therefore, the good resolution to live better in the future. If you have these three ideas well engraved upon your heart, you will be sure to have contrition.[98]

One should note how heaven was only briefly mentioned, whereas hell and the sorrow of Calvary were described with much more detail. Although the memory's casting of the Old Regime as a golden age may explain the propensity for such spirituality, there very well may have been another reason for it as well. Since one implication of the memory was that unmitigated evil stemming from the Revolution was still present in the nineteenth century, it followed that such malevolence had to be met with the uncompromising spiritual force seemingly found only within the confines of Tridentine Catholicism.

Aside from instilling Tridentine rigor within organizations, the clergy could impart lessons drawn from memory through turning parish organizations into cells of counterrevolutionary resistance. This may be why, for example, Marc Sagnier's democratic Le Sillon movement failed to make significant inroads among rural Catholics in the diocese of Nantes and some other areas of the west; many in the clergy remained suspicious of democracy and other manifestations of "modernism."[99] As for those organizations that were established, the memory's teaching about a depraved present reinforced their counterrevolutionary character. When the diocesan director of the ACJF came to the town to establish the parish chapter, for example, he remarked that "for some years we have seen our [religious] freedoms fall one by one and our enemies, not content with their success, are again promising next to smother the little amount of Catholicism that remains in France." He contended that young Catholic men needed to unite and become "an army of generous and valiant hearts, capable of resisting the fierce sectarians who pledge our death."[100] The registry of the Christian Mothers states that the rationale for starting the association was to confront "the dangers to which [mothers] are exposed, above all in our time where every attempt is made to destroy the family."[101] In 1913, on the occasion of a boys' gymnastic rally held in the town, Machecoul's *curé* of Trinité was quick to compare the parish's gymnasts to the heroic Vendéens in the *Semaine religieuse*:

> Machecoul is full of souvenirs of these heroes who gave their blood for their king and their God. We would like our gymnasts to be the proud sons of these heroes through their endurance and faith. It seems to me that the souls of our old Vendéens must tremble today at the sound of the bugle and the drums; that they pray to God to put into the souls of our youth their holy zeal and faith.[102]

Parish organizations were affiliated with a memory of holy war, therefore, in a number of ways. As in the case of sermons, missions, and catechisms, these organizations frequently became a means of promoting Tridentine Catholicism. They offered occasions, moreover, for the clergy to reiterate the lesson informed by the memory: they were living in an irresolute time in which revolutionary evil was continuing to spread. But parish organizations were likely linked to the memory in another way as well. They allowed the Machecoulais to become comrades in arms in the ongoing struggle against evil in the nineteenth century—a notion that most parishioners seemed to embrace, if their overwhelming participation in these organizations is any indication. Such organizations enabled the town's Catholics to build a solidarity that, according to the memory, was desperately needed in the ongoing struggle. With the forces of liberalism, republicanism, and *libre pensée* increasingly arrayed against them in the nineteenth century, parishioners found in these organizations the strength to sustain themselves for their fight, and the means by which they could fulfill the heroic roles suggested by the memory.

Parish organizations were also intended to encourage devotional rites among the Machecoulais, which in themselves had affiliations with a memory of holy war. Trinité was home to many different devotions practiced by lay people in the nineteenth century: the so-called Month of Adoration, the Way of the Cross, the Forty Hours, and later Benediction and Exposition of the Eucharist.[103] But probably the most popular devotion in the parish was that of the Sacred Heart of Jesus, one of the most indispensable parts of a memory of holy war. Given that the Sacred Heart was the symbol adopted by Vendéen insurgents, devotion to it became a symbolic and ritualistic expression of saintly resistence in 1793.[104] But the Sacred Heart was not just the relic of a heroic past; it was also a devotion meant to battle evil in the present. As Raymond Jonas showed, devotion to the Sacred Heart became enormously popular in the 1860s when another counterrevolution, Pope Pius IX's struggle against nationalist forces in Italy, was under way.[105] By no accident, abbé Bouron established the Month of the Sacred Heart devotion in May 1868 at Machecoul—the same time when many bishops throughout France were consecrating their dioceses to this devotion.[106]

But even after the Papal States were lost, devotion to the Sacred Heart continued, especially whenever area Catholics felt they were under siege by evil forces. The Month of the Sacred Heart devotion was later established, for example, in the girls' Catholic primary school in 1881—precisely when Catholic education was under assault by republican politicians in Paris.[107] In 1895 the Machecoul Confraternity of the Most Holy Sacrament and the Holy Virgin changed its name to the Confraternity of the Most Holy Sacrament and the Sacred Heart of Jesus.[108] The name change coincided with anticlerical politicians' ongoing denunciation of intransigent Catholics, who by that point had chosen the Sacred Heart as both religious and political symbol.[109] Parish iconography also hints at the strong allegiance to the Sacred Heart during the second half of the nineteenth century, for the church at Machecoul had an altar dedicated to it from 1854 to 1906. It remains there to this day, as can be seen in Figure 5.2.[110] Some Machecoulais, moreover, likely participated in national pilgrimages dedicated to the

Figure 5.2
The Nineteenth-Century Altar of the Sacred Heart in the Church of Trinité at Macheco.
(Two photographs by the author, 1994-1995)

Sacred Heart, specifically to Paray-le-Monial (Saône-et-Loire), and later to the national shrine at Montmartre in Paris.[111]

Given the mnemonic insinuation that the postrevolutionary era was in the throes of revolutionary evil, the conclusion of the nineteenth century held great spiritual significance for the priests and parishioners at Trinité. It also offered the occasion to invoke the Sacred Heart in the struggle against Satan. The *curé* or a *vicaire* saw the moment as so important that he wrote down how the parish commemorated the very first night of the twentieth century:

> From 28 December 1900 to 1 January 1901, a triduum was preached in the church of Machecoul by a Redemptorist Father from the convent of Sables with the goal of offering to the Sacred Heart of Jesus reparations for the offenses committed toward his adorable majesty over the course of the nineteenth century and to consecrate the century that was about to begin. . . The church scarcely contained the large

throng of faithful, of whom a number took Holy Communion. After an instruction whose goal was to increase devotion to the Divine Heart of Jesus present in the Eucharist, a magnificent procession of the Most Holy Sacrament was made to the altar of the Sacred Heart in order to make an act of consecration there. The splendor and the piety of the ceremonies of this first night of the twentieth century will leave a great and edifying memory within the parish.[112]

That the clergy would make a connection between the depravity of the nineteenth century and a consecration of the twentieth century to the Sacred Heart was a logical outcome of a memory of holy war. France had abandoned the Sacred Heart in the century that had just ended, yet believers had the chance to help renew the nation by consecrating themselves and the new century to the Sacred Heart, just as the Vendéen heroes had allegedly done in 1793.

Many other acts of piety were observed within the parish aside from that of the Sacred Heart. Devotions to Mary in small towns like Machecoul certainly increased in number, thanks to the incidence of Marian apparitions at La Salette, Lourdes, and Pointmain—especially after these became centers of national pilgrimage in France during the nineteenth century.[113] Many Machecoulais likely participated in national pilgrimages during the second half of the nineteenth century, for Catholics from diocese of Nantes traveled often and in great numbers to the Marian shrines or churches at La Salette (Isère), Chartres (Eure-et-Loire), and, of course, the most important of all, Lourdes (Hautes-Pyrénées). Like most other dioceses in France, the diocese of Nantes's favorite national pilgrimage during the late nineteenth and early twentieth centuries was that to Lourdes.[114] Between 1872 and 1914 the diocese of Nantes sponsored and organized approximately fifty-eight pilgrimages to the celebrated site in the Pyrenees.[115] Exactly how many parishioners from Trinité took part in such pilgrimages is uncertain. Yet we do know that during the 1908 pilgrimage one *curé* of Machecoul, abbé Leroux, was given the privilege to say a mass at Lourdes for the pilgrims from his diocese.[116]

These national pilgrimages consistently show a memory of holy war's influence. A case in point was a manual of canticles distributed to those making the eighth pilgrimage to Lourdes from the diocese of Nantes in 1877. The police in the Loire-Inférieure seized a copy of the manual precisely because it was found to be politically volatile.[117] A canticle to be sung when the pilgrims arrived at the shrine included verses that captured the lessons about the nineteenth century stemming from the memory:

> Impiety is tossing with fury
> And the demon makes a supreme effort;
> Save the world, Oh divine Mary,
> It is seated at the shadow of death.
>
> Proud of its vain science,
> This century is deaf to the threats of heaven;
> Mary, Oh you who cherish innocence,
> Keep us in the faith of our fathers.
>
> Make it so your name is engraved on our soul;
> That for us it be a mark of honor,
> And that marshaled under your white banner,
> We will fight the battles of the Lord.[118]

But there were more to the songs than these suggestive lyrics. Many hymns within the manual possessed a marching rhythm and a parade-like melody; they were no less than battle hymns. Undoubtedly many pilgrims went to the Pyrenees to be cured of their ills, as Ruth Harris has made clear.[119] Maybe they had little interest in the memory's implications about the nineteenth century. Yet given both the music and the words, how could the message elude them? They were off to wage a war against evil, much in accord with their own roles arising from the memory.

True, such signs of piety indicated more than the lessons taken from a memory of holy war. Admittedly some of the themes discussed here were not unique to the Machecoul area; many Catholics throughout France looked on the nineteenth century as an irreligious epoch. One can find a plethora of themes, moreover, in the wide variety of religious practices and pronouncements in a very vibrant parish, let alone read too much into them. But even given these caveats, the manifestations of this parish's piety—especially the pronouncements of Catholics living in the midst of postrevolutionary evil—show how a memory of holy war permeated the town's religious culture. Merely applying the lessons of the past to the present, however, even if it was through provocative public ceremonies, religious rites, and politically suggestive symbolism, often was not enough for believers. Indeed, the memory suggested to many that a true battle had to be waged. In one sense, of course, the struggle was within one's heart: a contest to conquer one's vices and to live in accord with God's law. But for Catholics at Machecoul who adhered to a memory of holy war, the answer was not that simple. To join the battle demanded, at times, a fight in the flesh.

The Word Incarnate

The militancy among those possessing a memory of holy war during the nineteenth century first appeared in 1815, specifically when Napoleon returned to France after his brief exile to Elba. In response to his return, a popular uprising took place in virtually the same region in the west where hostilities had begun in 1793. Wealthy notables in the region such as Suzannet, several La Rochejaqueleins, and Louis de Charette began recruiting area peasants for the new Vendée. Yet in contrast to the situation in 1793, government troops and police responded immediately to the crisis. Begun in early April, the 1815 insurgency was over by the end of June (by which point the outcome was moot since Napoleon had been defeated at Waterloo). The differences between the insurgencies of 1815 and 1793, though, were appreciable. Compared with the 1793 rebellion, the 1815 version involved a much smaller number of participants, the rebels lacked what little organization and coordination had characterized the first Vendée, and the tendency for desertion among insurgents was much higher.[120] Yet a similarity existed between the revolts. Local officials again made accusations that the clergy was directly responsible for inciting rebellion. According to reports, the *curés* and *vicaires* were among the most defiant and outspoken individuals in the region during the One Hundred Days.[121]

Perhaps in concert with a different memory—that concerning the civil war among republicans—one military officer revealed that the insurgents consisted of "nobles, followed by all the priests except for one, nearly all the mayors of the communes, and some innkeepers." He added that "priests are those who do the most harm; they preach to all that religion forbids the recognition of Napoleon, that as ministers of God they would lose their lives rather than renounce the king."[122] Priestly defiance was reported to be especially noteworthy at Machecoul. A brigadier general reported that before his arrival on April 25, the *vicaire* abbé Chevalier had been calling for revolt and that he himself had arrived just in time to stop the agitation.[123] Similarly, when the prefect later asked who had been involved in the 1815 uprising, the town's mayor remarked that no one in the commune had taken up arms, but that many had expressed the desire for revolt through their words and correspondence.[124]

Was there any truth to such allegations? As in the case of the original insurgency, one can never be sure. If there was some exaggeration on the part of local government and police officials, it was likely a result of a republican memory of the first insurgency. But even given an element of republican memory implicit in the reports, there is no reason to discount them altogether. Area priests, in being faithful to their own perceived calling as holy warriors, conceivably felt that they had a divine obligation to be defiant, if not to join actively in the rebellion. In view of the mnemonic tendency to extol the Vendée as a sacred event, priests likely saw rebellion as a prophetic requirement in keeping with their office; they likely saw themselves as successors to the warriors and martyrs of 1793.

Priests and religious in western France had less of a reason to personify the lessons of memory during the Restoration, but the same could not be said for the July Monarchy, particularly in 1832. Early in that year Machecoul's mayor observed that citizens loyal to Louis-Philippe and isolated in the countryside were being ill treated by those resisting conscription and that royalist "nobles and bourgeois and above all the blackrobes" were the primary authors of the trouble.[125] About a week later the Machecoul mayor complained that royalist meetings were being held in and around the commune and that the resisters to conscription were starting to gather arms.[126] Shortly thereafter he reported that the explosive political situation in the Machecoul canton precluded conscription for the class of 1831.[127] The mayor also insisted that priests were largely responsible for draft resistance. He claimed that through the counsel in the confessional, priests were telling draft dodgers not to give in: "It is only in Latin conversations that [we], 'sometimes succeed in uprooting evil, many attempts often are necessary before success is achieved.'"[128] How the mayor was able to determine what was being said within the confessional is a mystery. Equally uncertain is how lowly military draftees could understand Latin.

Draft resistance and purported clerical support for it, however, soon had wider repercussions. The duchesse de Berry, who had been exiled from France shortly after the 1830 Revolution, saw in the tense situation an opportunity whereby the Bourbons could return to power. The mother of the Bourbon pretender entered France and began rallying support for a new insurrection in the west. Landing near Marseille, the duchesse covertly made her way across France and entered the west in May 1832. On hearing of the duchesse's impending return in early April, the "Green Cravats" in the Machecoul area began making plans for yet another rebellion. The duchesse subsequently ordered the insurrection to begin near the end of May, but the commencement of the uprising was poorly coordinated. On June 3 the government declared a state of siege in the Vendée and the Loire-Inférieure, and in the days that followed the police and the military quickly routed the paltry rebel bands.[129] In the Machecoul area only about three hundred men rose up in rebellion, and of those a mere thirty had firearms. The rest of western France refused to join in the insurgency, and so by June 8 the uprising of 1832 was all but over.[130]

With the revolt crushed, departmental authorities sought to determine the causes of the insurgency. The mayor of Machecoul claimed that four groups were responsible: legitimist notables, draft dodgers, fanatical priests, and "bigots of the lowest class." Authorities understood that economic dissatisfaction was a contributing factor, but they also believed that clergy and members of religious orders had played a part. When the prefect asked the town's mayor what measures should be enacted to maintain peace in his region, the mayor insisted on "the removal of the Brothers of Christian Doctrine from primary instruction."[131] As in 1815, it is impossible to tell from these 1832 reports what was really true: were they merely reflecting the republican memory about 1793, or were priests actively engaged in personifying a memory of holy war? In all likelihood, it was a little of both. Regardless of the reality, though, accusations against rebellious priests continued to abound. The commander of the gendarmerie at Machecoul concluded that aside from pro-Bourbon notables, the conduct of most parish priests in the canton "has always been in opposition to the government." He claimed that "the *vicaire* of Paulx was found in the [rebel] band at Caraterie," and that "many *curés* do not chant prayers for the King and his family, most notably those of Machecoul and Paulx."[132] In a different report, the officer was more specific in his allegations, some of which were admittedly tenuous. He charged that the *curé* of Saint-Même frequently visited with the principal leaders of the Bourbon royalists and that the discourse to his parishioners was frequently "dangerous." The *curé* of La Marne was accused of "mixing politics and religion" in his sermons and consorting with royalist leaders as well. The policed refused to believe the *vicaire* of Paulx who, when found among a rebel band, said that he was carrying the last sacraments to a man who lived nearby.[133]

The 1832 rebellion was the last of the major Vendéen insurgencies. But in another sense resistance to revolution remained as strong as ever, thanks in no small part to a memory of holy war. Its ongoing influence became no more obvious among Catholics in and around Machecoul than between 1858 and 1870, when events in Italy involving Pope Pius IX became a growing concern to a clergy and laity especially sensitive to nationalistic and liberal assaults on the church. True, a surging Ultramontanism felt throughout the French church at midcentury somewhat underlay this response. Yet the introduction of the Roman liturgy in the diocese of Nantes and Napoleon III's 1859 intervention in Italy (indirectly against Pope Pius IX and supporters of the Papal States) alone cannot adequately explain why Catholics in the west responded to the crisis as they did.[134] The clergy and laity in and around Machecoul came to the assistance of Pope Pius IX in primarily two ways. First, a great many priests and laypeople gave financial aid to the pope from 1860 to 1870. This funding mostly came in the form of the *Denier de Saint Pierre*, otherwise known as Peter's Pence. Pope Pius IX also received funds from other sources originating in the department, namely in the form of loans, money raised in lotteries, and military subscriptions.[135]

The second and most critical aid came in the form of volunteers from the diocese of Nantes who joined papal military forces in the fight against Italian nationalists and republicans. Most belonged to a multinational force known as the pontifical *zouaves*. Approximately 30 percent of all papal *zouaves* came from France, with about one-third of those (about one thousand) originating from eight dioceses in the western part of the country. A total of 343 *zouaves* came from the diocese of Nantes alone, the most of any diocese in France. The force was first commanded by the celebrated General de Lamoricière, himself a native of the Nantes region, but the *zouaves* eventually came under the command of Athanase de Charette, the great-nephew of the Vendéen general who had fought in the 1793 insurrection.[136] Other *zouave* military leaders similarly came from affluent legitimist families in the west, namely Henri Cathelineau, Alain de Kersabiec, Arthur Bougrenet de la Tocnaye, and Alain de Charette (the brother of Athanase).[137] Prosopographic research into the volunteers from the diocese has revealed that the *zouaves* came from all social segments: notables, landowners, merchants, artisans, and agricultural laborers.[138] The largest mass of volunteers came from the city of Nantes (122), but many came from the rural parishes surrounding it. Indeed, one *zouave* hailed from Machecoul and another from nearby Saint-Même.[139]

The memoirs the *zouaves* left behind indicate that the motivations for joining the pontifical army were multifarious. Many *zouaves* of the west had a strong belief in the principle of legitimacy, as they recognized the divine right of the pope to rule the Papal States while simultaneously opposing republicanism. There also was a strong sense of fidelity to family obligations, particularly among affluent royalists. The six Charette brothers who fought in the war felt it their duty to maintain the political military reputation surrounding their great uncle. Alliances were forged, moreover, between classmates in Catholic *collèges* within the department, like the one at Machecoul: so much so that if one man volunteered for service, many of his friends would follow. But perhaps the primary reason why volunteers agreed to fight for the pope was a sense of religious obligation implicit in a memory of holy war. *Zouaves* like Louis Gicquel later wrote, "I spilled my blood for my religion in defending the temporal power of the Holy Father, I am content and happy and I take my last breath while thinking I did my duty."[140] Further proof of the memory's influence among volunteers from western France is that many sewed the insignia of the Sacred Heart to their uniforms.[141]

In keeping with the memory, parish priests were also instrumental in the recruitment of papal volunteers. This is why between 1858 and 1869 fifty-five complaints were made against priests or religious in the diocese of Nantes over the Roman question, most of which concerned exhortations given from the pulpit. These pronouncements proved particularly alarming to communal and departmental authorities because the call to help Pope Pius IX was often accompanied by criticism of Napoleon III's Italian policy. One gendarme reported that a *vicaire* at Legé spoke not only of the sacking and pillaging of churches and monasteries in Italy but also had predicted that the churches would be closed in France and that civil war would erupt. Similarly, an official reported that at Vieillevigne a priest proclaimed that the emperor "will be punished in this world before being punished in the next" and that "the scenes of the Terror will return in a short while. Priests will be tied to the altars and the churches burned, religion destroyed."[142] Even the bishop of Nantes, Monseigneur Jaquemet, declared in November 1869 that Catholics were living in a "moment of greatest danger" that required ardent prayer on behalf of all the faithful in the diocese. He warned that "the catastrophe that the hatred, violence, and trickery of the wicked makes us anticipate appears imminent." Characterizing the fall of the Papal States as "the greatest crime of modern times," Jaquemet also proclaimed that those who stood by as the pope lost his temporal power would be subject to "the greatest punishments."[143] Analogies made between papal *zouaves* and Vendéen insurgents were rife in religious and royalist newspapers. One *zouave* killed in 1859 was described as shedding his "Vendéen blood" for the pope and as being a descendant of an insurgent who miraculously escaped death in 1794.[144]

After Pope Pius IX's loss of the Papal States, opportunities to rebel continued to present themselves to the Machecoulais. During the early Third Republic Catholics in the west saw, albeit more figuratively, additional Vendées. The new fields of honor included the ballot boxes during national and regional elections as democratization in France grew, as area public schools after the Ferry laws imposed laicization in public education, and as the republic formally abolished houses of religious orders in France.[145] To be sure, the contests in these spaces never approached the violence seen in the three Vendéen insurgencies, to say nothing of the nationalist siege of papal Rome. The decline of civil violence in the nineteenth century, after all, was felt as much in the communities of western France as almost everywhere else in the nation. But they did offer opportunities whereby believers could express their resistance and seemingly engage enemies for the same reasons that their ancestors, at least according to a memory of holy war, had done in 1793.

While many anticlerical measures confronted Catholics in the early Third Republic, among the most impassioned for the faithful at Machecoul was the 1905 Law of the Separation of Church and State, which abrogated the 1801 Napoleonic Concordat. Much of the controversy over the legislation stemmed from Article Four, which called for the government to take an inventory of church property in each and every parish before it was turned over to "religious associations" composed of laypeople. After passage of the legislation these inventories were scheduled to begin in January 1906 and be completed in only a few months.[146] For his part, the bishop of Nantes issued a statement in the mid-January edition of his *Semaine religieuse* calling for Catholics to remain calm during the inventories. Still, many of his instructions reflected a familiarity with a memory of holy war. He announced that the *curés* must be present during the taking of inventories, for they were the "Guardians of the holy place and the sacred treasures" and had "the serious obligation of not abandoning them in this sorrowful circumstance."[147] Area legitimist papers went much further in their advice to area Catholics; one even called for physical resistance against government officials responsible for taking the inventories.[148]

Catholics within the diocese of Nantes, like many of those throughout the west, the Massif-Central, the Pyrenees, and Flanders, heeded the call for both symbolic and physical resistance.[149] Beginning in early February and continuing into March, the most politically active parishioners, together with parish priests, frequently showed up at the churches to protest the taking of inventories. The diocese of Nantes saw varying degrees of protest against the inventories. In a few isolated communes, inventories were taken without incident. In many other communes, however, symbolic protests or moderate protests characterized by nonviolent resistance unfolded. Some parishes in Nantes, along with other parishes in the extreme southeast, were locations for strong protests, which usually involved about three hundred to five hundred demonstrators, some of whom were armed with clubs and barricaded the doors of parish churches. The most serious demonstrations took place in the southwestern sector of the department—where much of the War of Vendée had been fought. Typically the strongest protests attracted anywhere from eight hundred to two thousand (usually peasants) armed with clubs, scythes, and pitchforks. The protestors often sang religious canticles, cried out "Down with Freemasons" and "Down with Jews," insulted the police and government officials, and solidly blocked the parish church doors.[150]

The attempt to take an inventory at Machecoul was one of the most violent demonstrations within the diocese of Nantes.[151] On January 28 two gendarmes came to the Machecoul *curé*, abbé Leroux, to notify him that the property receiver for the department would take an inventory of the parish church on February 6 in the midafternoon. The notification gave abbé Leroux the opportunity to notify area royalists and many parishioners so that the protest could be prepared. In early February the property receiver arrived on schedule, together with several gendarmes. At precisely two o'clock the church bells rang and a large crowd gathered at the church. When the receiver arrived, he found about seven hundred women assembled within the church saying prayers and singing canticles, while approximately five hundred men stood outside the church doors behind the *curé*, the *vicaires*, the *fabrique* (the parish funding committee), and legitimist notables from the countryside. As the receiver tried to begin the inventory, the *curé* stepped forward and recited a protest: one in which echos of the myth of the holy war could be heard. The protest called the priest and parishioners of the parish "guardians and defenders of this property" who were bound "by a sacred obligation" not to turn over anything to the government. It called the taking of the inventory "an attack upon the sacred rights of the Church, a violation of the formal will of the contributors, a preparation for future confiscation." The *curé* further depicted the protest as "a refusal to participate in the grievous proceedings" as well as a "resolution to defend and claim" the parish's property. After the declaration, the *curé* told the receiver that he could enter the church.[152]

But when the receiver proceeded toward the doors, he was surrounded by a crowd composed of, in his words, "hostile peasants at the head of which were reactionary leaders from neighboring communes" who rained kicks and punches down on him. About eight gendarmes with rifles moved forward and tried to calm the crowd by formally declaring that it was in violation of the law. The presence of the police, however, only seemed to excite parishioners more, many of whom started yelling "Long live [religious] liberty" and "Down with the burglars." The gendarmes found that all the doors of the church were closed and detected that there was a large group of people inside. The receiver, "fearing serious trouble" and suffering from numerous bruises, felt it best to withdraw from the premises and take the inventory at a later date. Two of the gendarmes escorted the receiver out of town and the others returned to the barracks, while the crowd resorted to cries of victory.[153] Ultimately, the receiver took the inventory later in the year and the *fabrique* was officially dissolved near the end of 1906.[154]

Though the protest was a seeming success for the Machecoulais, those who violated the law on that day did not go unpunished. When the police later investigated the incident, they concluded that "the movement, although locally generated, was a royalist maneuver provoked by the *châtelains* of the countryside and nearby who, after having cast the crowd against the authorities, took shelter behind the demonstrators." The police made similar judgments for inventory protests at nearby Paulx and Saint-Etienne-de-Mer-Morte.[155] Still, the parish's lowly protestors bore the brunt of the punishment, which included short stints of imprisonment and substantial fines. Perhaps the assailants were mere lackeys of local royalist politicians, as the police report indicates. Even so, the passion evident in the protestors seemed to reflect a memory of holy war. Given the staying power of that memory, tensions between the Catholic Machecoulais and state authorities probably remained palpable between 1906 and 1914. With the coming of World War I and the formation of the "*union sacrée*," however, local church-state squabbles must have appeared diminutive compared with the nation's overwhelming military crisis—a context in which a memory of holy war likely lost much of its poignance.

Why did nineteenth-century Catholics at Machecoul respond, at least from time to time, with these acts of rebellion? Here again, a memory of holy war looms large. Most instances of defiance by fervent Machecoulais erupted whenever they believed that the state was violating the rights or stature of the Catholic Church. Believers tended to see various state regimes as enemies of the church in 1815, 1832, the 1850s and 1860s (albeit in Italy on that occasion), and 1906. In all cases the perception was that a desecration of the sacred, a direct assault on God, was taking place. Those who subscribed to the memory rebelled at these times on account of their impression that the divine struggle allegedly ignited in 1793 was, in essence, still being fought. Given that the memory held that the first insurgency was fought for God and against unbelief, it followed that any and all attempts to limit the rights and influence of the Catholic Church in the nineteenth century constituted a return of revolution and, with it, another obligation to battle against it.

Overall, this chapter shows why a memory of holy war was among the most far-reaching repercussions of the Machecoul massacres; it remained a powerful political and cultural force in the town through-out the nineteenth century. It pervaded the clergy's teachings, parish organizations, collective prayers and devotions, liturgical symbols, and rituals—in addition to informing the political actions and reactions of the town's clergy and laity at several critical junctures. Still, the memory's permeation of all these phenomena was just one manifestation of its impact. Another was how it facilitated much-needed unification in the town and thereby created a common local identity. Through the memory, most Machecoul Catholics became, as it were, holy warriors. Their schools became bastions consecrated to God, just as their parish church became a divine fortress. Their organizations served as sacred battalions, the teachings received there and elsewhere were tactical in-structions, their priests commanders in the field. Their rites, symbols, and devotional practices offered occasions for spiritual combat, just as their occasional political militancy was a way to fight in the flesh. All of these elements were a result of the one memory, and all had the effect of coalescing a community that, by 1914, was thoroughly Catholic in identity.

So can it be said, then, that a memory of holy war served to dissipate the social, political, and cultural hostility that exploded at Machecoul in the 1790s? To a degree this was the case, for the memory seemed to channel the violent impulses of the 1790s into less destructive paths.[156] Much remembrance, after all, came in the form of words, rites, and symbols. Compared with 1793 there was relatively little violence that erupted in and around the town in the nineteenth century. Undoubtedly a good share of this trend was attributable to a growing sensitivity and revulsion to popular violence in the nineteenth century, not to mention the state's increased capability to control its citizens.[157] Yet it may be that the nature of memory assured that the battles of belief at Machecoul would be waged more in the parish church and in the minds of the faithful than in the town's streets.

Though the memory's tendency to displace violence may be deemed a positive development for the town in the nineteenth century, it nonetheless came with a certain price—an expenditure particularly significant to historians. A case can be made that a memory of holy war had the effect of obfuscating what had really happened in the town in 1793, namely by accentuating the role of the town's counterrevolutionary martyrs, while neglecting the roles of the counterrevolutionary murderers and their republican victims. It was altogether forgotten that, at least in Machecoul's case, the civil war was more of a struggle *between* Catholics than a fight *against* them. Truth be told, many republicans massacred in the town in 1793 had been more devoted to their religion than the insurgent killers had been to theirs. Since a memory of holy war could never concede this point, the subtleties of the town's cultural conflict during the Revolution became lost to future generations. Such an omission was seemingly reinforced by a republican memory of civil war, which, given its virulent anticlericalism in the nineteenth century, conveniently neglected the facts of the massacres as well. Thus a memory of holy war has been responsible not only for the denial of historical reality among the Machecoulais in the nineteenth century but also for the need to set the record straight through what has been written here.

Notes

[1]See Martin, "La Vendée: région mémoire: Bleus et Blancs," in Nora, 1: 519-34.

[2]Elsewhere I have made the case that the town remained culturally isolated during the nineteenth century, despite ongoing economic and political modernization in France as a whole. Much of this immutability was probably due to the ongoing land-ownership scheme in western France, whereby numerous tenant farmers continued to rent from a few privileged proprietors. See Edward J. Woell, "Counterrevolutionary Catholicism in Western France: The Battle of Belief at Machecoul, 1774-1914," Ph.D. Dissertation (Ann Arbor: University Microfilms, 1997), 133-150.

[3]In the nineteenth century Machecoul had numerous primary and secondary schools for both boys and girls established and administrated by religious orders, in addition to possessing an impressive number of *vicaires* working under the *curé*. See Woell, "Counterrevolutionary Catholicism," 347-423. This imposing array of religious institutions and personnel was by no means unique for the diocese of Nantes during the nineteenth century. See Launay, *Le diocèse de Nantes sous le second empire*, 1: 267-454, 2: 481-564. The important role of religious orders in the formation of nineteenth-century French society, including the educational system, is underscored in Sarah Curtis, *Educating the Faithful: Religion, Schooling, and Society in Nineteenth-Century France* (DeKalb: Northern Illinois University Press, 2000).

[4]During most of the nineteenth century the town's mayors and municipal council members in the commune were generally from the urban elite and were politically liberal or moderate, since they were either elected by a very narrow franchise or were appointed by the prefects of the Loire-Inférieure. Of the fifteen members who constituted the municipal council of 1807, for example, five were *rentiers*, three were agriculturalists, two were artisans, one was a merchant, one an innkeeper, one a municipal agent, and one a retired military officer. But after 1871, when local administrators began to be elected through universal male suffrage, the mayors and municipal council members were mostly royalists and came from the agricultural sector. This was because during the early Third Republic the vast majority of agriculturalists in and around Machecoul were solidly in the royalist camp, as Andre Siegfried illustrated. Siegfried himself attributed this predominant political sentiment in western France to the land scheme in which the many tenants grossly outnumbered the rather few landlords, who together with the local priests convinced these tenants to vote as they did, whether in national or local elections. See ADLA, 1 M 296. Table Containing Information about Members of the Machecoul Municipal Council, 25 September 1807; Table of Municipal Councilors Elected on May 1, 1892, May 3, 1892; André Siegfried, *Tableau politique de la France de l'Ouest sous la troisième république* (Paris: Librairie Armand Colin, 1913), 195.

[5]It is important to note here that due to the Napoleonic Concordat, French bishops reserved the right to name *curés* and other local clerics to their positions. Readers should also be aware that most of the local clergy had agricultural and artisanal backgrounds, and therefore they were well familiar with those to whom they ministered. See Marius Faugeras, "Vocations sacerdotales séculières au XIXe siècle (1803-1814) dans le diocèse de Nantes," *Mémoires de la Société archéologique et historique de Nantes et de Loire-Atlantique* 117 (1981), 101-04.

[6]These sermons are similar in structure to those belonging to Yves-Michel Marchais and those examined by Thomas Kselman in the diocese of Angers. See Lebrun, *Parole de Dieu et révolution*; Kselman, *Death and the Afterlife in Modern France*. To put these sermons in chronological perspective, of the 106 approximately 78 had dates on them. The majority of these fell between 1820 and 1880, with the median date standing at approximately midcentury. Some sermons had two dates on them, like "1841" and "1865," suggesting that they were used multiple times.

[7]Gibson, 17-29.

[8]Launay, *Le diocèse de Nantes sous le second empire*, 2: 541-43.

[9]APM, Sermons. The Work of Lent, Summary of Instructions, 1848, 1860.

[10]Ibid., "Carême," 1832.

[11]Ibid., "Courte Instruction pour le jour des morts," 1803.

[12]Gibson, *A Social History of French Catholicism*, 27-28.

[13]APM, Sermons, "Sacrilège," no date.

[14]Ibid., "Discours sur les devoirs des enfants envers leurs pères et mères," no date.

[15]*Catéchisme de Nantes, imprimé par ordre de Monseigneur de Guérines, Evêque de Nantes* (Nantes: Imprimerie Bourgeois, 1826). Catechisms used in the nineteenth century in the diocese of Nantes are available at ADLA.

[16]Marius Faugeras, *Le diocèse de Nantes sous la monarchie censitaire (1813-1822-1849)*, 2 vols. (Fontenay-le-Comte: Imprimerie Lussaud Frères, 1964), 2: 224-25.

[17]Launay, *Le diocèse de Nantes sous le second empire*, 2: 539.

[18]*Catéchisme de Nantes, imprimé par ordre de Monseigneur de Guérines, Evêque de Nantes: Nouvelle édition revue et autorisée par Monseigneur Fournier* (Nantes: Imprimerie Bourgeois, 1870); *Catéchisme de Nantes, imprimé par ordre de Monseigneur de Guérines, Evêque de Nantes: Nouvelle édition revue et autorisée par Monseigneur LeCoq* (Nantes: Imprimerie Bourgeois, 1888).

[19]For more on the religious vibrancy of the diocese of Nantes, see Fernand Boulard, "Matériaux pour l'histoire religieuse du peuple français: Aspects de la pratique religieuse en France 1802-1939: L'exemple des pays de Loire," *Annales économies, sociétés, civilisations* 31 (1976), 782-88.

[20]The breakthrough study in feminization was Claude Langlois, *Le catholicisme au feminin: Les congrégations françaises à supérieure générales au XIXe siècle* (Paris: Editions du Cerf, 1984).

[21]Ralph Gibson, "Hellfire and Damnation in Nineteenth-Century France," *Catholic Historical Review* 74 (1988), 383-402. See also Kselman, *Death and the Afterlife in Modern France*, 83-88.

[22]No one has made this more clear than Fernand Boulard in his pioneering work on the religious sociology of modern France. Boulard's map suggests wide variations in practice and belief from one region of the nation to the next. See Boulard, ed., *Matériaux pour l'histoire religieuse du peuple français, XIXᵉ-XXᵉ siècles*, 2 vols. (Paris: Centre Nationale des Recherches Scientifique, 1982).

[23]This point is emphasized particularly well and convincingly by Tessie P. Liu in *The Weaver's Knot: The Contradictions of Class Struggle and Family Solidarity in Western France, 1750-1914* (Ithaca: Cornell University Press, 1994), 10-21.

[24]Launay, *Le diocèse de Nantes sous le second empire*, 2: 591-608.

[25]See note 5.

[26]APM, Pastoral Visit Reports, 1854, 1863, 1876, 1881, and 1889.

[27]APM, Parish Journal, May 16, 1850.

[28]Ibid., December 3, 1838.

[29]Ibid., January 14, 1846.

[30]APM, Nantes bishop to Machecoul *curé*, April 8, 1853.

[31]APM, Parish Journal, May 16, 1846, May 16, 1850, May 14, 1854, May 16, 1876, May 16, 1881, May 16, 1885, May 15, 1889, May 15, 1894, May 16, 1898; "La fête de Saint-Honoré à Machecoul," *SRN*, May 23, 1874, "Les fêtes de Machecoul, Consécration de l'église, Procession de Saint-Honoré," *SRN*, May 25, 1889, "La Confirmation et la fête de Saint-Honoré à Machecoul," *SRN*, 26 May 1894, "La fête de Saint-Honoré à Machecoul," *SRN*, May 23, 1896.

[32]For example, when Monseigneur Jaquemet was very ill in 1869, Monseigneur Celestin Guymener, the former bishop of Vincennes, Indiana (USA), was asked to attend the procession and administer the sacrament of confirmation. See APM, Parish Journal, May 16, 1869.

[33]APM, Parish Journal, May 16, 1850.

[34]Yveline Bernard, "L'épiscopat nantais de Monseigneur Rouard, évêque de Nantes, 1896 à 1914," Mémoire de maîtrise, directed by Marcel Launay (Nantes: Université de Nantes, 1989), 139.

[35]Gibson, 152-53.

[36]APM, Parish Journal, May 16, 1898.

[37]APM, Parish Journal, May 16, 1894.

[38]Launay, *Le diocèse de Nantes sous le second empire*, 2: 599.

[39]"Mandement de Monseigneur l'Évêque de Nantes pour le saint temps du Carême de l'an de grâce 1867," *SRN*, March 10, 1867.

[40]For more on the concept of *lieux de mémoire*, see Pierre Nora, "Between Memory and History: *Les lieux de Mémoire*," in Revel and Hunt, 631-643.

41Launay, *Le diocèse de Nantes sous le second empire*, 1: 470-71; Bernard, 121; Faugeras, *Le diocèse de Nantes sous la monarchie censitaire*, 1: 255-87.

42APM, Parish Journal, November 1895, December, 1905; Faugeras, 2: 261. Faugeras notes that more than 2,600 people were confirmed at Machecoul in 1820 following a mission there. The number of candidates was so high because the sacrament had not been administered in the parish since the late Old Regime.

43Gwénaël Bareau, "L'épiscopat nantais de Monseigneur LeCoq (1877-1892)," Mémoire de maîtrise, directed by Marcel Launay (Nantes: Université de Nantes, 1993) 31.

44Faugeras, *Le diocèse de Nantes sous la monarchie censitaire*, 2: 261.

45Launay, *Le diocèse de Nantes sous le second empire*, 1: 466-70.

46APM, Parish Journal, November, 1894. An excerpt from the *Semaine religieuse* was inserted into the parish journal.

47Martin, *La Vendée de la mémoire*, 65; Faugeras, *Le diocèse de Nantes sous la monarchie censitaire*, 1:199-201.

48Sheryl Kroen, *Politics and Theater: The Crisis of Legitimacy in Restoration France, 1815-1830* (Berkeley: University of California Press, 2000), 39-75.

49APM, Parish Journal, 16 May 1889.

50"Triduum en l'honneur du à. P. de Montfort à Machecoul," *SRN*, 15 December 1888.

51Louis Pérouas, "La piété populaire au travail sur la mémoire d'un saint, Grignion de Montfort," *Actes du 99e congrès national des sociétés savantes, Besançon* (1976), 269-70.

52"Le pèlernage au calvaire de Pontchateau," *SRN*, October 4, 1873,

53Pérouas, "La piété populaire," 270.

54"Le pèlerinage de la Garnarche," *SRN*, October 13, 1888.

55Launay, *Le diocèse de Nantes sous le second empire*, 1: 301-11, 2: 650-56.

56Faugeras, *Le diocèse de Nantes sous la monarchie censitaire*, 2: 296-98.

57Launay, *Le diocèse de Nantes sous le second empire*, 2: 605-6.

58Pérouas, "La piété populaire," 261-62.

59"Pèlerinage au calvaire de Pontchâteau: Presidé Par Monseigneur l'Evêque de Nantes, le 24 septembre 1873," *SRN*, September 13, 1873; "Pèlerinage au calvaire de Pontchâteau, 24 septembre," *SRN*, Septembre, 20, 1873; "Pèlerinage au calvaire de Pontchâteau," *SRN*, October 4, 1873.

60"Pèlerinage du 8 septembre 1888 au calvaire du bienheureux de Montfort à Pontchâteau," *SRN*, September 15, 1888.

61"Triduum en l'honneur du à. P. de Montfort à Machecoul," *SRN*, December 15, 1888.

[62] The legend of Bluebeard is based on the heinous crimes allegedly committed by Gilles de Retz. Despite the claims that he had tortured children, for which he was later burned at the stake, Gilles de Retz remained a hero within local memory at Machecoul, particularly among those who maintained his innocence. For a dated yet elemental biography of Gilles de Retz, see A. L. Vincent and Clare Binns, *Gilles de Rais: The Original Bluebeard* (London: A. M. Philpot, 1936).

[63] APM Registry of Gilles de Retz, February 1911. The club changed the name to Gilles de Retz not only because of his association with Joan of Arc, who became tremendously popular among French Catholics at the beginning of the twentieth century, but also because the club's members felt that he better embodied the physical attributes that they esteemed.

[64] APM, Pastoral Visit Reports, 1854, 1876; ADLA, 92 V 98. Property Inventory of the Machecoul Fabrique, 17 May 1906. Note that a new parish church was built between 1854 and 1876, for which new altars and statues were erected.

[65] Martin, *La Vendée de la mémoire*, 65; Faugeras, *Le diocèse de Nantes sous la monarchie censitaire*, 1: 199-201.

[66] Martin, *La Vendée de la mémoire*, 69-70.

[67] Ibid., 56-59. An important element of Vendéen memory in the nineteenth and twentieth centuries was the hagiography of those notables in western France who had assumed leadership roles in the 1793 insurgency. François-Athanase Charette de la Contrie was the most important to a memory of holy war in and around Machecoul, but also remembered in western France were Henri Rochejaquelein, Louis-Marie Lescure, Jacques Cathelineau, Nicolas-Jean Stofflet, Charles-Henri-Felicité Sapinaud, and Charles de Bonchamps. For more on these notables and their background, see Augris.

[68] Martin, *La Vendée de la mémoire*, 65-68.

[69] Faugeras, *Le diocèse de Nantes sous la monarchie censitaire*, 1: 200-201.

[70] ADLA, 2 V 2. Prefect to Minister of Public Instruction and Religion, March 25, 1831.

[71] Martin, *La Vendée de la mémoire*, 92-93.

[72] Ibid., 99-105, 110, 112-15.

[73] Ibid., 126-28; Launay, *Le diocèse de Nantes sous le second empire*, 678-87.

[74] AN, F[19] 6000. Two newspaper articles on this ceremony can be found in this dossier: "Un curé factieux," *Nation*, September 9, 1887; "Bulletin politique," *Le phare de la Loire*, September 15, 1887.

[75] Michel Lagrée, "Le clergé Breton et le premier centenaire de la Révolution française," *Annales de Bretagne et des pays de l'Ouest* 91 (1984), 255-61; Martin, *La Vendée de la mémoire*, 142-58, 171-81.

[76]General Charette's repudiation of the *ralliement* evokes one of the three celebrated political developments in which the French Catholic church played a vital role during the first thirty years of the Third Republic. The other two were Boulangism and the Dreyfus Affair. Few if any Catholics in and around Machecoul rallied to the republic. Boulangism and the Dreyfus Affair had implications for the Church in the diocese of Nantes, but they mostly took a back seat to more local concerns within rural communes, like the laicization of public communal schools. See Michael Burns, *Rural Society and French Politics: Boulangism and the Dreyfus Affair* (Princeton: Princeton University Press, 1984), 30, 130, 148, 166.

[77]AN, F[19] 6000. Special Commissioner of Nantes to Minister of the Interior, Royalist Manisfestation at Couffé, August 27, 1896.

[78]For more on counterrevolutionary ritual and the spiritual story that it told, see Edward J. Woell, "Waging War for the Lord: Counterrevolutionary Ritual in Rural Western France, 1801-1906," *Catholic Historical Review* 88 (January 2002), 17-41. The salience of symbolism was apparent not only among Catholics in western France but among many republicans as well. See Maurice Agulhon, *Marianne into Battle: Republican Imagery and Symbolism in France 1780-1880*, trans. Janet Lloyd (Cambridge: Cambridge University Press, 1981).

[79]The notion that the Revolution represented quintessential evil was a common one throughout the French Catholic church in the nineteenth century. As François Pie, the long-time bishop of Poitiers, expressed it, "the Revolution of 1789 is the original sin of public life." See Jonas, 147.

[80]Note that Thomas Kselman describes a somewhat similar narrative, which he attributes to the "prophetic tradition" of Catholicism in modern France. See Kselman, *Miracles and Prophecies*, 113-40.

[81]APM, Pastoral Visit Reports, 1854, 1863, 1876, 1881, and 1889.

[82]Launay, *Le diocèse de Nantes sous le second empire*, 2: 554.

[83]APM, Registry of the Holy Rosary Confraternity, October 6, 1861; AEN, Boîte de Machecoul. Machecoul *curé* to bishop of Nantes, May 19, 1861; Machecoul *curé* to bishop of Nantes, May 9, 1861; Launay, *Le diocèse de Nantes sous le second empire*, 2: 551-59.

[84]APM, Registries for Enfants de Marie, Patronage de Saint-Joseph, and Jeunesse Catholique.

[85]Launay, *Le diocèse de Nantes sous le second empire*, 2: 616-22.

[86]Michel Lagrée, *Religion et cultures en Bretagne, 1850-1950* (Paris: Fayard, 1992), 197-98.

87 APM Registry of Enfants de Marie, 36. For more on the moral rigor of the nineteenth-century French clergy, see Gibson, *A Social History of French Catholicism*, 31.

88 See, for example, Jean-Clément Martin, "Le clergé vendéen face à l'industrialisation (fin XIXe - début XXe)," *Annales de Bretagne et des pays de l'Ouest* 89 (1982), 357-68.

89 Lagrée, *Religion et cultures*, 157-209, 405-33.

90 APM, Registry of the Jeunesse Catholique, November 17, 1905.

91 Launay, *Le diocèse de Nantes sous le second empire*, 1: 470-75; Lagrée, *Religion et cultures*. 322-26; Faugeras, *Le diocèse de Nantes sous la monarchie censitaire*, 2: 274-83.

92 APM, Registry of Enfants de Marie, 52 (circa 1863).

93 Ibid., December 8, 1863.

94 "La retraite des conscrits à Machecoul," *SRN*, November 14, 1896; "Retraite des conscrits à Machecoul," *SRN*, October 26, 1901.

95 Lagrée, *Religion et cultures*, 326-27.

96 "La retraite des conscrits à Machecoul," *SRN*, November 14, 1896.

97 Lagrée, *Religion et cultures*, 327-28.

98 APM, Registry of the Enfants de Marie, 51-56.

99 Lagrée, *Religion et cultures*, 183-92. To be sure, other parts of western France did embrace Sillon and other elements of Social Catholicism. For how and why this occurred in departments like the Finistère, see Caroline Ford, *Creating the Nation in Provincial France: Religion and Political Identity in Brittany* (Princeton: Princeton University Press, 1993).

100 APM, Registry of the Jeunesse Catholique, October 28, 1906.

101 APM, Registry of Mères Chretiennes. November 21, 1909.

102 "Chronique des oeuvres: Les concours gymnastique de Machecoul," *SRN*, August 16, 1913.

103 APM, Parish Journal, Pastoral Visit Report, 1881.

104 Faugeras, *Le diocèse de Nantes sous la monarchie censitaire*, 2: 234.

105 Jonas, 147-71.

106 APM, Parish Journal, May 8, 1868.

107 APM, Parish Journal, 1 May 1881.

108 AEN, Boîte de Machecoul. Regulations of the Confraternity of the Most Holy Sacrament and of the Sacred Heart of Jesus, December 5, 1895.

109 Jonas, 233-43.

110 APM, Pastoral Visit Reports, 1854, 1876. ADLA, 92 V 98. Property Inventory of the Machecoul Fabrique, May 17, 1906.

111 Jonas, 185, 230-31, 204-08, 215-20.

112 APM, Parish Journal, January 1, 1901.

[113]Launay, *Le diocèse de Nantes sous le second empire*, 2: 553-57; Bareau, 35; Bernard, 120.

[114]Bernard, 130-37.

[115]"58ᵉ Pèlerinage à Notre-Dame de Lourdes," *SRN*, May 16, 1914. The diocese always kept count of the number of its pilgrimages to Lourdes.

[116]"47ᵉ Pèlerinage à Notre-Dame de Lourdes," *SRN*, October 17, 1908.

[117]*Manuel des Pèlerins de la ville et du diocèse de Nantes à Notre Dame de Lourdes, 27 Aoft 1877* (Nantes: Bourgeois, 1877). A copy of this songbook is available at ADLA, 1 M 522.

[118]Ibid., 6.

[119]Ruth Harris, *Lourdes: Body and Spirit in the Secular Age* (New York: Viking, 1999).

[120]Martin, *La Vendée de la mémoire*, 37-50.

[121]ADLA, 1 M 495, Machecoul Mayor to Prefect, May 18, 1815.

[122]ADLA, 1 M 495, Anonymous to Prefect, April 23, 1815.

[123]ADLA, 12 V 3, *Maréchal de camp* to Prefect, April 25, 1815.

[124]ADLA, 1 M 495. Nantes Sub-prefect to Prefect, June 18, 1815.

[125]ADLA, 1 M 509. Machecoul Mayor to Prefect, January 25, 1832.

[126]Ibid., Machecoul Mayor to Prefect, February 2, 1832.

[127]Ibid., Machecoul Mayor to Prefect, February 16, 1832.

[128]ADLA, 2 V 2. Machecoul Mayor to Prefect, March 2, 1832.

[129]For more on the uprising of 1832, see H. A. C. Collingham, *The July Monarchy: A Political History of France 1830-1848* (New York: Longman, 1988), 126-27.

[130]Martin, *La Vendée de la mémoire*, 96-97.

[131]ADLA, 1 M 512, Machecoul Mayor to Prefect, July 14, 1832.

[132]ADLA, 1 M 512. Report, Canton of Machecoul, July 12, 1832.

[133]ADLA, 13 V 1. Notes on Some *Curés* in the Arrondissement of Nantes, circa 1832.

[134]Launay, *Le diocèse de Nantes sous le second empire*, 2: 689-90.

[135]Marius Faugeras, "Un aspect local de la question romaine: L'aide nantais au Saint-Siège (1860-1870)," *Annales de Bretagne et des pays de l'Ouest* 90 (1983), 47-72.

[136]Martin, *La Vendée de la mémoire*, 129-30.

[137]Launay, *Le diocèse de Nantes sous le second empire*, 2: 733-35.

[138]Marius Faugeras, "Les fidèlités en France au XIXᵉ siècle: les zouaves pontificaux (1860-1870)," *Enquêtes et documents (Université de Nantes)* 11 (1985): 277.

[139]Launay, *Le diocèse de Nantes sous le second empire*, 2: 740-42.

[140]Faugeras, "Les fidèlités en France," 278-97.

[141]Jonas, 157-64.

[142]Launay, *Le diocèse de Nantes sous le second empire*, 2: 721-22.

[143]ADLA, 1 M 519. "Invitation to Prayers for the Faithful of the Diocese of Nantes," November 21, 1866.

[144]Martin, *La Vendée de la mémoire*, 130-31.

[145]The 1901 Law on Associations, which banned many religious orders in France, was viewed as a particularly grievous assault on Catholics in the vocation-rich west. See Ford, 135-69.

[146]Jean-Marie Mayeur, *La séparation des églises et de l'état* (Paris: Editions Ouvrières, 1991), 91-92.

[147]"L'inventaire des biens d'Eglise," *SRN*, January 13, 1906.

[148]Lyonel Michel Pellerin, *Bloc agraire et comportement paysan: Les réactions aux inventaires en Loire-Inférieure (Fevrier-Mars 1906)* (Nantes: Centre de Recherches Politique, 1976), 26-27.

[149]Mayeur, 182. The map of inventory protests coincides both with Tackett's map of the Ecclestiatical Oath of 1791 and Boulard's map of Catholic observance after World War II. The most serious inventory incidents took place where the majority of priests had rejected the Civil Constitution of the Clergy and where Catholic vitality was the strongest after 1945.

[150]Pellerin, 28-46.

[151]For a more detailed description of this incident, see Edward J. Woell, "Reviving the Vendée: The Separation of Church and State in a Western Rural Parish," in Barry Rothaus, ed., *Proceedings of the Western Society for French History: Selected Papers of the Annual Meeting*, vol. 25 (Greeley: Colorado University Press, 1998), 110-119.

[152]APM, Parish Journal, February 6, 1906.

[153]ADLA, 1 M 526. "Tribune Publique. L'inventaire cultuel à Machecoul," *Le Populaire*, 9 February 1906; ADLA, 92 V 98. Report of the Machecoul Fabrique, February 6, 1906.

[154]APM, Parish Journal, December 11, 1906.

[155]AN, F⁷ 12402. Machecoul Report, March 24, 1906.

[156]The demise of religious violence through ritual seems to complement Claude Langlois's argument that the Napoleonic Concordat was particularly effective in dissipating if not eliminating religious violence. See Langlois, "La disparition de la violence religieuse en France au 19e siècle," *French Historical Studies* 21 (Winter, 1998), 4-25.

[157]For more on popular perceptions of violence in nineteenth-century France, see Alain Corbin, *The Village of the Cannibals*.

Epilogue

In one sense this story concludes in the early twenty-first century—more than two hundred years after it began. But in another sense the narrative has come full circle by returning, as was done in Chapter One, to my first journey to Machecoul. One day after arriving in the town, the sound of church bells rudely interrupted my research in the parish archives. Taking a break from my efforts in the late morning, I wandered over to the church of Trinité to observe the mass commemorating the feast of All Saints. There I did my best to play the anthropologist by observing the rites of the natives and discerning their beliefs. Many sensations from that mass made an impression on me, but among the most striking was seeing the church absolutely full of parishioners: a stunning phenomenon in a nation renowned for empty Catholic churches and massive indifference toward organized Christianity. Having only attended a French mass a few times before, I was also taken aback by a higher degree of pastoral formality than was the custom in a parallel liturgy in the United States. The celebrant read his sermon, for example, from a prepared, written text and consistently stood at an elevated lectern while giving his address. In contrast, I had grown up accustomed to priests imparting remarks based on a few notes or an outline, which they usually delivered while standing on the same level where the laity was seated. But perhaps my most lasting memory of that mass was the serious demeanor of most parishioners. It was apparent to this stranger in town that the Machecoulais still took the proceedings as a sacred rite worthy of their earnest mental concentration and bodily discipline.

As noteworthy as the attendance and demeanor of parishioners at that liturgy were, it was also obvious that even within a town in France well known for an extraordinary degree of Catholic practice and belief, religious culture was less influential among the Machecoulais than was the case before World War I. This became more clear only a few days later during an ordinary Sunday mass; whereas the parish church was chock full on All Saints' Day, relatively few could be found there on the following Sunday. The most recently compiled data regarding mass attendance and communion reception (albeit in the 1950s and

1960s) confirmed the impression. According to the data, attendance at Sunday mass in the canton of Machecoul was appreciably lower than it had been in the nineteenth century—a trend that had obviously continued in the intervening forty years.[1] The parish's finances, particularly parishioners' contributions, likewise reflected a growing divide between the total number of Catholics in the parish and those attending mass on a regular basis; donations were down significantly during the early 1990s. In 1989 parish contributions averaged 1,094 francs per month, but in 1994 they averaged only 800 francs a month. The drop was even more considerable when the 1994 contributions were compared with those of 1985: a 41 percent decrease over nine years.[2]

The personal experience of mass attendance may seem to have little to do with massacres that took place two hundred years earlier, but the absence of any apparent connection stands as a testament to how much Machecoul had changed, especially after World War I. In other words, this one segment of the town's religious culture suggested a significant rupture with the past, for there was absolutely no hint of the town's previous troubles. Yet elsewhere, that same culture reflected remarkable continuity. While religion certainly was no longer the mover and shaker that it had been at Machecoul in the eighteenth and nineteenth centuries, neither had it disappeared. There continued to be a formidable institutional presence responsible for fostering the Catholic faith. Three Catholic schools were thriving in the town: the *École maternelle de Notre-Dame* (a preschool/daycare facility), the *École primaire de Saint-Honoré*, and the *Collège et Lycée de Saint-Joseph*. The *collège* boasted 890 students, while the *lycée* had 676 during the 1994-1995 academic year. Religious education remained a major priority at the *écoles*, but less so at the *collège* and the *lycée*. At the two latter institutions the emphasis was on foreign languages (English, Spanish, and German), vocational training, math, and science.[3] In terms of personnel, the fall in the number of priests had forced remaining clerics to pool their resources and become more mobile in their pastoral work. A community of five priests worked together at Machecoul in an *équipe pastoral*, performing pastoral duties not only at the parish of Trinité but also at other area parishes in La Marne, Fresnay, and Saint-Même. The priests took turns at different sacramental ministries: daily mass, preparations for marriage or baptism, or the occasional funeral. They continued to inhabit the nineteenth-century *presbytère* and lived well, though by no means lavishly. There also was much less of a presence of regular clergy in the commune than there had been during the previous century. A very small community of the Monfortian Brothers of Saint Gabriel resided within the town, with its few members teaching at the Catholic schools.

The institutional presence of the Catholic Church in the town, however, was only one aspect of this religious culture's staying power. Although the liturgical reforms of the Second Vatican Council did much to transform the rituals practiced by the Catholic Machecolais, from a long-term perspective the sacraments largely remained what they had been in the nineteenth century. Many popular devotions—most notably recitation of the Rosary—were still practiced, though admittedly to a much lesser degree. An additional indicator that the town maintained some traditional religious observance was found in an advertisement for various pilgrimages in the foyer of the parish church. In 1995 the diocese of Nantes sponsored numerous religious pilgrimages. Five separate pilgrimages to Lourdes were proposed: two exclusively for the diocese in the spring and summer, the first to be dedicated to Saint Grignion de Montfort in April, and the second in conjunction with the national pilgrimage on the feast of the Assumption. The diocese also advertised eight pilgrimages to other shrines as well: three to Israel; one to Lisieux; another to Pointmain; another to Assisi and Rome; and still others to Nevers, Ars, Le Puy, and Fatima.[4]

The noteworthy continuity of such ritual from the nineteenth century was somewhat offset by a marked contrast in the clergy's pastoral, social, and political points of view. By 1994 the parish clergy had all but discarded the old God of fear, fire, and brimstone, opting instead for a God of love and mercy. The priests seemed much more interested, moreover, in focusing on the problems of the here and now than on the implications for the afterlife. This new approach was apparent, for example, in a 1995 pamphlet issued by the Pastoral Council for the Machecoul Sector of the diocese on the then-upcoming elections for president and municipal council members. The council stated that Catholics should keep in mind three convictions as they went to the polls:

DEMOCRACY is a valuable yet fragile commodity. SOLIDAR-
ITY must increase in proportion to the growth of poverty and the
worsening of exclusion. RESPECT FOR THE OBLIGATION OF
HELPING those who, throughout the world, suffer persecution for
doing what is just.

In affirming the Catholic notion of human dignity, the council called
for parishioners to be mindful of the important role that work plays
in human life. It acknowledged that "our region has a certain need for
economic growth," but added that this growth could not be based on
the "sole law of profit." The council emphasized the need for a government to be conscious of "bioethical" questions and to embrace a genuine
respect for human life. Although not citing abortion, euthanasia, or
birth control *per se*, it advised against supporting a "science without
conscience"—one that failed to consider the ethical implications of its
progress. The council seemed to support the idea of a united Europe,
yet it warned that France should be "faithful to the sources of [Europe's]
authentic unity, which is spiritual." The council also expressed concern
about any future policy of emigration (and deportation) in France, particularly one that did not take into consideration the value of sustaining
and maintaining families.[5]

The teaching and preaching at Trinité, as at other parishes in the
region, suggested that the church in the diocese of Nantes had assumed
a moderate pastoral and cultural orientation by the end of the twentieth
century. Its clergy remained faithful to the teachings of the Pope and
the Magisterium, but at the same time was not totally unsympathetic
to Catholics who disagreed with the hierarchy in some matters. The
diocese's bishop in 1995, Monseigneur Emile Marcus, personified such
moderation. His temperance became evident during a controversy within
the French church in 1995. Early that year Pope John Paul II removed
Monseigneur Jacques Gaillot from his position as bishop of Evreux, in
part because of his public stands on a variety of issues, including his
advocacy of the use of prophylactics to prevent the spread of the HIV
virus and thus AIDS. The pope's decision generated much consternation among Catholics in France, in effect splitting clergy and laity down
the middle. For his part, Monseigneur Marcus issued a statement to
Catholics in his diocese, praising Monseigneur Gaillot for his advocacy
on behalf of those who suffer. Yet simultaneously he declared, "I am no

less in communion with the pope than is the entire diocese of Nantes. The day of my episcopal ordination, I engaged myself 'to work at building up the body of Christ, which is the Church, and to remain in its unity, with the college of bishops, under the authority of the successor of Peter.'"[6]

These statements are helpful for understanding the current religious culture fostered by the clergy, yet by themselves they tell us little about the beliefs and practices of the Machecoul laity. True, rates for clerical recruitment, mass attendance, and Easter communion can assist the scholar in gauging popular religious mentalities.[7] But these are merely superficial indicators of what the religious culture of laypeople may be, particularly at a time when the rates for all of these have considerably diminished throughout France. Fortunately, other kinds of documentation available in the parish archives lent themselves to a more thorough assessment of popular belief. In 1988 Monseigneur Marcus conducted a pastoral visit to the parish of Trinité, just as his predecessors had done in compliance with Tridentine reform. But in the more recent case, the clergy and the bishop prepared the parish for the visit in a fundamentally different way. Instead of holding a mission or marking the festival of Saint Honoré, Catholics assembled according to the neighborhoods in which they lived, reflected on a number of questions, and offered their views on the church and its role in their own lives.

The bishop of Nantes and Machecoul's clergy specifically asked the laity to think how life had changed over the past twenty to forty years, especially with regard to personal relationships, material conditions, and working conditions, and to consider how these changes influenced their views of the church, the family, and their community. In effect, the meetings served the purpose of fostering an ongoing dialogue between clergy and laity in France: a discourse somewhat indicative of the Second Vatican Council's conception of the Church as "the people of God." Although all parishioners were invited to these meetings, admittedly only a minority attended and participated in the discussion. In the *quartier* of those living along the route to Pornic, for example, seventy-two families were invited to participate, but only fifteen families were represented by the twenty individuals attending. Still, in the twenty-five neighborhood meetings held, more than four hundred families were represented, thereby making it a respectable sample.[8]

When considering the new conditions of life in the town, parishioners responded that television was perhaps the most important technological change, in part because it deterred individuals from establishing relationships with others outside the home and discouraged dialogue within the household. Yet many acknowledged that television enabled children to be more aware of the world in general. Another major change in life in and around the town, according to the parishioners, came in the area of work. Many commented that the rhythm of work was being accelerated and that it was now being done under a fear of unemployment and its consequences.[9] One reflection from a neighborhood group was typical in this sense:

> Rhythms are very accelerated. The machine did not liberate the person. We became somewhat of a slave to modernization. We work in order to have more comfort, through some sacrifice of our freedom. The type of work is dependent on the type of education. Movement is necessary for work. The fear of unemployment changes the ambiance of work, it increases the power of the employer, and diminishes the rights of workers.[10]

Parishioners also remarked that recreation had a more important role in their life than before. This, too, had implications for the family, life within the home, and ultimately the Church:

> Recreation, sports, the organizations to which we belong assume a large role in our life, sometimes to the detriment of our family life: all of this organizational activity requires participation in meetings since planning and preparation take time. Parents are often occupied by sports or the different activities of their children. In times past, many generations lived under the same roof and work was divided. Progress has provided a lot of comfort in the homes but also a lot of new constraints: more than housekeeping work, today cuisine is more elaborate.[11]

The remarks show that social cohesion was still a reality at Machecoul. But as opposed to the situation in the nineteenth century, the parish no longer was the primary source of that solidarity; it had been somewhat supplanted by sporting clubs and similar organizations.

When parishioners were asked about the Church sacraments, almost all said that they wished for a return to "collective absolution," apparently a liturgical rite that took the place of individual confession. Not long after this ritual was instituted, however, Pope John Paul II forbade its use. The parish clergy revealed that "in all the groups they regretted the suppression of collective absolution and they unanimously asked that it be reestablished. . . . the celebration provided the occasion for a very serious familial orientation. . . . It was vibrant for an examination of both conscience and our state of sin."[12] With regard to the Church's catechism, a few groups remarked that it was not as good as the catechism of the past since many children were ignorant of prayer, feast days, and the sacraments. Many believed that the notion of sin was not taught anymore, and that something new had to assume the motivational role that fear played in the past:

> Values change. The Church remains attached to the old values. The youth reproach [the Church] for being more attached to the letter of the law than the spirit. They have had more education and understand things differently than their parents. Their faith is not the same. For example, in our childhood, they inculcated us with the notion of sin, the fear of hell. What does that represent in our time?[13]

Parishioners realized that they now had to play a larger role of responsibility in the Church, especially since the number of priests was declining. More than a few groups felt that the priests needed to be more congenial and familiar: that they should visit parishioners more often and use language that is more accessible to the congregation. Still, most considered that the current relationship between priest and people was better than it had been in the past since there was more reciprocity. As one neighborhood phrased it, "One finds the priests truly 'trainers' whose message is well received. In the past they were considered as notables of society. Today they are a lot more accessible to their parishioners."[14] Most critically, many groups regretted the intransigence of the Church when it came to certain ethical questions, such as sexuality and reproduction. More than a few parishioners felt that the Church should take a position on social issues, but that it should not delve into politics and confine itself more to the spiritual implications of the teaching. One group explained that "the history of the Church shows that in the taking of official positions, the Church can be mistaken. Thus we do not accept [Church] positions on subjects of the day as the gospel truth. For example, in that which concerns sexuality, the official positions of the Church are too rigid. Why refuse the use of the pill? In-vitro fertilization?"[15] A few groups complained that all bishops did not take the same positions on matters, which to them was not only unfair but also made Church teaching unclear. This was especially the case on the issue of whether the divorced and remarried could participate in sacramental practice.[16]

Though the comments of the Machecoulais affirmed that religious culture was no longer as integral to their identity as had been the case in the eighteenth and nineteenth centuries, by no means did they indicate that the values, morals, and cultural principles of the Church had been abandoned. Indeed, this part of western France remained a socially and politically conservative part of the country, where traditional notions of family and community were still maintained in the late twentieth century. Despite the upheavals created by the fast pace of contemporary life, the traditional familial structure remained relatively intact in this region. Divorce rates were generally lower there, and inhabitants still tended to marry at a relatively later age. The political tendencies of the region remained—as they did throughout the nineteenth century—to the right of France's center, albeit the center of the nation's political spectrum had significantly shifted. Indeed, western dyed-in-the-wool royalists at the end of the twentieth century were few and far between. Still, the majority of inhabitants in and around Machecoul have consistently been, since the inception of the Fifth Republic, supporters of Gaullist parties and similar center-right political movements.[17]

The voting results of several of the most recent presidential elections offer good evidence of this region's continuing penchant for right-of-center conservatism. The second round of the 1981 French presidential election, for example, provided a clear choice between the Socialist François Mitterrand and the center-right's Valéry Giscard d'Estaing. The vast majority of cantons in the west, including that of Machecoul, opted for Giscard over Mitterand by a margin of about 10 to 20 percentage points. Over 80 percent of the people in one northern canton in the Vendée department, in fact, voted for the center-right candidate.[18] The same kind of results were seen during the second round of the French presidential elections in 1995, which again offered a clear choice between right and left: the Gaullist Jacques Chirac against the Socialist Lionel Jospin. Once more the west was among the regions most supportive of the Chirac candidacy once he was pitted against Jospin. In the administrative sector known as the Pays de la Loire, which includes the departments of the Loire-Atlantique, the Vendée, the Maine-et-Loire, the Mayenne, and the Sarthe, Chirac emerged victorious over Jospin by a margin of 54.29 to 45.7 percent.[19] This narrow margin of victory was somewhat misleading, though, because it failed to indicate the degree to which Chirac enjoyed widespread support among the rural inhabitants in the west (especially since their votes were offset by those of the leftist urbanites in Nantes, Saint-Nazaire, Laval, Le Mans, and La Roche-sur-Yonne).[20] When just the rural regions are viewed apart from the urbanized areas of the west, these elections suggested that the rural regions of the west continued to be one of the most solid center-right strongholds in France. A convincing argument can be made that such political preference has a clear correlation to the region's traditional religious culture. In a sociological profile done during the first round of the presidential elections in 1995, the French newspaper *Le Monde* found that those who identified themselves as *Catholiques pratiquants* had voted for Chirac or another center-right candidate over Jospin by a margin of more than four to one.[21]

All in all, the reflections made by the parishioners as well as the voting patterns in the west at large show that, from a long-term perspective, Catholic belief and practice among the Machecoulais have not been in decline so much as they have been in transition. Otherwise put, the town's religious culture may be in the process of moving "from one Catholicism to another," as Yves Lambert argued. In his study of sociological change and continuity in western France, Lambert emphasized that changes taking place in the realm of religious culture may not spell the end of organized religion or the disappearance of Catholicism in the west, but rather indicate that the Church was in the process of assuming a new role in the lives of individuals. According to Lambert, many remnants of Tridentine Catholicism were slowly disappearing, but in its place a new kind of Catholicism, emphasizing tolerance, pluralism, personal autonomy, and lay involvement, as well as fully embracing republican ideals in France, was increasingly taking root.[22] Such a transition, one can argue, may be leading to an even stronger commitment to the Church on behalf of families and individuals, especially since their participation in ritual and belief is no longer motivated by the social pressures and constraints that in the past sometimes prompted people living in small communities. Despite Lambert's optimism, however, the jury is still out on what religious culture may look like in the future at Machecoul. Given that the papacy of John Paul II was characterized by a refusal to accommodate those in the Church who disagreed with some of its teachings, it remains unclear whether many Catholics in France, including those at Machecoul, will conform to such teachings or perhaps part ways with the Church.

But what, if anything, does this current religious culture at Machecoul have to do with this story about "martyrs and murderers" in the eighteenth and nineteenth centuries? Admittedly—on the face of it—very little. Aside from the statue of Grignion de Montfort, the altar dedicated to the Sacred Heart in the Church of Trinité, and the small luncheon still held to commemorate the feast of Saint Honoré every May 16, there seemed to be very little evidence of the "culture wars" fought in the town in the eighteenth and nineteenth centuries. But therein lies a critical point that can be made about the phenomenon of memory. By the end of the twentieth century most Machecoulais had forgotten about the massacres. No doubt there were many reasons for this. Given the dynamic nature of contemporary society, historical consciousness is a rare find, even within a country with as storied a past as France. But this aside, one can argue that the process of forgetfulness essentially began in the nineteenth century, when a republican memory about what had happened there in 1793 increasingly disappeared from the minds of the Machecoulais. Meanwhile, a memory of a holy war—often ignoring the massacres altogether—increasingly gained acceptance, particularly in and through the town's religious culture. Perhaps the townspeople purposely denied the reality of an episode that devastated and divided the community. Perhaps this pursuit was relatively spontaneous, even unconscious. It is even conceivable that a certain degree of forgetfulness was all but necessary if inhabitants ever wanted to restore some semblance of civility within their town after the Revolution.

Yet such a rationale does little to explain the seeming disappearance of one of the most important long-term repercussions of the massacres, a memory of holy war. Why was this memory, which Chapter Five showed was so prominent within the town during the nineteenth century, largely unknown to the town's Catholics by 1994? In all likelihood much of this memory lost its meaning after World War I, not so much because of increasing secularization but rather because that war dictated a loss of one's local identity in preference to a national counterpart. In other words, once the Machecoulais defined themselves as "French," being "Vendéen" meant much less. The demise of royalism as a viable political option in France, moreover, likely demythologized the Old Regime, and to a degree the Vendéen insurgency as well. With the monarchy out of any political equation, the Old Regime was less likely to be seen as a golden age, let alone the insurgency as a fight for God and king. Finally, the comprehensive changes occurring within the French church itself in the nineteenth century—the transition from a God of fear to a God of love, the reconciliation with a democratic and republican political tradition—were finally felt in the rural parishes of western France, if not between the world wars, then most certainly after 1945. Thus Tridentine Catholicism, so integral to a memory of holy war, seemingly failed to resonate among new generations of townspeople.

This is not to say, however, that this particular memory, much less the contest over republican and insurgent memories that arose immediately after the massacres, disappeared altogether. On the contrary, there remains a small but very vocal minority in western France that continues to contest how the Revolution is remembered, and perhaps a smaller number there strives to maintain a memory of holy war as it was understood in the nineteenth century. Indeed, several organizations in the region have made it a point to preserve a largely insurgent memory of the War of Vendée. The largest and most important of these is the Souvenir vendéen, which was first established in 1932 and remains active to this day. The mission statement of the organization points to its obligation of clarifying not only what happened during the 1790s but also what these events purportedly represented:

> We are not neutral in the combat, which since 1793 has never ceased between the Revolution and Christian civilization. . . . The Revolution not only consisted of a change in the political regime. It made a *tabula rasa*. It prevented necessary reforms. . . . It crushed natural

liberties and bequeathed to us centralized institutions and the entire yoke that is choking us.[23]

The organization's rhetoric seemingly justifies the historian Jean-Clément Martin's description of the War of Vendée, two hundred years after it began, as a "guerre interminable."

Another regional organization dedicated to maintaining a mostly insurgent memory is the Association Vendée militaire, whose members continue to hold memorial services, erect placards and statues, and sponsor commemorations of the civil war. An example of their handiwork is the cross erected at the place Viarme in Nantes that marks the execution of Charette de la Contrie there on March 29, 1796. The cross, as seen in Figure E.1, has a fleur-de-lis at the end of each of the crosses' arms and a symbol of the Sacred Heart at its center. This association claims to remain above the polemical fray, but its own mission statement reflects a desire to perpetuate an insurgent memory:

> The Association Vendée militaire always chooses to venture in places marked by Vendéen history or by the personality of a leader. This association, which edits a review entitled Savoir [to know] wants to remain without ideological baggage. Its goal is to return to the true Vendée, the real Vendée that history and sentiment deformed over the previous century through a number of works judged too often as partisan.[24]

True, such groups represent a small minority standing on the political and cultural margins of modern society. But even within the context of the spatial mainstream, Vendéen symbols and signs abound, thus indicating that there has been an ongoing effort to maintain an insurgent memory, if not a memory of holy war. Among them is a prominent mosaic located on the floor in the exact center of the parish church of Trinité at Machecoul, as seen in Figure E.2 (see page 252). The mosaic depicts the *double-coeur*, signifying the devotions of the Sacred Heart of Jesus and the Immaculate Heart of Mary. Although this symbol is a relatively new one (emerging, according to Jean-Clément Martin, after World War II), it has become synonymous not only with the department of the Vendée but with the 1793 insurgency as well.[25]

Figure E.1
The Memorial to Charette de la Contrie at the Place
Viarme in Nantes, 1995.
(Two photographs by the author, 1994-1995.)

The bicentenary of the French Revolution in 1989 saw yet more confrontations between competing memories, particularly with regard to the civil war in western France. When the Socialist city council of La Roche-sur-Yon, the departmental seat of the Vendée, appropriated three thousand francs for a bicentennial celebration, a critic of the council suggested that "it should pay for some guillotines as well." On three separate occasions the municipality had to replant its tree of liberty, no doubt due to the actions of politically inspired vandals. On the other side, some proponents of an insurgent memory in the Maine-et-Loire complained that a Vendéen war sanctuary was desecrated and that the heads of statues depicting two Vendéen generals were broken off. At Nantes the local historical association ostracized a schoolteacher for serving as a prefect's correspondent for the commemoration. Some partisans also condemned the decision of the Nantes city council to celebrate the bicentennial at a place within viewing distance of the site where Carrier had sent Machecoul's abbé Hervé de la Bauche and other

Figure E.2
The Double-Coeur Symbol in the Church of Trinité at Machecoul, 1994.
(Photograph by the author, 1994-1995.)

priests to their death in the Loire River back in 1793. Looking ahead to the two-hundred-year anniversary of the insurrection in 1993, the conservative-led General Council of the department of the Vendée called for creation of a center devoted to the study of counterrevolution.[26]

Those dreams became a reality in 1994, when partisan scholars created the Centre Vendéen de recherches historiques. From the very beginning the center has staked a claim to scholarly legitimacy, largely by associating itself with academic historians in France. The center's website, for example, explains that the idea for the center was conceived by Emmanuel Le Roy Ladurie, and that the center's "scientific council" was first led by François Furet and Pierre Chaunu (though it is not clear exactly how active they had been in the organization). The center itself is directed by Alain Gérard who, as suggested in Chapter Four, is one of the leading contemporary purveyors of an insurgent memory and has written about the Machecoul massacres. The center also claims an academic legitimacy because it "organizes colloquia and publishes books concerning the Vendée, in addition to the *Revue recherches vendéenes*," apparently a journal sent to its members and regional depositories. The center declares itself, moreover, a "laboratory of ideas and the place of exchanges between researchers who work on the Vendée."[27] True to its word, it has published numerous books, including *Christianisme et Vendée*, *Les vendéens des origines à nos jours*, and *D'une grande guerre à l'autre: La Vendée, 1793-1914*.[28]

But while the center suggests an openness to varying perspectives of the civil war, even a superficial examination of its website exposes a decidedly insurgent memory. On the map showing the various incidents in the War of Vendée from March to September 1793, for instance, there is no indication of Machecoul, where—even the most ardent insurgent sympathizer must acknowledge—atrocities were done to republicans in March and April 1793.[29] The center's historical time line posted on its website only suggests that "many parishes" revolted on March 11 and 12, but again with no reference to the massacres at Machecoul.[30] Yet at the same time, the time line goes into much detail regarding atrocities committed by republican troops in 1794. The entry for the massacre at Lucs by the infernal columns of the republican army states that 564 persons were killed there, "including 110 children less than eight years old."[31] Thus, while the center claims that it is telling the true story of civil war (though admittedly in this case directed toward the casual websurfer), it fails to document the Machecoul massacres, likely in a conscious effort to minimize any kind of insurgent culpability. In this way an insurgent memory of those events continues.

Similarly, key elements of a memory of holy war still can be found, particularly among conservative Catholics in western France. On February 26, 1984, the Catholic Church beatified ninety-nine martyrs killed during the Revolution. Jean-Clément Martin found it significant that among those attending were Polish priests, suggesting that analogies were being made between the persecution of Catholic Poles by Communists in the 1980s and that of Catholics of western France by republicans in 1793 and 1794. As Martin himself put it, "Lech Walesa is the new Cathlineau." For Martin such a commemoration represented both the persistence and the plasticity of the region's memory of the insurgency.[32] If seen within a context including a memory of holy war, however, the historical continuities become more clear.

Recent manifestations of the memory did not end there. In 1989, with the blessings of Pope John Paul II, the primate of Poland, Joseph Cardinal Glemp, traveled to western France at the invitation of the politician who most identified himself with an insurgent memory, Philippe de Villiers. At one mass the Polish cardinal paid homage to those who, he claimed, had died for their faith in the 1790s, and he took the occasion to condemn the French Revolution for creating the "illusion of a perfect world that did not require salvation and thus had no need of God, of a moral order, or of the Church of Christ."[33] Many Catholic bishops in France, moreover, initially were reluctant about allowing Catholics to join in the bicentenary celebration, although they ultimately gave their approval.[34] No doubt the manifestations of a memory of holy war are increasingly rare. All the same, there may be much presumption in writing its obituary.

Bringing the contest of memories about revolution and counterrevolution as well as a memory of holy war up to date provides yet another illustration of how arduous and illusive the study of an episode like the Machecoul massacres can be. As if the lack of documentation and conflicting accounts of what happened during the civil war were not enough, such difficulties are exacerbated by ongoing bickering over the past, particularly among some who persist in embracing either one of the two opposing memories of the 1790s. Those seeking to study any aspect of the War of Vendée are therefore likely to find themselves caught in a complicated web of history and memory in which it is exceedingly difficult to determine where one ends and the other begins. And even if scholars are freed from such tangled constraints, awaiting them is a complexity that flies in the face of simplifications too often made by the contested memories documented here.

What simplifications? What complexity? This story shows that during the late Old Regime, Machecoul was neither a completely peaceful and religiously obedient community marked by a just and well-ordered hierarchy, nor an oppressed town dominated by clerical greed, institutional corruption, and religious repression. Rather, the town was home to a pronounced cultural divide involving religious beliefs, practices, and institutions. Similarly, the French Revolution in this small town represented neither an atheistic campaign to eliminate Catholic belief and practice nor a selfless effort at democratization that later became derailed by a deceptive and superstitious clergy, a perfidious nobility, and their blind and recalcitrant sycophants. Instead, the Revolution—above all its religious reforms—activated a dialectic in the town that, in and of itself, produced unprecedented political, economic, and religious disaffection among its inhabitants, both rich and poor.

Just as significant to the story, the Machecoul massacres constituted neither a legitimate defense against the genocidal rage of a totalitarian republic nor a zealous, sadistic bloodletting encouraged, if not led, by vengeful priests and their fanatical followers. Rather, the massacres typified a civil war in the truest sense of the term: one in which brutal killings and similar atrocities done to innocents were committed and ideologically justified by revolutionaries and counterrevolutionaries alike. For that matter, during the nineteenth century the Catholic Machecoulais had little interest in propagating polemical falsehoods about the massacres and the reprisals that followed. More accurately, they subscribed to a valuable, self-sustaining memory: one that accentuated some parts of their troubled past while overlooking others. Overall, this narrative suggests that the two sides that clashed at Machecoul in 1793—contrary to the contested memories that arose from the massacres and are still prevalent—had their fair share of both martyrs and murderers. Such a story will remain repugnant, though, to all who persist in remembering the same episode in completely contradictory ways.

Notes

[1] In the 1950s regular mass attendance at Machecoul stood at 74 percent, while Easter communion stood at 70 percent. It is very rare in post-World War II France to see areas with even strong religious adherence having mass attendance and Easter communion rates above 80 percent, whereas in the nineteenth century the same areas reported mass attendance at 90 or 95 percent. See François-André Isambert and Jean-Paul Terrenoire, *Atlas de la pratique religieuse des catholiques en France* (Paris: Éditions du C.N.R.S., 1980), 29, 34, 51.

[2] APM, "Moyenne des billets et pièces de monnaie à la quête des dimanches ordinaires," ca. January 1995 (provided by the *curé*, Monsieur l'abbé Jean Garaud).

[3] ACM, "Structure pédagogique du collège, année scolaire 1994-1995," ca. November 1994, "Structure pédagogique du lycée, année scolaire 1994-1995," ca. November 1994 (furnished by the principal of the institution).

[4] Advertisements for the pilgrimages and lectures were posted on the bulletin board within the parish church of Trinité.

[5]APM, "Conseil pastoral du secteur de Machecoul. Les élections," January 1995.

[6]Émile Marcus, "Qu'allons-nous faire de cette épreuve?" ca. March 1995. Photocopies of this statement apparently were distributed to all of the parishes in the diocese.

[7]Imambert and Terrenoire, 34-36.

[8]Approximately 1,500 families belonged to the parish, meaning that about 27 percent of all families participated in the meetings.

[9]APM, "Synthèse de réflexions en quartiers pour la visite du P. Marcus," January 1988.

[10]Ibid., "Rénunion de quartier route de Challans," December 21, 1987.

[11]Ibid., "Réunion de quartier route de Pornic," December 18, 1987.

[12]Ibid., "Rencontres des quartiers, paroisse de Machecoul," no date.

[13]Ibid., "Réunion de Quartier, route de Pornic," December 18, 1987.

[14]Ibid., "Rencontre du quartier des Basclotières," December 17, 1987.

[15]Ibid., "Rencontre lotissement des Moulins," January 12, 1988.

[16]Ibid., "Synthèse," no date.

[17]Yves Lambert, "Famille, Politique et Religion," in *L'Ouest bouge-t-il? Son changement social et culturel depuis trente ans* (Nantes: Reflets du passé, 1983), 195-222.

[18]Ibid., 208-13.

[19]"Les résultats du second tour de l'élection présidentielle: Pays de la Loire," *Le Monde*, May 9, 1995, 42.

[20]Note that the Socialist, Communist, and other leftist parties control many of the municipal governments in the west, including those of Nantes as well as its working-class suburbs such as Bougenais, Carquefou, Rezé, and Saint-Herblain. See "Le premier tour des élections municipales: Loire-Atlantique," *Le Monde*, June 13, 1995, 41-42.

[21]The percentage of votes that the candidates received from those who identified themselves as practicing Catholics were as follows: Laguiller, 4; Hue, 3; Jospin, 15; Voynet, 2; Balladur, 37; Chirac, 26; de Villiers, 5; Le Pen, 8; and Cheminade, 0 percent. See "Tableau 1: Profil sociologique," *Le Monde*, April 25, 1995, 10.

[22]Lambert, 230.

[23]Jean-Clément Martin, *Une guerre interminable, la Vendée deux cents ans après* (Nantes: Reflets du passé, 1985), 44-49.

[24]Ibid., 49-56.

[25]Ibid, 31-39.

[26]Ibid., 106-7.

27"Presentation du centre vendéen de recherches historiques," http://www.histoire-vendée.com/present.htm (Accessed January 15, 2004).

28"Catalogue de publication du centre vendéen de recherches historiques," http://www.histoire-vendée.com/catalog.php (Accessed January 15, 2004).

29"Le pré-carré vendéen (mars-septembre 1793)," http://www.histoire-vendée.com/images/P8_gformat.jpg (Accessed January 15, 2004).

30"Le Vendée des origines à nos jours," http://www.histoire-vendée.com/histoire4.php (Accessed January 15, 2004).

31"Le Vendée des origines à nos jours," http://www.histoire-vendée.com/histoire5.php (Accessed January 15, 2004).

32Martin, *Une guerre interminable*, 146. Martin also observed that comparisons were drawn between the 1790 Civil Constitution of the Clergy and François Mitterrand's attempt to restrict parochial schools in France in 1984. The initiative failed in part because of popular protest, most notably in the west.

33Kaplan, 101-5.

34Kaplan illustrates divisions within the church over the bicentenary. While integrists condemned the commemoration and conservative Catholics viewed it with much apprehension, moderate and liberal Catholics (led by Monseigneur Gaillot, the bishop of Evreux) took part in many of the celebrations. See Kaplan, 112-33.

Bibliography

Primary Sources

Archival Material

Archives nationales (CARAN)
Series F⁷. Police générale; Series F¹⁹. Cultes; Series K. Villes et provinces.

Archives départementales de la Loire-Atlantique
Series E. État civil; Series Fi. Cartes et plans; Series G. Clergé séculier; Series
   H. Clergé régulier; Series L. Administration révolutionnaire; Series M.
   Administration générale et économie; Series O. Administration et compt-
   abilités communales; Series Q. Domaines; Series T. Instruction publique,
   sciences et arts; Series V. Cultes; Series X. Bienfaisance, assistance, et
   prévoyance sociale.

Archives épiscopales du diocèse de Nantes
Boîte de Machecoul.

Archives paroissiales de Machecoul (Trinité)
Cantique à Saint-Honoré; Pastoral Visit Reports, 1854, 1863, 1876, 1881, 1889,
   1988; Parish Journal; Agendae ecclésiastique; Order of Procession for Saint-
   Honoré, 1848; Bishop of Nantes to Machecoul Curé, 8 April 1853; "Vie
   paroissiale;" Registry of the Christian Mothers; Registry of the Machecoul
   Catholic Youth; Registry of the Children of Mary; Registry of the Gilles
   de Retz; Registry of the Saint Vincent de Paul Society; Sermons; Hubert
   Breheret, "Signes de Croix sur nos routes de Machecoul;" Cemetery Plan.

Archives collégiales de Machecoul (Saint-Joseph)
"Annales du pensionnat des frères de Saint-Gabriel, Machecoul." ca. 1869-
   1912.

Printed Sources

Adresse à l'Assemblée Nationale. Nantes: Gigougeux, 1790

Almanach nantais et journalier. Nantes: Imprimerie de Mme. Hérault, 1811.

*Archives parlementaires de 1787 à 1860; recueil complêt des débats législatifs et
   politiques des chambres françaises, première série (1787-1799).* Vols. 60-92.
   Paris: Centre national de la recherche scientific, 1869.

Bethuis, Germain. *Les massacres de Machecoul et considérations générales sur la
   guerre de la Vendée.* Nantes: Imprimerie Mangin et Giraud, 1873.

Briand, P.-M. *Notices sur les confesseurs de la foi dans le diocèse de Nantes pendant la Révolution.* Nantes: Librairie Lanoë-Mazeau, 1903.

Catéchisme à l'usage des fidèles, dans les circonstances actuelles. 1791.

Catéchismes (premier et second) du diocèse de Nantes, imprimé par ordre de Monseigneur Jean Augustin Frétat de Sarra, évêque de Nantes. Nantes: Bourgeois, 1781.

Catéchisme de Nantes, imprimé par ordre de Monseigneur de Guérines, évêque de Nantes. Nantes: Imprimerie Bourgeois, 1826.

Catéchisme de Nantes, Imprimé par ordre de Monseigneur de Guérines, évêque de Nantes: Nouvelle édition revue et autorisée par Monseigneur Journier. Nantes: Imprimerie Bourgeois, 1870.

Catéchisme de Nantes, Imprimé par ordre de Monseigneur de Guérines, évêque de Nantes: Nouvelle édition revue et autorisée par Monseigneur LeCoq. Nantes: Imprimerie Bourgeois, 1888.

Dumas, Alexandre. *The She-Wolves of Machecoul.* Boston: Little, Brown, and Company, 1894.

Eutrope de la Laurencie, Charles. *Ordonnance de Monseigneur l'Évêque de Nantes, au sujet de l'election faite par les electeurs du département, du Sieur Julien Minée, pour Évêque du département de la Loire-Inférieure.* Gand: Imprimerie de Crapart, 1791.

Hacquet, Pierre (Frère). *Mémoire des missions des Monfortains dans l'Ouest (1740-1779): Contribution à la sociologie religieuse historique.* Edited by Louis Pérouas. Fontenay-le-Comte: Université de Poitiers, 1964.

Huet, J.-B. *Statistiques du département de la Loire-Inférieure.* Paris: Imprimerie des Sourds-Muets, an X (1801-02).

⁻ *Recherches économiques et statistiques sur le département de la Loire-Inférieure.* Nantes: M. Malassis, an XI (1802-03).

Manuel des pèlerins de la ville et du diocèse de Nantes à Notre Dame de Lourdes, 27 Aoft 1877. Nantes: Bourgeois, 1877.

Michelet, Jules. *Histoire de la Révolution française.* 2 Vols. Paris: Gallimard, 1952.

Le Monde. April, May, June, 1995.

Moniteur Universel (also entitled *Gazette National*). Paris, 1789-1810.

Reglement pour l'école secondaire à Machecoul. Nantes: Forest, 1807.

Semaine religieuse du diocése de Nantes. 1865-1914, 1924.

Young, Arthur. *Travels in France during the Years 1787, 1788, and 1789.* Edited by Constantia Maxwell. Cambridge: Cambridge University Press, 1950.

Secondary Sources

Works of Reference

Abbad, Fabrice, ed. *La Loire-Atlantique des origines à nos jours*. Saint-Jean d'Angély: Éditions Bordessoules, 1984.

Ashley, Percy. *Local and Central Government: A Comparative Study of England, France, Prussia, and the United States*. College Park: McGrath Publishing, 1969.

Augris, Frédéric. *Vendéens et républicains dans la guerre de Vendée 1793-1796*, 2 vols. Cholet: Éditions du Choletais, 1993.

Berranger Henri (de). *Guide des archives de la Loire-Atlantique*. 2 Vols. Nantes: Imprimerie de Bretagne, 1962.

Boulard, Fernand. *An Introduction to Religious Sociology: Pioneer Work in France*. Translated by M. J. Jackson. London: Darton, Longman and Todd, 1960.

Deville, Raymond. *The French School of Spirituality: An Introduction and Reader*. Translated by Agnes Cunningham. Pittsburgh: Duquesne University Press, 1994.

Furet, François, and Mona Ozouf. *A Critical Dictionary of the French Revolution*. Translated by Arthur Goldhammer. Cambridge, Mass: Harvard University Press, 1989.

Imbert, Jean, ed. *Administration et église du concordat à la séparation de l'église et de l'état*. Geneva: Libraire Droz, 1987.

Isambert, François-André, and Jean-Paul Terrenoire, *Atlas de la pratique religieuse des catholiques en France*. Paris: CNRS, 1980.

Ladame, Jean. *Les saints de la piété populaire*. Paris: Éditions S.O.S., 1991.

Marion, Marcel. *Dictionnaire des institutions de la France aux XVIIe et XVIIIe siècles*. Paris: Éditions A. et J. Picard et compagnie, 1969.

Répetoire des visites pastorales de la France. Première série: *Anciens diocèses (Jusqu'en 1790)*. 4 Vols. Paris: CNRS, 1983.

Schmidt, Vivian A. *Democratizing France: The Political and Administrative History of Decentralization*. Cambridge: Cambridge University Press, 1990.

Scott, Samuel F., and Barry Rothaus, eds. *Historical Dictionary of the French Revolution*. 2 Vols. Westport: Greenwood Press, 1985.

Vincent, A. L. and Clare Binns, *Gilles de Rais: The Original Bluebeard*. London: A. M. Philpot, 1926.

Books, Articles, and Unpublished Studies

Adams, Thomas McStay. *Bureaucrats and Beggars: French Social Policy in the Age of Enlightenment.* New York: Oxford University Press, 1990.

Agulhon, Maurice. *Marianne into Battle: Republican Imagery and Symbolism in France 1780-1880*, trans. Janet Lloyd (Cambridge: Cambridge University Press, 1981).

Aoustin, Jean. "Répercussions démographiques et économiques de la Révolution dans la région insurgée de Machecoul." Mémoire principal pour le diplome d'études supérieures d'histoire. Directed by J. Bois. Nantes: Université de Nantes, 1966.

Arnold, Odile. *Le corps et l'âme: La vie des religieuses au XIXe siècle.* Paris: Éditions du Seuil, 1984.

Aston, Nigel. *Religion and Revolution in France, 1780-1804.* Washington, D. C.: Catholic University Press, 2000.

Bachelier, A. *Le jansénisme à Nantes.* Paris: Nizet and Bastard, 1934.

Baecque, Antoine (de). *Glory and Terror: Seven Deaths under the French Revolution.* Translated by Charlotte Mandell. New York: Routledge, 2003.

Bak, János M. and Gerhard Benecke, eds. *Religion and Rural Revolt.* Manchester: Manchester University Press, 1984.

Baker, Keith M. *Inventing the French Revolution: Essays on French Political Culture in the Eighteenth Century.* New York: Cambridge University Press, 1990.

————., ed. *The French Revolution and the Creation of Modern Political Culture.* 4 vols. Oxford: Pergamon Press, 1994.

Bareau, Gwénaël. "L'épiscopat nantais de Monseigneur LeCoq (1877-1892)." Mémoire de maîtrise. Directed by M. Launay. Nantes: Université de Nantes, 1993.

Baynast, Anne (de). "La vente des biens nationaux du première origine dans le district de Machecoul, 1790-1793." Mémoire de maîtrise. Directed by P. Bossis. Nantes: Université de Nantes, 1988.

Bazin, Jean-Pierre. "Les origines géographiques et sociales du clergé nantais au XVIIIe siècle." Mémoire de maîtrise. Directed by Y. Durand. Nantes: Université de Nantes, 1975.

Bernard, Yveline. "L'épiscopat de Monseigneur Rouard, évêque de Nantes de 1896 à 1914." Mémoire de maîtrise. Directed by M. Launay. Nantes: Université de Nantes, 1989.

Berthelot du Chesnay, Charles. *Les prêtres séculiers en Haute-Bretagne au XVIIIe siècle.* Rennes: Université de Rennes, 1984.

Blanning, T. C. W. *The French Revolutionary Wars, 1787-1802.* London: Arnold Publishers, 1996.

Bloch, Marc. *French Rural History: An Essay on its Basic Characteristics*. Translated by Janet Sondheimer. Berkeley: University of California Press, 1966.

———. *The Royal Touch: Sacred Monarchy and Scrofula in England and France*. Translated by J. E. Anderson. London: Routledge and Kegan Paul, 1973.

Bois, Paul. *Paysans de l'Ouest: Des structures économiques et sociales aux options politiques depuis l'époque révolutionnaire dans la Sarthe*. Paris: Flammarion, 1971.

Boucard, Victor. *Saint Honoré patron des boulangers: Son culte à Machecoul et dans le pays de Retz*. Nantes: Imprimerie Saint-Clément, 1938.

———. "Les anciens moulins de Machecoul." *Bulletin de la société archéologique et histoirique de Nantes et de la Loire-Inférieure*, 87 (1948): 98-107.

Boulard, Fernand. "Matériaux pour l'histoire religieuse du peuple français: Aspects de la pratique religieuse en France 1802-1939: L'exemple des pays de Loire." *Annales économies, sociétés, civilisations*, 31 (1976): 782-88.

———, ed. *Matériaux pour l'histoire religieuse du peuple français, XIXᵉ-XXᵉ siècles*. 2 Vols. Paris: CNRS, 1982.

Bourrigaud, René. *Le développement agricole au 19ᵉ siècle*. Nantes: Centre d'Histoire du Travail de Nantes, 1994.

Bradley, James E. and Dale Van Kley, eds. *Religion and Politics in Enlightenment Europe*. Notre Dame: University of Notre Dame Press, 2001.

Braudel, Fernand. *The Identity of France*. Translated by Siân Reynolds. 4 Vols. New York: Harper Perennial, 1993.

Brégeon, Jean-Joël. *Carrier et la terreur nantais*. Paris: Librairie académique Perrin, 1987.

Breguet, Marie. *L'avant-guerre de Vendée: Les questions religieuses à l'Assemblé législative*. Paris: Téqui, 2004.

Burke, Peter. *Popular Culture in Early Modern Europe*. 2d ed. Aldershot: Ashgate, 1994.

Burns, Michael. *Rural Society and French Politics: Boulangism and the Dreyfus Affair*. Princeton: Princeton University Press, 1984.

Chartier, Roger. *The Cultural Origins of the French Revolution*. Translated by Lydia G. Cochrane. Durham: Duke University Press, 1991.

Chassin, Charles-Louis. *La préparation de la guerre de Vendée 1789-1793*. 3 vols. Paris: Imprimerie Paul Dupont, 1892.

Châtellier, Louis. *The Religion of the Poor: Rural Missions in Europe and the Formation of Modern Catholicism, c. 1500-c. 1800*. Translated by Brian Pearce. New York: Cambridge University Press, 1997.

Chéneau, Yves. *Les marches commune du Poitou et de Bretagne et leur paroisses au XVIIIᵉ siècle*. Cholet: Imprimerie Farré et Freulon, 1950.

Cholvy, Gérard. "'Du Dieu terrible au Dieu d'amour:' Une évolution dans la sensibilité religieuse au XIXᵉ siècle." *109ᵉ Congrès de la société savantes, Dijon, 1984* 11 (1984): 141-54.

———, and Yves-Marie Hilaire. *Histoire religieuse de la France contemporaine.* 3 Vols. Toulouse: Éditions Privat, 1985.

———. *La religion en France de la fin du XVIIIᵉ siècle à nos jours.* Paris: Hachette, 1991.

Chotard, Jean-René. "L'apport des procès-verbaux de visite pastorale à la connaissance de la société rurale dans le diocèse de Nantes sous la restauration." *Annales de Bretagne et des pays de l'Ouest* 80 (1973): 345-57.

Cobban, Alfred. *The Social Interpretation of the French Revolution.* Cambridge: Cambridge University Press, 1964.

Collingham, H. A. C. *The July Monarchy: A Political History of France 1830-1848.* New York: Longman, 1988.

Corbin, Alain. *The Village of Cannibals: Rage and Murder in France, 1870.* Translated by Arthur Goldhammer. Cambridge, Mass.: Harvard University Press, 1992.

Cousin, Bernard, Monique Cubells, and René Moulinas. *La pique et la croix: Histoire religieuse de la Révolution française.* Paris: Centurion, 1989.

Croix, Alan and François (Fanch) Roudat. *Les bretons, la mort et dieu de 1600 à nos jours.* Paris: Messidor Temps Actuels, 1984.

Crouzet, Denis. *Les guerriers de Dieu: La violence au temps des troubles de religion (vers 1525-vers 1610).* 2 Vols. Seysell: Champ Vallon, 1990.

Curtis, Sarah. *Educating the Faithful: Religion, Schooling, and Society in Nineteenth-Century France.* DeKalb: Northern Illinois University Press, 2000.

Dansette, Adrien. *Religious History of Modern France.* 2 Vols. Translated by John Dingle. New York: Herder and Herder, 1961.

Darnton, Robert. *The Great Cat Massacre and Other Episodes in French Cultural History.* New York: Random House, 1985.

———. *The Forbidden Best-Sellers of Pre-Revolutionary France.* New York: W. W. Norton and Company, 1995.

Delhommeau, Louis. *Le clergé vendéen face à la Révolution.* La Roche-sur-Yon: Siloë, 1992.

Delumeau, Jean. *Histoire vécue du peuple chrétien.* 2 Vols. Toulouse: Privat, 1979.

———. *Sin and Fear: The Emergence of a Western Guilt Culture 13th-18th Centuries.* Translated by Eric Nicholson. New York: St. Martin's Press, 1990.

Devlin, Judith. *The Superstitious Mind: French Peasants and the Supernatural in the Nineteenth Century.* New Haven: Yale University Press, 1987.

Doyle, William. *The Oxford History of the French Revolution*. New York: Oxford University Press, 1989.

———. *Jansenism: Catholic Resistance to Authority from the Reformation to the French Revolution*. New York: St. Martin's Press, 2000.

Dumarcet, Lionel. *François-Athanase Charette de La Contrie: Une histoire véritable*. Paris: Éditions Les 3 Orangers, 1997.

Dupâquier, Jacques, ed. *Histoire de la population française*. 4 Vols. Paris: Presses universitaires de France, 1988.

Dupuy, Roger. *De la Révolution à la Chouannerie: Paysans en Bretagne 1788-1794*. Paris: Flammarion, 1988.

———. *Les chouans*. Paris: Hachette Littératures, 1997.

Durand, Yves, ed. *Le diocèse de Nantes*. Paris: Beauchesne, 1985.

———. "Anticlericalisme et politique dans l'Ouest de la France à la fin du XVIIIᵉ siècle." *Histoire, économie, société* 9 (1990): 243-58.

Durkheim, Émile. *The Elementary Forms of Religious Life*. Translated by Karen E. Fields. New York: The Free Press, 1995.

Evans, Richard J. *In Defense of History*. New York: W. W. Norton, 1999.

Faucheux, Marcel. *L'insurrection vendéene de 1793: Aspects économiques et sociaux*. Paris: Imprimerie Nationale, 1964.

Faugeras, Marius. *Le diocèse de Nantes sous la monarchie censitaire (1813-1822-1849)*. 2 Vols. Fontenay-le-Comte: Imprimerie Lussaud Frères, 1964.

———. "Les vocations religieuses des femmes dans le diocèse de Nantes au XIXᵉ siècle (1803-1914)." *Enquêtes et Documents (Université de Nantes)* 1 (1971): 239-81.

———. "Vocations sacerdotales séculières au XIXᵉ siècle (1803-1914) dans le diocèse de Nantes." *Mémoires de la société archéologique et historique de Nantes et de Loire-Atlantique* 117 (1981): 101-32.

———. "Vocations religieuses d'hommes dans le diocèse de Nantes au XIXᵉ siècle." *Mémoires de la société archéologique et historique de Nantes et de Loire-Atlantique* 118 (1982): 39-59.

———. "Un aspect local de la question romaine: L'aide nantais au saint-siège (1860-1870)." *Annales de Bretagne et des pays de l'Ouest* 90 (1983): 47-72.

———. "Les fidèlités en France au XIXᵉ siècles: Les zouaves pontificaux (1860-1870)." *Enquêtes et documents (Université de Nantes)* 11 (1985): 275-303.

———. "Le diocèse de Nantes à la veille de la Révolution." *Mémoires de la société archéologique et historique de Nantes et de Loire-Atlantique* 124 (1988): 34-45.

Favret-Saada, Jeanne. *Deadly Words: Witchcraft in the Bocage*. Translated by Catherine Cullen. Cambridge: Cambridge University Press, 1980.

Fitzsimmons, Michael P. *The Night the Old Regime Ended: August 4, 1789 and the French Revolution.* University Park: Penn State University Press, 2003.

Ford, Caroline. *Creating the Nation in Provincial France: Religion and Political Identity in Brittany.* Princeton: Princeton University Press, 1993.

Furet, François. *Interpreting the French Revolution.* Translated by Elborg Forster. New York: Cambridge University Press, 1981.

Gabory, Émile. *La Révolution et la Vendée d'après des documents inédits: Les deux patries janvier 1789 à août 1793.* Paris: Libraire académique Perrin, 1941.

Geertz, Clifford. *Negara: The Theater State in Nineteenth-Century Bali.* Princeton: Princeton University Press, 1980.

Gerard, Alain. *La Vendée, 1789-1793.* Paris: Champ Vallon, 1992.

Gernoux, Alfred. "Maires de Machecoul." *Annales de Nantes et du pays nanatis,* 64 (1971): 27-28.

Gibson, Ralph. "Hellfire and Damnation in Nineteenth-Century France." *Catholic Historical Review* 74 (1988): 383-402.

———. *A Social History of French Catholicism 1789-1914.* New York: Routledge, 1989.

Gildea, Robert. *Education in Provincial France 1800-1914: A Study of Three Departments.* Oxford: Clarendon Press, 1983.

Ginzburg, Carlo. *The Cheese and the Worms: The Cosmos of a Sixteenth-Century Miller.* Translated by Johan and Anne Tedeschi. Baltimore: Johns Hopkins University Press, 1980.

———. *Clues, Myths, and the Historical Method.* Translated by John and Ann Tedeschi. Baltimore: Johns Hopkins Press, 1989.

Godechot, Jacques. *Les institutions de la France sous la Révolution et l'Empire.* Second Edition. Paris: Presses universitaires de France, 1968.

———. *La Contre-Révolution.* 2d ed. Paris: Presses universitaires de France, 1984.

Golden, Richard. *The Godly Rebellion: Parisian Curés and the Religious Fronde, 1652-1662.* Chapel Hill: University of North Carolina Press, 1981.

Gough, Hugh. *The Terror in the French Revolution.* New York: St. Martin's Press, 1998.

Grandmaison, Henri (de). *Machecoul et ses deux clochers.* La Guerche-de-Bretagne (Ille-et-Vilaine): Imprimerie Raynard, 1981.

Gras, Yves. *La guerre de Vendée.* Paris: Economica, 1994.

Greer, Donald. *The Incidence of Terror during the French Revolution.* Gloucester, Mass: Peter Smith, 1966.

Guillerand-Champenier, Marie-Claude. "Le diocèse de Nantes et la Révolution 17, 94-1801." *L'église de Nantes et la Révolution*. Edited by Jean Garaud. Nantes, 1989: 19-23.

Hales, E. E. Y. *Revolution and the Papacy 1769-1846*. South Bend: University of Notre Dame Press, 1966.

Halévi, Ran. *Les loges maçonniques dans la France d'ancien régime: aux origines de la sociabilité démocratique*. Paris: A. Colin, 1984.

Harris, Ruth. *Lourdes: Body and Spirit in the Secular Age*. New York: Viking, 1999.

Higonnet, Patrice. *Pont-de-Montvert: Social Structure and Politics in a French Village, 1700-1914* (Cambridge, Mass: Harvard University Press, 1971).

Hilaire, Yves-Marie. *Une chrétienté au XIX\u1d49 siècle? La vie religieuse des populations du diocèse d'Arras (1840-1914)*. 2 Vols. Villeneuve-Ascq: Université de Lille, 1977.

Hoffman, Phillip T. *Church and Community in the Diocese of Lyon 1500-1789*. New Haven: Yale University Press, 1984.

Hufton, Olwen. *The Poor of Eighteenth-Century France 1750-1789*. London: Oxford University Press, 1974.

⸻. "Counter-revolutionary Women." In *The French Revolution in Social and Political Perspective*. Edited by Peter Jones. London: Arnold, 1996.

Hunt, Lynn. "The Many Bodies of Marie Antoinette: Political Pornography and the Problem of the Feminine in the French Revolution." In *Eroticism and the Body Politic*. Edited by Lynn Hunt. Baltimore: The Johns Hopkins University Press, 1991.

⸻. *The Family Romance of the French Revolution*. Berkeley: University of California Press, 1992.

Huppert, George. *After the Black Death: A Social History of Early Modern Europe*, 2d ed. Bloomington: Indiana University Press, 1998.

I.N.S.E.E.-Direction régionale de Nantes. *Population par communes de 1801 à 1962: Département de la Loire-Atlantique*. Nantes, 1966.

Irvine, William D. *The Boulanger Affair Reconsidered: Royalism, Boulangism, and the Origins of the Radical Right in France*. New York: Oxford University Press, 1989.

Jarnoux, Alphonse. *La Loire leur servit de linceul: Les prêtres victimes de la première noyade, Nantes 16 novembre 1793*. Quimper: Imprimerie Cornouillaise, 1972.

⸻. "Monseigneur Duvoisin, évêque de Nantes, rebâtit son diocèse sur les ruines (1802-1813)." *Mémoires de la société archéologique et historique de Nantes et de Loire-Atlantique* 116 (1979-1980): 59-83.

Jonas, Raymond. *France and the Cult of the Sacred Heart: An Epic Tale for Modern Times*. Berkeley: University of California Press, 2000.

Jones, Colin. *The Charitable Imperative: Hospitals and Nursing in Ancien Régime and Revolutionary France*. New York: Routledge, 1989.

Jones, P. M. *Reform and Revolution in France: The Politics of Transition, 1774-1791*. New York: Cambridge University Press, 1995.

Jones, Peter, ed. *The French Revolution in Political and Social Perspective*. London: Arnold, 1996.

————. *Liberty and Locality in Revolutionary France: Six Villages Compared, 1760-1820*. New York: Cambridge University Press, 2003.

Kale, Stephen D. *Legitimism and the Reconstruction of French Society, 1852-1883*. Baton Rouge: Louisiana State University Press, 1992.

Kaplan, Stephen Laurence. *Farewell Revolution: Disputed Legacies, France, 1789/1989*. Ithaca: Cornell University Press.

Kennedy, Michael L. *The Jacobin Clubs in the French Revolution: The First Years*. Princeton: Princeton University Press, 1982.

Kertzer, David. *Ritual, Politics, and Power*. New Haven: Yale University Press, 1988.

Kreiser, B. Robert. *Miracles, Convulsions, and Ecclesiastical Politics in Early Eighteenth-Century France*. Princeton: Princeton University Press, 1984.

Kroen, Sheryl. *Politics and Theater: The Crisis of Legitimacy in Restoration France, 1815-1830*. Berkeley: University of California Press, 2000.

Kselman, Thomas A. *Miracles and Prophecies in Nineteenth-Century France*. New Brunswick: Rutgers University Press, 1983.

————. *Death and the Afterlife in Modern France*. Princeton: Princeton University Press, 1993.

Lafon, Jacques. *Les prêtres, les fidèles et l'état: Le ménage à trois du XIX*[e] *siècle*. Paris: Beauchesne, 1987.

Lagrée, Michel. *Mentalités, religion, et histoire en Haute-Bretagne au XIX*[e] *siècle: Le diocèse de Rennes, 1815-1848*. Paris: Librairie C. Klincksieck, 1977.

————. "Prêtres et laics dans le légendaire contre-révolutionnaire ou les rôles inverses." *Annales de Bretagne et des pays de l'Ouest* 89 (1982): 229-35.

————. "Le clergé Breton et le premier centenaire de la Révolution française." *Annales de Bretagne et des pays de l'Ouest* 91 (1984): 249-67.

————. *Religion et cultures en Bretagne, 1850-1950*. Paris: Fayard, 1992.

————, and Jehanne Roche. *Tombes de mémoire: La dévotions populaires aux victimes de la Révolution dans l'Ouest*. Rennes: Apogée, 1992.

Lallié, Alfred. *Le district de Machecoul, 1788-1799: Études sur les origines des débuts de l'insurrection vendéene dans le pays de Retz*. Nantes: Vincent Forest et Émile Grimaud, 1869.

———. *Le diocèse de Nantes pendant la Révolution.* 2 Vols. Nantes: B. Cier, 1893.

Lambert, Yves. "Famille, politique et religion." In *L'Ouest bouge-t-il? Son changement social et culturel depuis trente ans.* Nantes: Reflets du Passé, 1983.

Langlois, Claude. *Le catholicisme au féminin: Les congrégations française à supérieure générale au XIXᵉ siècle.* Paris: Éditions du Cerf, 1984.

———. "La rupture entre l'Eglise catholique et la Révolution." In *The French Revolution and the Creation of Modern Political Culture,* vol. 3, *The Transformation of Political Culture, 1789-1848.* Edited by Francois Furet and Mona Ozouf. Oxford: Pergamon Press, 1987.

———. "La disparition de la violence religieuse en France au 19ᵉ siècle," *French Historical Studies* 21 (Winter, 1998): 4-25.

Latteux, Patricia. "Les réfugiés du sud du district de Machecoul à Nantes pendant la guerre de Vendée." Mémoire de maîtrise. Directed by J.-C. Martin. Nantes: Université de Nantes, 1991.

Launay, Marcel. "Les procès-verbaux des visites pastorales dans le diocèse de Nantes au milieu du XIXᵉ siècle." *Annales de Bretagne et des pays de l'Ouest* 82 (1975): 179-93.

———. *Le diocèse de Nantes sous le second empire: Monseigneur Jaquemet, 1849-1869.* 2 Vols. Nantes: CID Éditions, 1982.

———. "Un évêque de Nantes à la découverte de son diocèse au XIXᵉ siècle: Les visites pastorales de Monseigneur Jaquemet sous le Second Empire." *Mémoires de la société d'histoire et d'archéologie de Bretagne* 61 (1984): 245-52.

———. "Chronique d'un épiscopat nantais: Monseigneur Rouard (1896-1914)." *Annales de Bretagne et des pays de l'Ouest* 91 (1984): 581-92.

———. *Un seul pasteur, un seul troupeau: La Brière catholique au XIXᵉ siècle (journal de l'abbé Allain).* Nantes: Reflets du Passé, 1984.

LeBras, Gabriel. *L'église et le village.* Paris: Flammarion, 1976.

Lebrun, François. *Les hommes et la mort en Anjou aux 17ᵉ et 18ᵉ siècles: Essai de démographie et de psychologies historiques.* La Haye: Mouton et compagnie, 1971.

———. *Parole de Dieu et révolution: Les sermons d'un curé angevin avant et pendant la guerre de Vendée.* Toulouse: Privat, 1979.

———, ed. *Histoire des catholiques en France du XVᵉ siècle à nos jours.* 2 Vols. Toulouse: Privat, 1980.

———and Roger Dupuy, eds. *Les résistances à la Révolution: Actes du colloque de Rennes (17-21 septembre 1985).* Paris: Imago, 1987.

LeGoff, T. J. A., and D. M. G. Sutherland. "Religion and Rural Revolt in the French Revolution: An Overview." In *Religion and Rural Revolt.* Edited by

János M. Bak and Gerhard Benecke. Manchester: Manchester University Press, 1984.

———. *Vannes and its Region: A Study of Town and Country in Eighteenth-Century France*. Oxford: Clarendon Press, 1981.

Le Mené, Michel, and Marie-Hélène Santrot, eds. *Cahiers des Plaintes et Doléances de Loire-Atlantique: Texte intégral et commentaires*. 4 Vols. Nantes: Éditions du Conseil Général de Loire-Atlantique, 1989.

Lewis, Gwynne. *The French Revolution: Rethinking the Debate*. London: Routledge, 1993.

Librec, H. *La franc-maçonnerie dans la Loire-Inférieure 1744-1946*. Nantes, 1946.

Ligou, Daniel, ed. *Histoire des francs-maçons en France*. Second Edition. Toulouse: Privat, 2000.

Liu, Tessie P. *The Weaver's Knot: The Contradictions of Class Struggle and Family Solidarity in Western France, 1750-1914*. Ithaca: Cornell University Press, 1994.

Loupès, Philippe. *La vie religieuse en France au XVIII siècle*. Paris: SEDES, 1993.

Lucas, Colin. "The Crowd in Politics." In *The French Revolution in Social and Political Perspective*. Edited by Peter Jones. London: Arnold, 1996.

Lusson-Houdemon, Patricia. "La vie sacramentelle des fidèles dans l'Ouest à travers les registres clandestins." In *Pratiques religieuses dans l'Europe révolutionnaire*. Edited by Bernard Plongeron. Turnhout: Brepols, 1988.

Marcilhacy, Christianne. *Le diocèse d'Orléans au milieu du XIX siècle: Les hommes et leur mentalités*. Paris: Sirey, 1964.

Martin, Jean-Clément, ed. *Vendée-Chouannerie*. Nantes: Reflets du Passé, 1981.

———. "Le clergé vendéen face à l'industrialisaton (fin XIXe - début XXe)." *Annales de Bretagne et des pays de l'Ouest* 89 (1982): 357-68.

———. *Une guerre interminable; la Vendée deux cents ans après*. Nantes: Reflets du passé, 1985

———. *La Vendée et la France*. Paris: Éditions du Seuil, 1987.

———. *La Vendée de la mémoire*. Paris: Éditions du Seuil, 1989.

———. "Est-il possible de compter les morts de la Vendée?" *Revue d'histoire moderne et contemporaine* 1 (1991): 105-21.

———. "Histoire et polémique: Les massacres de Machecoul." *Visions contemporaines* 7 (1993): 156-91.

———, ed. *Religion et Révolution: Colloque de Saint-Florent-le-Vieil 13-14-15 Mai 1993*. Paris: Anthropos, 1994.

———. *Révolution et contre-révolution en France 1789-1989: Les rouages de l'Histoire.* Rennes: Presses Universitaires de Rennes, 1996.

———. "La Vendée, région mémoire: Bleus and blancs." In *Les lieux de mémoire: La république, la nation, les France.* Edited by Pierre Nora. 3 Vols. Paris: Gallimard, 1997.

———, ed., *La Contre-Révolution en Europe XVIIIe-XIXe siècles: Réalités politiques et sociales, résonances culturelles et idéologiques.* Rennes: Presses Universitaires de Rennes, 2001.

Mayer, Arno J. *The Furies: Violence and Terror in the French and Russian Revolutions.* Princeton: Princeton University Press, 2000.

Mayeur, Jean-Marie. *La vie politique sous la troisième République, 1870-1940.* Paris: Editions du Seuil, 1984.

———. *La séparation des églises et de l'état.* Paris: Éditions Ouvrières, 1991.

McMahon, Darrin M. *Enemies of the Enlightenment: The French Counter-Enlightenment and the Making of Modernity.* New York: Oxford University Press, 2001.

McManners, John. *The French Revolution and the Church.* London: SPCK, 1969.

———. *Church and State in France, 1870-1914.* London: SPCK, 1972.

———. *Death and the Enlightenment: Changing Attitudes to Death among Christians and Unbelievers in Eighteenth-Century France.* New York: Oxford University Press, 1981.

———. *Church and Society in Eighteenth-Century France.* 2 Vols. Oxford: Oxford University Press, 1999.

McPhee, Peter. *The French Revolution 1789-1799.* New York: Oxford University Press, 2002.

Merrick, Jeffrey. *The Desacralization of the French Monarchy in the Eighteenth Century.* Baton Rouge: Louisiana State University Press, 1992.

Mille, Fabien. "La population de Machecoul pendant la Révolution d'apres l'état civil." Mémoire de maîtrise. Directed by J.-C. Martin. Nantes: Université de Nantes, 1997.

Minois, Georges. *Les religieux en Bretagne sous l'ancien régime.* Luçon: Éditions Ouest-France, 1989.

Mitchell, Harvey. "The Vendée and Counterrevolution: A Review Essay." *French Historical Studies* 5 (1968): 405-29.

Mousnier, Roland. *Peasant Uprisings in Seventeenth-Century France, Russia, and China.* Translated by Brian Pearce. New York: Harper and Row, 1970.

Muchembled, Robert. *Popular Culture and Elite Culture in France 1400-1750.* Translated by Lydia Cochrane. Baton Rouge: Louisiana State University Press, 1985.

Muir, Edward and Guido Ruggiero, eds. *Microhistory and the Lost Peoples of Europe.* Baltimore: Johns Hopkins University Press, 1991.

―――. *Ritual in Early Modern Europe.* New York: Cambridge University Press, 1997.

Naud, Danielle. "Les structures familiales en Vendée au XIXe siècle." Mémoire de maîtrise. Directed by Y. Durand. Nantes: Université de Nantes, 1976.

Nora, Pierre, ed. *Les lieux de mémoire: La république, la nation, les France.* 3 Vols. Paris: Gallimard, 1997.

Ormières, Jean-Louis. "Politique et religion dans l'Ouest." *Annales: économies, sociétés et civilisations* 40 (1985): 1041-66.

Oury, Louis. "La second mort de Joseph Bara." *Révolution,* March 10, 1989: 58-63.

―――. "Les chapelets de Machecoul." *Révolution,* July 7, 1989: 20-24.

Ozouf, Mona. *Festivals and the French Revolution.* Translated by Alan Sheridan. Cambridge, Mass: Harvard University Press, 1988.

―――. *L'école, l'église et la République, 1871-1914.* Paris: Éditions du Seuil, 1992.

Paré, O. *Quelques documents sur la paroisse de Machecoul.* Tarbes (Pyrénées Hautes): Imprimerie Saint-Joseph, 1973.

―――. *Les pasteurs de Machecoul.* Tarbes: Imprimerie de Saint-Joseph, 1975.

Pellerin, Lyonel Michel. *Bloc agraire et comportement paysan: Les réactions aux inventaires en Loire-Inférieure (fevrier-mars 1906).* Nantes: Centre des recherches politiques, 1976.

Pérouas, Louis. "La piété populaire au travail sur la mémoire d'un saint, Grignion de Montfort." *Actes du 99e congrès national des sociétés savantes, Besançon* (1976): 259-72.

―――. *Grignion de Montfort et la Vendée.* Paris: Éditions du Cerf, 1989.

―――. "Grignion de Montfort, un prédicateur vraiment populaire?" *Annales de Bretagne et des pays de l'Ouest* 98 (1991): 205-10.

Perriard, Pierre. *Histoire des curés de campagne: de 1789 à nos jours.* Paris: Plon, 1986.

―――. *La vie quotidienne du prêtre français au XIXe siècle, 1801-1905.* Paris: Hachette, 1986.

Perroys, Joseph. *Les Bénédictines de Notre Dame du Calvaire à Machecoul, 1673-1958.* Rezé (Loire-Atlantique): Séquences, 1993.

Petitfrère, Claude. "Les causes de la Vendée et de la Chouannerie: Essai d'historiographie." *Annales de Bretagne et des pays de l'Ouest* 84 (1977): 75-101.

―――. *Les vendéens d'Anjou (1793).* Paris: Bibliothèque Nationale, 1981.

———. "The Origins of the Civil War in the Vendée." In *The French Revolution in Social and Political Perspective*. Edited by Peter Jones. New York: Arnold, 1996: 340-58.

Phayer, J. Michael. "Politics and Popular Religion: The Cult of the Cross in France, 1815-1840." *Journal of Social History* 11 (1978): 346-65.

Plongeron, Bernard. *Théologie et politique au siècle des lumières (1770-1820)*. Geneva: Librairie Droz, 1973.

———. *La vie quotidienne du clergé français au XVIIIe siècle*. Paris: Hachette, 1974.

———, ed. *Pratiques religieuses, mentalités et spiritualités dans l'Europe révolutionnaire (1770-1820)*. Turnhout: Brepols, 1988.

Poulat, Émile. *Les "Semaines religieuses:" Approche socio-historique et bibliograhphie des Bulletins diocésains français*. Lyon: Centre d'histoire du catholicisme, 1972.

———. *Église contre bourgeoisie: Introduction au devenir du catholicisme actuel*. Tourai: Casterman, 1977.

Renard, Jean. *Les évolutions contemporaines de la vie rurale dans la région nantaise: Loire-Atlantique, bocages vendéens, mauges*. Les Sables d'Olonne: Éditions Le Cercle d'Or, 1975.

Revel, Jacques. "Micoranalysis and Construction of the Social." In *Histories: French Reconstructions of the Past*. Edited by Jacques Revel and Lynn Hunt. New York: The Free Press, 1995.

Roudat, François (Fanch). "Le message politique des sermons en Breton à la fin de l'ancien régime." *Annales de Bretagne et des pays de l'Ouest* 89 (1982): 143-52.

Schwartz, Robert M. *Policing the Poor in Eighteenth-Century France*. Chapel Hill: University of North Carolina Press, 1988.

Secher, Reynald. *La génocide franco-française: La Vendée-Vengé*. Paris: Presses universitaires de France, 1986.

———. *A French Genocide: The Vendée*. Translated by George Holoch. Notre Dame: University of Notre Dame Press, 2003.

Sedgwick, Alexander. *Jansenism in Seventeenth-Century France: Voices in the Wilderness*. Charlottesville: University Press of Virginia, 1977.

Shapiro, Gilbert and John Markoff, eds. *Revolutionary Demands: A Content Analysis of the Cahiers de Doléances of 1789*. Stanford: Stanford University Press, 1998.

Sheehan, Jonathan. "Enlightenment, Religion, and the Enigma of Secularization: A Review Essay." *American Historical Review* 108, no. 4 (October 2003): 1061-80.

Sheppard, Thomas. *Loumarin in the Eighteenth Century: A Study of a French Village.* Baltimore: Johns Hopkins University Press, 1971.

Siegfried, André. *Tableau politique de la France de l'Ouest sous la troisième République.* Paris: Librairie Armand Colin, 1913.

Société des Etudes Robespierristes. *Joseph Bara (1779-1793): Pour le deuxième centenaire de sa naissance.* La Couronne: Sopan, 1981.

Sutherland, Donald. *The Chouans: The Social Origins of Popular Counter-Revolution in Upper Brittany, 1770-1796.* Oxford: Clarendon Press, 1982.

————. *France 1789-1815: Revolution and Counterrevolution.* New York: Oxford University Press, 1985.

Tackett, Timothy. *Priest and Parish in Eighteenth-Century France: A Social and Political Study of the Curés in a Diocese of Dauphiné, 1750-1791.* Princeton: Princeton University Press, 1977.

————, and Claude Langlois. "Ecclesiastical Structures and Clerical Geography on the Eve of the French Revolution." *French Historical Studies* 11 (1980): 352-70.

————. "The Social History of the Diocesan Clergy in Eighteenth-Century France." In *Church, State, and Society under the Bourbon Kings.* Edited by Richard Golden. Lawrence: Coronado Press, 1982.

————. "The West in France in 1789: The Religious Factor in the Origins of the Counterrevolution." *Journal of Modern History* 54 (1982): 715-45.

————. *Religion, Revolution and Regional Culture in Eighteenth-Century France: The Ecclesiastical Oath of 1791.* Princeton: Princeton University Press, 1986.

————. "Women and Men in Sommières [Gard] and the Ecclesiastical Oath of 1791." In *Pratiques religieuses, mentalités et spiritualités dans l'Europe révolutionnaire.* Edited by Bernard Plongeron. Turnhout, Brepols, 1988.

————. *Becoming a Revolutionary: The Deputies of the French National Assembly and the Emergence of a Revolutionary Culture (1789-1790).* Princeton: Princeton University Press, 1996.

————. "Conspiracy Obsession in a Time of Revolution: French Elites and the Origins of the Terror, 1789-92," *American Historical Review* 105, no. 3 (June 2000): 690-713.

————. *When the King Took Flight.* Cambridge, Mass: Harvard University Press. 2003.

Taylor, George V. "Noncapitalist Wealth and the Origins of the French Revolution." *American Historical Review* 72 (1967): 469-96.

————. "Revolutionary and Nonrevolutionary Content in the *Cahiers*: An Interim Report." *French Historical Studies*, 7 (1972): 479-502.

Tilly, Charles. *The Vendée: A Sociological Analysis of the Counterrevolution of 1793*. Cambridge, Mass.: Harvard University Press, 1964.

Truant, Cynthia. *The Rites of Labor: Brothers of Compagnonnage in Old and New Regime France*. Ithaca: Cornell University Press, 1994.

Valeri, Valerio. Review of *The Cheese and the Worms*, by Carlo Ginzburg. In *Journal of Modern History* 54 (1982): 139-43.

Van Kley, Dale. *The Jansenists and the Expulsion of the Jesuits from France*. New Haven: Yale University Press, 1975.

————. *The Damiens Affair and the Unraveling of the Ancien Régime 1750-1770*. Princeton: Princeton University Press, 1984.

————. *The Religious Origins of the French Revolution: From Calvin to the Civil Constitution, 1560-1791*. New Haven: Yale University Press, 1996.

————. "Christianity as Causality and Chrysalis of Modernity: The Problem of Dechristianization in the French Revolution." *American Historical Review* 108 (October 2003): 1081-104.

Vovelle, Michel. *Piété baroque et déchristianisation en Provence au XVIII* siècle*. Paris: Seuil, 1978.

————. *The Revolution against the Church: From Reason to Supreme Being*. Translated by Alan José. Columbus: Ohio State University Press, 1991.

Weber, Eugen. *Action Française: Royalism and Reaction in Twentieth-Century France*. Stanford: Stanford University Press, 1962.

————. *Peasants into Frenchmen: The Modernization of Rural France 1870-1914*. Stanford: Stanford University Press, 1976.

Woell, Edward J. "Counterrevolutionary Catholicism in Western France: The Battle of Belief at Machecoul, 1774-1914," Ph.D. Dissertation. Ann Arbor: University Microfilms, 1997.

————. "Prelude to a Massacre: The Ecclesiastical Oath Crisis at Machecoul [Loire-Atlantique], 1790-1791." In *Proceedings of the Western Society for French History: Selected Papers of the Annual Meeting*, Vol. 24. Edited by Barry Rothaus. Greeley: University Press of Colorado, 1997: 233-44.

————. "Reviving the Vendée: The Separation of Church and State in a Western Rural Parish." In *Proceedings of the Western Society for French History: Selected Papers of the Annual Meeting*, Vol. 25. Edited by Barry Rothaus. Greeley: University Press of Colorado, 1998: 110-19.

————. "Waging War for the Lord: Counterrevolutionary Ritual in Rural Western France, 1801-1906." *Catholic Historical Review* 88 (January 2002): 17-41.

Index